D1144116

UNDERSTANDING *of* SUICIDAL BEHAVIOUR

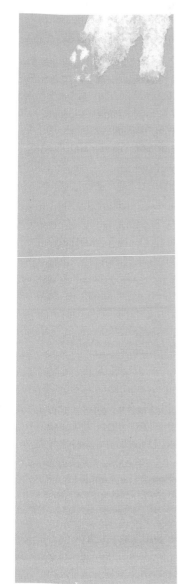

The Wiley Series in

CLINICAL PSYCHOLOGY

Titles published under the series editorship of:

J. Mark G. Williams — *School of Psychology, University of Wales, Bangor, UK*

A list of earlier titles in the series follows the index.

UNDERSTANDING SUICIDAL BEHAVIOUR

The Suicidal Process Approach to Research, Treatment and Prevention

Edited by

Kees van Heeringen
Unit for Suicide Research
Department of Psychiatry
University of Gent
Belgium

JOHN WILEY & SONS, LTD
Chichester · New York · Weinheim · Brisbane · Singapore · Toronto

Copyright © 2001 by   John Wiley & Sons Ltd,
Baffins Lane, Chichester,
West Sussex PO19 1UD, England

National 01243 779777
International (+44) 1243 779777
e-mail (for orders and customer service enquiries):
cs-books@wiley.co.uk
Visit our Home Page
on http://www.wiley.co.uk
or http://www.wiley.com

Reprinted November 2001. Paperback edition 2002

Other Wiley Editorial Offices

John Wiley & Sons, Inc., 605 Third Avenue,
New York, NY 10158-0012, USA

WILEY-VCH Verlag GmbH, Pappelallee 3,
D-69469 Weinheim, Germany

John Wiley & Sons, Australia Ltd, 33 Park Road, Milton,
Queensland 4064, Australia

John Wiley & Sons (Asia) Pte Ltd, 2 Clementi Loop #02-01,
Jin Xing Distripark, Singapore 129809

John Wiley & Sons (Canada) Ltd, 22 Worcester Road,
Rexdale, Ontario M9W 1L1, Canada

Library of Congress Cataloging-in-Publication Data

Understanding suicidal behaviour : the suicidal process approach to research, treatment, and prevention / edited by Kees van Heeringen.
     p. cm. — (The Wiley series in clinical psychology)
   Includes bibliographical references and index.
   ISBN 0–471–98803–0
   1. Suicidal behaviour.   I. Title: Understanding suicidal behaviour.   II. Heeringen, Kees van
   III. Series.
   RC569.U54 2001
   616.85'8445—dc21   00–069697

British Library Cataloguing in Publication Data

A catalogue record for this book is available from the British Library

ISBN 0–471–98803–0 (cloth)
   0–471–49166–7 (paper)

Project management by Originator Publishing Services, Gt. Yarmouth (typeset in 10/12 Palatino)
Printed and bound in Great Britain by Biddles Ltd, Guildford and King's Lynn
This book is printed on acid-free paper responsibly manufactured from sustainable forestry, in which at least two trees are planted for each one used for paper production.

CONTENTS

LIST OF CONTRIBUTORS

Lawrence Amsel

MHCRC for the Study of Suicidal Behavior, Department of Neuroscience, New York State Psychiatric Institute, 1051 Riverside Drive, New York, NY 10032, USA

Alan Apter

Department of Child and Adolescent Psychiatry, Sackler School of Medicine, Tel Aviv University, Geha Hospital, PO Box 102, Petah Tikva 49100, Israel

Ella Arensman

Department of Clinical and Health Psychology, Leiden University, PO Box 9555, 2300 RB Leiden, The Netherlands

Unni Bille-Brahe

Centre for Suicidological Research, Tietgens Allé, DK-5230 Odense M, Denmark

Robert D. Goldney

The Adelaide Clinic, 33 Park Terrace, Gilberton, South Australia 5081, and Department of Psychiatry, University of Adelaide, South Australia 5005, Australia

Keith Hawton

Centre for Suicide Research, University Department of Psychiatry, Warneford Hospital, Oxford OX3 7JX, UK

Ad J.F.M. Kerkhof

Department of Clinical Psychology, Vrije Universiteit, De Boelelaan 1109, 1081 HV Amsterdam, The Netherlands

Ineke Kienhorst

Lupineoord 63, 3991 VH Houten, The Netherlands

Kevin M. Malone

Department of Adult Psychiatry, Mater Misericordiae Hospital, University College Dublin, 63 Eccles Street, Dublin 7, Ireland

| J. John Mann | *Department of Neuroscience, New York State Psychiatric Institute, 1051 Riverside Drive, Box 42, New York, NY 10032, USA* |

Konrad Michel — *Psychiatrische Poliklinik, Universitätsspital, Mürtenstrasse 21, CH-3010 Berne, Switzerland*

Maeve Moran — *Department of Adult Psychiatry, Mater Misericordiae Hospital, University College Dublin, 63 Eccles Street, Dublin 7, Ireland*

Hadas Ofek — *Department of Child and Adolescent Psychiatry, Sackler School of Medicine, Tel Aviv University, Geha Hospital, PO Box 102, Petah Tikva 49100, Israel*

Leslie R. Pollock — *Institute of Medical and Social Care Research, University of Wales, Wheldon Building, Bangor LL57 2UW, UK*

Lil Träskman-Bendz — *Section of Psychiatry, Department of Neuroscience, University Hospital, SE-22185 Lund, Sweden*

Ladislav Valach — *Bürgerspital, Medizinische Klinik, CH-4500 Solothurn, Switzerland*

Kees van Heeringen — *Unit for Suicide Research, Department of Psychiatry, University Hospital Gent, De Pintelaan 185, B-9000 Gent, Belgium*

Herman M. van Praag — *Department of Psychiatry and Neuropsychology, Maastricht University, PO Box 5930 Maastricht, The Netherlands*

Åsa Westrin — *Section of Psychiatry, Department of Neuroscience, University Hospital, SE-22185 Lund, Sweden*

J. Mark G. Williams — *Institute of Medical and Social Care Research, University of Wales, Wheldon Building, Bangor LL57 2UW, UK*

INTRODUCTION

Suicidal behaviour occurs at the crossroads of the past and the future. The past exerts its influence in relation to recent, as well as more distant past, life events. As will be described in various chapters in this book, the past is particularly important in the development of suicidal behaviour by determining how these adverse events are perceived, and thus how individuals react. In other words, our past determines how we see the future, and thus determines to a large extent whether we will develop hopelessness when confronted with adverse events. An important impetus for editing this book is the fact that suicidal phenomena are commonly regarded as related to emotional problems, whether or not in the context of a psychiatric disorder, at a certain moment in a person's life. In this book it will be argued that this approach to the understanding of suicidal behaviour can only partially explain why suicidal behaviour occurs, and thus leads to the difficulties in predicting and preventing the occurrence of suicide with which clinicians are all familiar.

In spite of major research efforts to describe risk factors, develop treatment approaches and implement prevention strategies, suicidal behaviour continues to be an important public health problem. As far as the effectiveness of these approaches and strategies has been evaluated the results have not been particularly encouraging. Among the many potential reasons for this discrepancy there may be a lack of understanding of the causes and precipitants of (the repetition of) suicidal behaviour because of the fact that the process leading to suicidal behaviour has not been taken into account. This book will review the epidemiological, psychological and biological aspects of the suicidal process, thus providing potential new approaches to risk assessment, research and treatment.

The assessment of the risk of suicide is one of the most difficult and demanding skills, which (mental) health professionals have to acquire. Risk assessment is among the most difficult tasks because of the limited specificity of currently known risk factors, but also one of the most risk-factor research and its implications for the assessment of suicide risk, with an emphasis on the benefits of including a trait-like predisposition to suicidal behaviour in risk assessment. The following chapter describes the role of society in triggering and shaping the suicidal process, thus providing a description of which societal factors have to be taken into account when strategies to change the course of the suicidal process are developed. Based on a review of the current treatment strategies, Chapter 11 indicates the need for new approaches to the treatment of suicidal behaviour and the challenges for adequate prevention, which may be provided by the suicidal process approach. The following chapter addresses suicidal behaviour as a goal-directed action (i.e. the consequence of a developmental process), and points at the need for health-care professionals to create the opportunity to listen to the narrative of the patient. Chapters 13 and 14 describe the consequences of the suicidal process approach for the psycho-pharmacological and psychotherapeutic treatment of suicidal ideation and behaviour, respectively. Implications for future research on the causes of suicidal behaviour and for its treatment and prevention are described in the final chapter.

Although the process approach to suicidal behaviour is not new, its conceptualization still remains to a certain extent at the level of hypotheses, in particular with regard to the description of its biological and psychological underpinnings and their course over time. However, this book has taken an evidence-based approach as much as possible, and it thus shows that many of these hypotheses now have a much firmer theoretical base than at the time of the early descriptions of the process. Our knowledge of the role of factors, which may determine the initiation and course of the suicidal process, has not yet reached a steady state, and, because of rapidly increasing diagnostic possibilities (e.g. in the area of neural science), it can be expected that our knowledge of such factors may increase rapidly, with the implicit danger that some or many of the hypotheses may seem naive in the light of further evidence. However, the convergent nature of findings from diverging research approaches to the study of the process, such as epidemiology, psychology and biology, indicates that the field has reached some coherence, which provides a firm ground for the description of implications for the treatment, prevention and further study of suicidal behaviour.

Part I

THE SUICIDAL PROCESS:
AN OVERVIEW OF
RESEARCH FINDINGS

Chapter 1

THE SUICIDAL PROCESS AND RELATED CONCEPTS

Kees van Heeringen

INTRODUCTION

A vast amount of epidemiological data shows considerable differences in sociodemographic and psychopathological characteristics between individuals who communicate suicidal ideation, those who attempt suicide and those who commit suicide. Evidence is, however, accumulating in support of an association between these phenomena. This evidence is provided mainly by longitudinal studies of attempted suicide patients and by retrospective psychological autopsy studies of individuals who died as a result of suicide. These studies will be discussed in more detail in the next chapter, but some of the main findings will be used here to describe the different concepts or models that have been developed to understand the relationship between these suicidal phenomena. These concepts or models include the "suicidal pyramid", the "suicidal career" and the "suicidal process".

In this chapter these concepts will be introduced, thus providing the basis for the description of the epidemiological, biological, psychological and psychiatric underpinnings of these concepts, which will be elaborated in the first part of this book. However, preceding these introductory descriptions of the suicidal process and related concepts, the definition of a number of terms as used throughout this book have to be addressed.

Understanding Suicidal Behaviour. Edited by Kees van Heeringen
© 2001 John Wiley & Sons Ltd.

DEFINITIONS OF RELEVANT TERMS

The term *suicidality* will be used in this book to describe cognitive and behavioural characteristics, which may become manifest as *suicidal ideation* or *suicidal behaviour*. The term suicidal ideation refers to the occurrence of any thoughts about self-destructive behaviour, whether or not death is intended. Such thoughts may range from vague ideas about the possibility of ending one's life at some point of time in the future to very concrete plans to commit suicide. In a similar way, the term suicidal behaviour may cover a wide range of self-destructive behaviours with a non-fatal or fatal outcome, described by the terms *attempted suicide* and *suicide*, respectively. A more detailed definition of attempted suicide will be given in the next chapter, but it should be noted here that the definitions as used in this book are purely descriptive, and that motives for the behaviour, or the level of *suicidal intent* (i.e. the wish to die) are not included in the definition. Related to intent are the *lethality* of the method used to attempt or commit suicide, and the *medical seriousness*, describing the physical consequences of the self-destructive act. The term *suicidal gesture* has been used to describe self-destructive acts that are considered "non-serious" because of the fact that the resulting condition is not life threatening, or that patients seek help after the act. In view of the fact that suicidal intent, the life-threatening nature of consequences and motivations for the behaviour are difficult to define in an unequivocal way, which may lead to inconsistent use of the concepts (Malone et al, 1995), the term suicidal gesture will not be used in this book. Instead, the term "attempted suicide" will be used to describe any forms of self-destructive behaviour which do not follow a typical pattern of habitual reactions to adverse life events, as is the case in self-mutilation.

The term "attempted suicide" has been criticized because it is used to describe a behaviour which, probably more often than not, lacks any serious suicidal intention (Hawton and Catalan, 1987). However, alternatives to replace this term, such as "parasuicide" or "deliberate self-harm" have their drawbacks too: "parasuicide" because it equally implies suicidal intentions, and "deliberate self-harm" because of the implication that physical harm always occurs. This latter consideration (i.e. that physical damage is an essential consequence of the behaviour), indicates a major distinction between the concepts of attempted suicide and self-mutilation, in addition to the three variables that Pattison and Kahan (1983) used to classify clinically different self-destructive behaviours. First, they describe a "direct/indirect" variable in terms of time and awareness: direct self-destructive behaviour occurs in a short period of time with personal awareness of the effect of one's actions, thus implying conscious intent to harm oneself. Second, the "lethality" variable classifies self-destructive behaviour on a continuum from high to low probability of death from the behaviour. Third, the "repetition" variable differentiates between single-event and multiple-event classes of self-destructive behaviour. In this way, a classification model of self-destructive behaviours was constructed in which deliberate self-harm is a distinctive class, characterized by direct self-harming behaviour with low lethality and in a repetitive pattern. In this classification model, "suicide attempts" are characterized as direct self-destructive behaviours, with high (single-event) or medium (multiple-event) lethality. Moreover, a single "atypical" direct self-harm episode was distinguished, which is difficult to classify because of the clinical ambiguity about the level of conscious intent of lethality in many cases. The term "attempted suicide" as used in this book thus includes the classes "deliberate self-harm" and "atypical self-harm" as described in Pattison and Kahan's classification.

More recently, O'Carroll and colleagues (1998) proposed a comprehensive nomenclature for self-injurious thoughts and behaviours in which a distinction is made between "risk-taking thoughts and behaviours" and "suicide-related thoughts and behaviours" (Table 1.1).

In this nomenclature the term "suicide attempt" is used to describe potentially self-injurious behaviours with a non-fatal outcome for which there is evidence (either explicit or implicit) that the person intended at some (non-zero) level to kill himself/herself. In contrast with the definition of "attempted suicide" as used in this book, suicidal intent is included in the definition of attempted suicide in this nomenclature, the drawbacks of which have been described above. Apart from this distinction, this nomenclature can be of particular relevance for the study and understanding of the suicidal process (e.g. as a result of inclusion of risk-taking thoughts and behaviours in the range of phenomena that may occur in the course of the process). For example, a significant association between smoking and suicidal behaviours has been found (Mann et al, 1999), which is independent of any association between smoking and psychiatric illness. As will be described below and in several chapters in this book, the early recognition of specific risk-taking behaviours as related to suicide may contribute substantially to its prediction and prevention.

Barber and colleagues (1998) recently introduced the term *aborted suicide attempts* to describe events in which an individual is one step away from attempting suicide with an intent to kill himself of herself, but in which the individual does not complete the act and thus incurs no physical injury, because of a change of mind immediately before the actual co-occurring schizophrenic or affective disorder. The term suicidality referred in this study to severe suicidal intention, plans, preparations and/or attempts. The syndrome was found to consist of ruminative thinking, social withdrawal and hopelessness, and included no symptoms which are typical of the underlying psychiatric disorder, such as positive symptoms in schizophrenia or a depressed mood in depression. The authors concluded that suicidality should be seen as a phenomenon that occurs independent of specific psychiatric disorders. The suicidality syndrome and the process approach may show to some extent overlapping characteristics, as the former syndrome includes symptoms which are not particularly related to a psychiatric disorder and even may occur in individuals without a current medical or psychiatric disorder. As hopelessness has indeed been found to have trait-like properties, the suicidality syndrome, at least partially, refers to what the authors call a predilection. Such a predilection may exist in a latent form without any overt signs of suicidality, but may become clinically important if triggered by a negative situation of living, such as a psychiatric disorder.

A third model, which may show overlapping characteristics when compared with the suicidal process approach, is the stress–diathesis model as recently described by Mann and colleagues (1999). In this model, stress-related psychopathological phenomena are separated from those related to a diathesis or trait-like predisposition. Mann and co-workers (1999) were able to show that neither the nature nor the severity of state-dependent-illness characteristics distinguished patients with a history of suicide attempts from those without such a history. This finding is of great importance for the assessment of the risk of suicide, as clinicians currently intuitively rely on (whether or not objective) measures of the severity of psychiatric illness as a guide to the risk for suicidal acts. However, as will be described in more detail in Chapter 4, a clear association was found between the occurrence of non-fatal suicidal behaviour and a trait factor reflecting aggression and impulsivity, indicating the importance of such a diathesis or trait-like predisposition in predicting suicidal behaviour.

The description of these models reveals that they share common characteristics, in particular by uncoupling suicidality and state-dependent symptoms of psychiatric disorders. These divergent approaches point in a similar way at the important role of trait-dependent characteristics in the explanation of the occurrence of suicidal behaviour. Such characteristics constitute a predilection or a predisposition, as labelled in the suicidality syndrome and the stress–diathesis model, respectively. According to Mann and co-workers (1999), psychiatric disorders may play a role in the development of suicidal behaviour, but as a stressor or a trigger of suicidal behaviour, and thus not as a direct causal factor. While the suicidal process model primarily focuses on the relationship between different aspects of suicidality, this model also implies the existence of trait-like dimensions, which determine the occurrence and course of the process. Mann and colleagues (1999) suggested on the basis of the results of their study of the stress–diathesis model that suicidal behaviour is the consequence of some degree of state–trait interaction. While further evidence is needed to demonstrate whether and how manifestations of the process are related to (exacerbations of) psychiatric disorders, it can be assumed that the inherent progression of suicidality over a prolonged period of time is not related to such state-like conditions, but more so to a trait-like predisposition.

However, as will become apparent in the first part of this book which is dedicated to a review of evidence in support of this hypothesis, the way in which such a predisposition manifests itself from a psycho-pathological point of view may change in the course of the suicidal process. For example, Williams and Pollock describe in Chapter 5 that symptoms related to anxiety or anger may predominate in the early phases of the process, while later stages may be characterized by symptoms of despair and hopelessness. Of utmost importance for the management and prevention of suicidal behaviour is the accumulating evidence showing that such a trait-like predisposition is amenable to change as a result of psychotherapeutic and/or psychopharmacological interventions. These interventions are described in detail in Part II of this book.

REFERENCES

Apter, A., Bleich, A., King, R.A., Kron, S., Fluch, A., Kotler, M. and Cohen, D.J. (1993) Deaths without warning? A clinical postmortem study of suicide in 43 Israeli adolescent males. *Archives of General Psychiatry*, **50**: 138–142.

Ahrens, B. and Linden, M. (1996) Is there a suicidality syndrome independent of specific major psychiatric disorders? Results of a split half multiple regression analysis. *Acta Psychiatrica Scandinavica*, **94**: 79–86.

Barber, M.E., Marzuk, P.M., Leon, A.C. and Portera, L. (1998) Aborted suicide attempts: a new classification of suicidal behavior. *American Journal of Psychiatry*, **155**: 385-389.

Eskin, M. (1999) Social reactions of Swedish and Turkish adolescents to a close friend's suicidal disclosure. *Social Psychiatry and Psychiatric Epidemiology*, **34**: 492–497.

Hawton, K. and Catalan, J. (1987) *Attempted Suicide: A Practical Guide to its Nature and Management* (Second Edition). Oxford, Oxford Medical Publications.

Hawton, K., Arensman, E., Wasserman, D., Hulten, A., Bille-Brahe, U., Bjerke, T., Crepet, P., Deisenhammer, E., Kerkhof, A., De Leo, D., Michel, K., Ostamo, A., vulnerability is only one part of the suicidal process. It has to be triggered to become manifest, after which several forces act upon its expression. Social relationships and mental-health care may have a strong impact upon the expression of the suicidal process. The suicidal process may thus be slowed down, temporarily stopped, or accelerated. However, changes in the expression of the suicidal process are not only due to such forces. The underlying vulnerability may also change (e.g. through a decrease in impulsivity in association with growing older). In some people the vulnerability to suicide may be a life-long characteristic. They may be substantially hopeless when not depressed, and their hopelessness may be activated during recurrent depressive episodes (Young et al, 1996). Socio-economical and cultural factors influence the prevalence and expression of the vulnerability to suicide, as is shown by epidemiological research.

This chapter deals with this epidemiological research by reviewing the empirical data on the suicidal process. Epidemiological findings will be presented which will address the following questions: what is the relationship between suicidal ideation and attempted or completed suicide, what are the characteristics of people showing suicide ideation or attempted suicide, and what is the relationship between attempted suicide and completed suicide? What is currently known about suicidal careers, what about repetition of suicidal behaviour, and what about different pathways to suicide? This overview will include the available data on the size of the problem of attempted suicide, and of patterns and trends of its occurrence in divergent countries. Moreover, social and demographic characteristics, and risk factors and risk moments associated with the expression of the suicidal process will be discussed.

SUICIDAL IDEATION

Suicidal ideation may be rather harmless, e.g. in adolescents who, for the first time in their lives, face emotional problems and interpersonal conflicts. It may be a transient thought, a mental representation of one of many possible solutions, a romantic fantasy, or an occasional nightmare. Many adolescents report having had suicidal ideation when asked for in questionnaires which are administered anonymously. Questions like "have you ever (seriously) considered committing suicide when you were confronted with troubles?" reveal up to 20 per cent affirmative answers in general adolescent-population samples, and sometimes in even larger proportions of selected samples (Goldney et al, 1989; Kienhorst et al, 1991). Findings like these suggest that considering suicide as one of the possible alternatives when confronted with problems is a rather normal and prevalent way of coping in adolescents. However, in adolescents who have been sexually abused and who have injured themselves repeatedly, suicidal ideation may have a different meaning and thus be considered harmful. The same suicidal thoughts in two persons may indicate different degrees of suicide risk depending on their problem histories.

When people grow older they seem to report suicidal ideation less commonly, even when they are asked for lifetime occurrence of suicidal ideation. With advancing age the remembered seriousness of previous suicidal ideation may become less intense, or such thoughts may have been forgotten. More recent cohorts of young people may show suicidal ideation more commonly than former young generations. Suicidal ideation, however, is difficult to assess by means of anonymous questionnaires, because there may be considerable variation in what respondents mean when they report suicidal thoughts, urges or tendencies. Even clinicians may have difficulties in assessing suicidal symptoms in adolescents and young adults, as there are considerable discrepancies between their judgements and self-rated suicidality of adolescents (Joiner et al, 1999).

Suicidal ideation appears to be rather common also in adults. The 1-year prevalence of ideation among adults ranges from 2.3 per cent (Paykel et al, 1974) to 5.6 per cent (Crosby et al, 1999), while the lifetime prevalence of suicidal ideation has been shown to be 13 to 15 per cent (Crosby et al, 1999; Paykel et al, 1974; Weissman et al, 1999). A recent epidemiological study in a community sample of respondents aged 15 to 54 years in the USA revealed self-reported life time suicidal ideation in 13.5 per cent, a suicide plan in 3.9 per cent, and a suicide attempt in 4.6 per cent (Kessler et al, 1999). The transition from ideation to a suicide plan occurred in 34 per cent, and from a plan to an attempt in 72 per cent. Moreover, 26 per cent proceeded from suicide ideation to an unplanned attempt. This is not the only study suggesting the importance of impulsivity in attempted suicide, because of which the phase of planning is skipped. In another large-scale telephone survey in the USA the 12-month prevalence of suicidal ideation was estimated at 5.6 per cent, while the 12-month prevalence for a suicide plan and for a suicide attempt was estimated at 2.7 per cent and 0.7 per cent, respectively (Crosby et al, 1999). In this study at least one-third of the adults who reported attempted suicide did not report a suicide plan. Suicide plans therefore are in most cases, but not always, a precursor of attempted suicide. The same might be true for suicidal ideation, as some people who attempt suicide do not contemplate suicide or attempted suicide before that act, but act impulsively upon emotional turmoil.

Risk factors related to suicidal ideation included female gender, being previously married, age below 25 years, poor education and a psychiatric DSM-III-R disorder (Kessler et al, 1999), although these factors were less strongly related to progression from ideation to a plan or an attempt. Crosby and colleagues (1999) identified being single, unemployed, on assistance or living below the poverty level as additional risk factors.

Suicidal ideation can be expressed in many ways and may reflect many different intentions or tendencies to act. Suicidal ideation may indicate discontent with present living conditions, or may act as a warning signal for individuals in situations which are perceived as stressful. It may also function as a kind of mental preparation for the act, in the same way as an athlete mentally rehearses his bodily movements before the high jump. Suicidal ideation reflects ambivalence, it reflects the hopes and illusions for the future, it reflects the evaluations of the quality of life which co-vary with life events and changing conditions of living. Suicidal ideation may reflect threats people perceive to their self-esteem, e.g. in people who are narcissistically hurt. The occurrence of suicidal ideation may thus reflect a long-term vulnerable self-esteem, which becomes manifest in times of interpersonal conflict.

The communication of suicidal intent may mobilize others, help the person to find mental-health-care treatment, and thus may help to overcome emotional problems. In patients with severe mental illness, communication of suicidal intent may elicit quite different reactions. In general, however, the communication of suicidal intent is a very powerful appeal to others. Family members, care givers or fellow patients mostly, but not always, will react with immediate compassion. Suicidal ideation and its expression therefore may be strengthened by social reinforcement.

Suicidal ideation commonly occurs in depression, in schizophrenia and among abusers of alcohol and drugs. The most important characteristic of suicidal ideation is that it is ambivalent and fluid, and that it may fluctuate. Therefore, it is a complicated matter to relate the intensity of suicidal ideation measured at any moment to eventual suicide. This point was clearly demonstrated by Beck and colleagues (1997). In a sample of psychiatric in-patients they asked for suicidal ideation in two ways—by means of the Scale for Suicide Ideation-Current and the Scale for Suicide Ideation-Worst (SSI)—thus assessing the level of suicidal ideation at the moment of the study and at its worst point in the patient's life, respectively. Both scales were studied in relation to subsequent suicides. The SSI-Worst had a much better predictive validity than the SSI-Current, indicating that asking a patient for current suicidal ideation may not be the best question in assessing suicide risk. This issue will be discussed further in Chapters 5 and 9.

The main conclusion from research on suicidal ideation in relation to actual suicidal behaviour is that planned or unplanned suicide attempts can be characterized by a rapid onset and a high level of unpredictability, and that even among high-risk persons suicidal ideation is fluctuating and not a reliable short-term indicator of the risk of suicide. The worst level of suicidal ideation in a person's history appears to to be a better long-term predictor of suicide. Sociodemographic characteristics of suicide ideators are similar to those of suicide attempters (Weissman et al, 1999).

ATTEMPTED SUICIDE

Attempted suicide probably is a very common mental-health problem in many countries, but exact national figures are lacking. Only recently standardized procedures for monitoring the occurrence and characteristics of attempted suicide have been used in international epidemiological research. In this section an overview of empirical findings on the size of the problem, social and demographic characteristics, risk factors and risk periods, and patterns and trends for separate countries are presented. The overview is based on results from individual epidemiological studies, collaborative studies and survey studies of self-reported suicide attempts. As far as possible, comparisons between nations will be presented and associations with social indicators will be described. To facilitate understanding of the phenomenon we start with a description and definition of attempted suicide.

Description and definition

The term "attempted suicide" is an umbrella term that covers a number of different behaviours. A common characteristic of these behaviours is that people inflict acute harm upon themselves, poison or injure themselves, or try to do so, with a non-fatal outcome. Also common to these behaviours is that they occur in conditions of emotional turmoil. Suicide attempts are undertaken with a view and expectation of acute self-harm or unconsciousness as a means of realizing changes through actual or intended consequences.

In many ways, however, non-fatal suicidal behaviours differ enormously. Some attempts are aimed at dying, but the majority will have different aims, which may include the mobilization of help or a temporary escape from stress, and other attempts may have ambiguous aims. Some attempts are well prepared, while others are carried out impulsively. Attempts may result in different physical consequences, depending upon intention, preparation, knowledge of the lethality of the chosen method, and upon purely coincidental factors.

It is often difficult to determine the meaning of a suicide attempt based on overt characteristics of the behaviour or on a person's self-report. Because of the fear of consequences—such as admission to a psychiatric hospital or stigmatization, or because of psychological defence mechanisms—people sometimes deny or conceal their intentions, reflecting dissimulation tendencies. Furthermore, sometimes people who show potentially lethal self-destructive behaviour do not in fact have any wish to die, but impulsively act out a wish to change their circumstances. On the other hand, people who present at a general hospital with minor self-injury or minor self-poisoning may have had strong intentions to die, but had insufficient knowledge of the lethality of the method. All this caused Kreitman and colleagues (1969) to state that "... the term attempted suicide is highly unsatisfactory, for the excellent reason that the great majority of patients so designated are not in fact attempting suicide". Other terms such as deliberate self-poisoning, self-harm or self-injury have disadvantages as well because they "... neglect the very real association that exists between attempted suicide and completed suicide (not only repetition, but also the coincidental actions of others which may influence the outcome)". Therefore they proposed the term "parasuicide", designating "an act which is like suicide, yet is something other than suicide". This proposal has received support from researchers, but clinicians never got used to the term. In clinical practice the term "parasuicide" can only be explained with reference to the term "attempted suicide". The term "parasuicide" suffers from a similar drawback: it implies suicidal intention, which in fact may be absent (Hawton and Catalan, 1987). In recent studies, and in this chapter, the two terms therefore are being used as synonyms. For convenience, the terms "parasuicide", "attempted suicide" and "deliberate self-harm" can each be conceived as the sum of "deliberate self-injury" and "deliberate self-poisoning" (Hawton et al, 1997a).

A definition was developed for the World Health Organization/European Union Study on Parasuicide, now called the WHO/EU Study of Suicidal Behaviour (see page 22). The terms "attempted suicide" and "parasuicide" are used as equivalents and are defined as (Platt et al., 1992):

> An act with non-fatal outcome, in which an individual deliberately initiates a non-habitual behaviour that, without intervention from others, will cause self-harm, or deliberately ingests a substance in excess of the prescribed or generally recognised therapeutic dosage, and which is aimed at realising changes which the subject desired via the actual or expected physical consequences.

Attempted suicides in some cases may be conceived as failed suicides. In the vast majority of cases, however, attempted suicide should not be viewed as failed suicides, because the dynamics are often very different. This difference is reflected in the characteristics of the actors. For example, completed suicides more often concern males who are relatively old, while attempted suicides more often concern young women.

Epidemiology

There was a sharp increase in the numbers of people treated in hospitals because of intentional overdose or self-injury in Europe, the USA and Australia during the 1960s and 1970s (Weissman, 1974; Hawton and Catalan, 1987). Several studies showed a stabilization in rates in the 1980s (Platt et al, 1988; Hawton and Fagg, 1992). In the early 1990s these numbers increased again in some catchment areas (Hawton et al, 1997b). The number of persons treated for attempted suicide in general hospitals does not, however, adequately reflect the size of the problem. These numbers should be calculated against the size and the characteristics of the population in the area that is being served by the hospital. Furthermore, in some countries suicide general practitioners treat attempters when there is no need for hospital admission. In many instances attendance of emergency service following self-poisoning is not even registered. There are no national registrations that reliably monitor trends in attempted suicide seen in general hospitals. Furthermore, differences in definition of non-fatal suicidal behaviour make it difficult to compare the results of epidemiological studies. And, of course, there probably are many attempted suicides that do not come to the attention of medical professionals. Also, studies on attempted suicide have mainly been conducted in the USA, Canada, Western Europe and Australia. Few studies have been carried out in other parts of the world.

Until recently, in very few places there have been continuous monitoring studies of attempted suicide during a long period of time, in which characteristics of persons attempting suicide were related to the

some communities meet the needs of their underprivileged youngsters better than others.

Classification

As stated on page 20, there is considerable variety in behaviours within the broad category of non-fatal suicidal behaviour. A review of classification studies (Arensman and Kerkhof, 1996) revealed three types of suicide attempt(er)s: a "mild" type, a "severe" type and a "mixed" type. The "mild" type of non-fatal suicidal behaviour is carried out most commonly by means of relatively non-violent methods leading to limited physical injury. Young age, living together, few precautions to prevent discovery, low level of suicidal preoccupation, low suicidal intent and interpersonal motivation are characteristics associated with mild forms of attempted suicide. The "severe" category consists mostly of suicide attempts, which are carried out using relatively violent methods leading to serious physical consequences. Relatively old age (i.e. 40 years or older), many precautions to prevent discovery, high level of suicidal preoccupation, high suicidal intent, self-directed motivation, frequent relocation, previous attempted suicides, depression, drug dependence, high degree of overall dysfunctioning, poor physical health and a history of psychiatric treatment are characteristics associated with the concept of "severe" attempted suicide. The risk of repetition is higher in the "severe" type. In the "mixed" type of attempted suicide the attempts and the attempters show mixed characteristics, which makes this type harder to identify in medical practice.

In a further refinement study of the classification of attempted suicide, Arensman (1997) studied psychological and personal history variables in relation to recurrent non-fatal suicidal behaviour during a follow-up period of 1 year. She validated the "mild" type, which constituted approximately 40 per cent of the total sample and was characterized by being predominantly younger than 29 years of age, single, living alone or with parents, and having minor injuries because of the index attempt. The mean number of previous attempts was 3.7. The repetition rate in the follow-up period for this group was 27 per cent. In the older age group, two further groups were distinguished (i.e. one with a moderate and the other with an extremely high risk for non-fatal repetition). The high-risk group, consisting of approximately 28 per cent of the total sample, suffered more physical injury as a consequence of their act. This group predominantly consisted of females in the age range 30–49 years who were divorced or separated, living alone and who were economically inactive. A majority had made previous attempts, the mean number of previous attempts being five. They had histories of traumatic life events and experiences that mostly started early in life. A high percentage reported physical, sexual and mental maltreatment by parents in childhood and early adolescence, followed by physical and mental maltreatment by partners later in life. The females in this group more often were divorced and the total number of times they were divorced or had cohabited with a partner was significantly higher. The high-risk group showed highest scores on depression, hopelessness and expression of state-anger. Two-thirds of this high-risk group could be diagnosed as having a borderline personality disorder, which accounts for the patterns of relational and affective instability. During follow-up at least 75 per cent engaged in repeated non-fatal suicidal behaviours.

The third, or 'moderate', group was characterized by low levels of physical injury following their suicidal behaviour. This group consisted of individuals who were predominantly older than 30 and married, and scored intermediate on measures of depression, hopelessness and anger. The mean number of previous attempts was 2.3, and 33 per cent made at least one repeated attempt during follow-up. Surprisingly, no association was found between this classification and levels of reported suicide intent or reported motivations such as a wish to die, to appeal, to stop consciousness or to revenge. This latter finding underlines the difficulty of classifying attempted suicide according to intentions.

REPETITION

Repetition is one of the core characteristics of suicidal behaviour. Among individuals who commit suicide up to 44 per cent have a history of attempted suicide. Females attempted suicide in the final year before committing suicide more frequently than males (39 versus 19 per cent; Isometsä and Lönnqvist, 1998). Among suicide attempters "repeaters" are probably more common than "first-evers". Several studies have shown that between 30 and 60 per cent of suicide attempters have made previous attempts, and between 15 and 25 per cent have done so within the year before an episode (Kreitman and Casey, 1988; Platt et al, 1988, 1992; Hawton and Fagg, 1995; Isometsä and Lönnqvist, 1998). The risk of repeated suicidal behaviour is highest during the first year after a suicide attempt, and especially within the first 3–6 months (Goldacre and Hawton, 1985; Hawton and Fagg, 1988, 1995). In the WHO/EU Multicentre Study on Parasuicide it was found that at least 54 per cent of attempters had attempted before, and that 30 per cent had a history of at least two attempts. This study also showed that 30 per cent of suicide attempters made another attempt during a 1-year follow-up (Kerkhof et al, 1998; Arensman et al, submitted).

These findings underline the obvious need for knowing how to prevent repetition. Better knowledge of antecedents or risk factors may lead to early identification of persons at risk and to more efficacious treatment. Many studies have aimed at identifying such risk factors or antecedents, and some of these are now well known. Sociodemographic risk factors associated with repetition include belonging to the 25–49 age group, and being divorced, unemployed and from a lower social class. Psychiatric and psychosocial characteristics of repeaters include substance abuse, depression, hopelessness, powerlessness, personality disorders, unstable living conditions or living alone, criminal records, previous psychiatric treatment and a history of stressful traumatic life events, including broken homes and family violence. From a prospective point of view, a history of attempts predicts future non-fatal suicide attempts (Buglass and Horton, 1974; Van Egmond and Diekstra, 1989; Sakinofsky et al, 1990; Kreitman and Foster, 1991; Arensman and Kerkhof, 1996; Sakinofsky, 2000).

SUICIDE FOLLOWING ATTEMPTED SUICIDE

Suicide attempters have a high risk of committing suicide. Between 10 and 15 per cent eventually die because of suicide (Maris, 1992). Mortality as a result of suicide is higher among suicide attempters who have made previous attempts (Hawton and Catalan, 1981; Hawton and Fagg, 1988). The risk of suicide following attempted suicide is nearly twice as high among males than among females, the risk being particularly high in the first year (Suokas and Lönnqvist, 1991; Nordström et al, 1995). Alcohol and drug abuse and the social deterioration in association with these disorders are particular risk factors for subsequent suicide (Cullberg et al, 1988). Risk factors further include other psychiatric disorders such as affective disorders, schizophrenia and personality disorders, and a highly lethal, non-impulsive index suicide attempt.

PATHWAYS TO SUICIDE

Based on this review of epidemiological data at least four different pathways to suicide can be described. These pathways reflect differences in the expression of the vulnerability to suicidal behaviour.

Pathway 1: Suicide after many years of persistent suicidal ideation, planning and non-fatal suicidal behaviour

This is a relatively frequent pathway to suicide, which may occur in individuals with long-term mental illnesses such as severe depression, schizophrenia, alcohol and drug abuse, and severe personality disorders. The history of these individuals is commonly characterized by traumatization, long-term relational problems, psychiatric treatment, life-long adversity and one or more suicide attempts. This pathway reflects the most outspoken and permanent vulnerability to suicide. Mental-health care can have a preventive effect on this pathway by providing adequate treatment according to good clinical practice. This mental-health care should be provided continuously and should be prolonged even when the patient is recovering and/or discharged from hospital. Intensive management is needed in these cases. The majority of individuals with this extreme vulnerability to suicide, with many recurrent periods of intense suicidality, will, however, probably not commit suicide but die because of another reason. This depends, among others, upon the quality of the mental-health-care system. It should be noted, however, that these individuals have an increased risk of death as a result of other causes (Neeleman, 1997).

Pathway 2: Suicide following periods of recurrent suicidal ideation, planning and non-fatal suicidal behaviour

A second, relatively frequent pathway consists of episodic expressions of the underlying vulnerability, followed by periods in which people are mildly or not at all suicidal. Thus, when not confronted with adversities the vulnerability becomes latent and lies beneath a threshold, which reflects a satisfactory quality of life. This pathway illustrates the on-and-off character of many suicidal careers. Recurrent suicidal planning and suicide attempts are being elicited by life events which may be part of a normal life, such as the death of a spouse, becoming unemployed or by the absence of a therapist. Crisis-intervention facilities are needed in this type of suicidal career in combination with aftercare services for patients admitted to a general hospital following a suicide attempt. General practitioners may be helpful in monitoring the mood changes of these vulnerable patients.

Chapter 3

STRESS AND SUICIDAL BEHAVIOUR

Lil Träskman-Bendz and Åsa Westrin

INTRODUCTION

As described in Chapter 1, longitudinal and psychological autopsy studies have provided evidence for a strong association between suicidal behaviour and psychiatric disorders. There are, however, a number of reasons to separate the study of suicidal behaviour from the study of psychiatric disorders.

First, the occurrence of suicidal behaviour is not bound to the borders of classical psychiatric disorders such as depression or schizophrenia, and it is more common in some somatic disorders, such as cancer, or neurological disorders than in others (Stenager and Stenager, 1998). Second, familial transmission of suicidal behaviour occurs independently of psychiatric disorders (Brent et al, 1996). Hence the existence of one or more suicidal syndromes independent of major psychiatric disorders has been proposed (Ahrens and Linden, 1996).

Evidence is accumulating that such a syndrome can be explained, at least partly, in terms of a "stress-vulnerability" model for suicidality and depression (Coccaro and Astill, 1990; Van Praag, 1996; Deakin, 1998). Increasing possibilities to study biological characteristics of psychopathological phenomena including suicidal behaviour have led to the identification of the role of monoamines and of mechanisms within the stress system in this vulnerability (Stratakitis and Chrousos, 1995). In the next chapter Van Praag will provide a detailed example of an interaction between stress and psychological characteristics by

Understanding Suicidal Behaviour. Edited by Kees van Heeringen
© 2001 John Wiley & Sons Ltd.

describing the impact of stress-induced neuro-endocrinological changes on the regulation of anxiety and aggression. Mann and colleagues (1999) have recently proposed a comprehensive stress–diathesis model in which suicidal behaviour is considered as the consequence of an interaction between acute phenomena—'stress'—and a 'diathesis', reflecting a persistent vulnerability because of genetic factors, childhood experiences and/or dietary factors. This chapter will focus on biological aspects of suicidal behaviour by describing the processes involved in the impact of stressors on the individual.

THE STRESS SYSTEM

Basic adaptive responses to stress include *fight and flight* (i.e. a state of sudden arousal) and *withdrawal* (i.e. a state of inactivity and reduced use of energy). The former reaction is associated with an autonomic or sympathetic drive, and thus with an increased activity in the noradrenaline–adrenaline system. The latter response is related to increased activity of the hypothalamic–pituitary–adrenal (HPA) axis, leading to changes in glucocorticoid regulation. Thus, within the stress system, autonomic and neuro-endocrine actions occur and are functionally intertwined. There is, for example, a high concentration of corticotropin-releasing hormone (CRH) in the locus coeruleus (LC), which contains almost 50 per cent of the norepinephrine neurons in the brain, and there is evidence for synaptic contacts between CRH terminals and LC dentrites (Van Bockstaele et al, 1996).

The HPA axis

Pre- and postnatal stressors may affect the HPA system with lifelong consequences. Long-term stress affects one of the two known CRH receptors (i.e. CRH-1), which is localized in the hippocampus, amygdala and hypothalamus. CRH-1 receptors mediate both neuro-endocrine and behavioural or autonomic responses to stress (Holsboer, 1999).

Cortisol binds to hippocampal mineralocorticoid receptors during normal conditions. During stress, cortisol also binds to glucocorticoid receptors. Several lines of evidence suggest that the hippocampus is involved in stress-related disorders, such as depression and post-traumatic stress disorder (PTSD; Gurvits et al, 1996; Sheline et al, 1996). The hippocampus exerts an inhibitory effect on the HPA axis. In both depression and PTSD, this inhibition is suggested to be associated with

STRESS, SEROTONIN AND TEMPERAMENT

Serotonin has a protective and inhibiting effect on noradrenaline in the brain. Individuals with "a low-serotonin trait" are thus often regarded as disinhibition prone. The noradrenergic system is activated during stress, and, if neither serotonin nor social support serve as buffers, this activation may lead to an aggressive outburst, which may result in self-destructive or violent behaviour (Coccaro and Astill, 1990).

Correlational patterns, as found in CSF studies, suggest the possibility of an "uncoupling" of monoamines from each other in depressive disorders (Geracioti et al, 1997). An association between a dysfunctional serotonin system and impulsive violent behaviour has been demonstrated in patients with various psychiatric disorders (Shalling et al, 1988). The most robust findings concerning impulsivity and low-serotonin function have been reported in violent offenders (Virkkunen et al, 1989), in people with alcoholism (Linnoila et al, 1983) and in people with personality disorders of the B cluster in DSM terms (Coccaro et al, 1989).

Apart from the association between low-CSF-5-hydroxyindoleacetic acid (5-HIAA) and violent suicidal behaviour (Träskman et al, 1981), low-CSF 5-HIAA has also been demonstrated in depressed patients who attempt suicide with a high suicidal intent and/or a high medical lethality score of their severe self-harming behaviour (Malone et al, 1995; Mann and Malone, 1997).

It has been hypothesized that different parts of the serotonin system in the brain are associated with different psychopathologies, which are all of importance for stress and suicidal behaviour (Deakin, 1998). Projections from the median-raphe nuclei terminate in postsynaptic serotonin 5-HT_{1a} receptors in the hippocampus and medial frontal cortex, where serotonin is supposed to have a protective role against stress. If this stress is long lasting, the resilient role of serotonin probably disappears, resulting in dysphoria and deteriorated cognition. The dorsal-raphe nuclei are connected with prefrontal 5-HT_2 postsynaptic receptors, which are of interest for suicidality, disinhibition and aggression (Stanley and Mann, 1983). A hyperactivity of these neuronal circuits is also associated with excessive anxiety. In one of our studies we found that trait anxiety was higher in suicidal patients with major depression than in matched non-suicidal patients or healthy controls (Pendse et al, 1999). In this study, 5-HT_2 binding or function was, however, not measured.

Comorbidity of psychiatric disorders in combination with cognitive and affective disturbances and/or disinhibition is regarded as a key phenomenon in the evaluation of suicidality. As described in more detail in Chapter 7, Apter and colleagues (1990) performed a study in psychiatric in-patients using self-rating scales. They found that suicidality, impulsivity, state and trait anxiety, mood and anger were interrelated, leading them to suggest that these characteristics shared a common serotonin-related malfunctioning.

Engström and co-workers (1997) performed cluster analyses of temperament scales rated by suicide attempters. The most "severe" cluster contained impulsiveness, trait anxiety and psychoticism. Patients belonging to this cluster often repeated their suicide attempts. CSF studies of this cluster did not, however, reveal a decreased serotonin function. A significant positive correlation between impulsivity (solidity) and CSF–5-HIAA was only found in alcoholics (Engström et al, 1996). Recently, Engström and co-workers (1999) compared temperament dimensions between violent offenders and suicide attempters The results showed high trait anxiety in both populations. A trait of "indirect aggression" was more common in suicide attempters, while violent offenders had more "social desirability".

STRESS, GENETICS AND ENVIRONMENTAL FACTORS

Stressors thus induce hormonal and neuro-chemical responses, which are determined by the genetic make-up, the ability to cope with stress, personality, and social support. The first episode of a mood disorder is commonly a reaction to a severely stressful event. It has also become clear that such events may become less important as triggers of repeated episodes (Post, 1992). According to Mann and colleagues (1999), suicide attempts occur in an early phase of psychiatric illnesses. A long-term follow-up study by Brådvik and Berglund (pers. comm.) among people with severe depressive disorders (i.e. melancholias) who committed suicide, showed that females start their "suicidal career" much earlier than males. Stressful life events thus seem to be of minor importance for completed suicide, while the contribution of long-lasting stress and genetic factors should be underlined.

Genetics

A controlled familial study of adolescent suicides showed that suicide runs in families, and that suicide is associated with aggression-related traits, but not with psychiatric disorders (Brent et al, 1996). Follow-up CSF studies (Träskman-Bendz et al, 1984) and animal studies (Higley et al, 1993) have similarly shown a genetic influence on serotonergic disturbances which are related to the regulation of aggression. In the search for genes of importance for suicidal behaviour, genes related to monoamine metabolism have been studied. So far, there is no conclusive evidence that genes coding for tryptophan hydroxylase or tyrosine hydroxylase play a major role (Mann et al, 1996; Kunugi et al, 1997; Persson et al, 1997; Furlong et al, 1998; Nielsen et al, 1994). However, the first molecular genetic studies have reported polymorphisms in the tryptophan hydroxylase gene, but it seems likely that further polymorphisms will be found in other neurotransmitter systems, which are involved in the multi-determined act of suicidal behaviour (Roy et al, 2000). A genetic susceptibility to suicide is only likely to manifest itself in an individual at times of severe stress or when ill with a psychiatric disorder.

A substantial proportion of patients showing suicidal behaviour have parents with depression (mothers), alcoholism (fathers) or suicidality. These patients often score high on trait anxiety (Mann et al, 1999; Öjehagen, pers. comm.). There are twin studies indicating that genetic factors are important for both suicidality and temperament dimensions related to suicidality, such as somatic anxiety and psychasthenia (Gustavsson et al, 1996a, 1996b). The propensity to be optimistic or pessimistic seems to have a substantial genetic component (Plomin et al, 1992), as does the ability to cope with stressful events (Kendler et al, 1991).

Even though social support is defined primarily by external resources, genetic components related to temperament are of importance (Kendler et al, 1993). One enduring vulnerability factor, which is commonly mentioned in relation to social support is negative affectivity, which means a pervasive negative mood marked by anxiety, depression and hostility. Because of this pervasive negative mood, individuals may be predisposed to experience stress and distress in their lives, which in turn may affect the occurrence and type of illness, and the illness behaviour including suicidality. A number of studies have indeed provided evidence of a relationship between negative affectivity and negative health outcomes, including suicidal behaviour (Cross and Hirschfeld, 1986).

Psychosocial or environmental factors

An individual's social network plays a potential stress-buffering role (Kaplan, 1996; Magne-Ingvar, 1999). Among a person's salient social identities are those based on differentiation according to gender, socio-economic status, marital status, race, religion and ethnicity. If a person fails to meet the standards that apply to the social identities in a particular situation, distress and feelings of self-rejection will be experienced.

Environmental factors cannot be separated from personality-related characteristics. An individual's temperamental make-up defines, among others, the characteristics of their social network. For example, hostile styles during childhood may lead to a tendency to create interpersonally stressful events later in life, and to a tendency to respond to such events with hostility or anger (Adler and Matthews, 1994). Some individuals are more sensitive to environmental factors than others. Social networks, migration and even dietary factors may have protecting or reinforcing influences on stress behaviours and feelings.

Dietary characteristics have indeed recently received increasing attention, particularly with regard to tryptophan, cholesterol, fatty acids and alcohol. A tryptophan-free diet can provoke a depressed mood or aggression in vulnerable persons (Benkelfat et al, 1994; Bjork et al, 1999). Stress, genetics and dietary factors influence the metabolism of cholesterol. The association between low cholesterol concentrations, on the one hand, and low serotonin and violent deaths, on the other, has been described by several authors (Muldoon et al, 1990; Fawcett et al, 1997; Kaplan et al, 1997; Kunugi et al, 1997; Golomb, 1998). Hibbeln and Salem (1995) recently pointed at the protective effect of diets containing omega-3 fatty acids on the occurrence of depressive disorders, and they even found a significant correlation between fatty-acid concentrations and CSF 5-HIAA levels in violent alcoholics (Hibbeln et al, 1998). Studies from, among others, Finland indicate that excessive intake of alcohol can be an important risk factor for violent and impulsive behaviour such as suicide (Berglund, 1984; Makela, 1996). Over-consumption of alcohol or drugs, with or without an established diagnosis of substance-abuse disorder, can also be regarded as a risk factor for repeated suicide attempts (Magne-Ingvar et al, 1997).

The relative importance of environmental influences was recently emphasized in a study of the effect of migration on mental health in general and suicidal behaviour in particular. This study clearly showed a two-fold increased risk of suicide in foreign-born individuals when compared with the native population, and demonstrated that the risk was higher in their new country than in their country of origin (Johansson, 1997). Moreover, suicide attempts were found to be more common among foreign-born people in Sweden than in the general Swedish population (Bayard-Burfield et al, 1999).

CONCLUSIONS

In conclusion, the impact of stress on vulnerability for suicidal behaviour could be viewed from different aspects spanning from genes to religion. Within each sphere, both protecting and facilitating factors could be described, and often various systems or dimensions modulate or balance each other—all for the purpose to survive.

ACKNOWLEDGEMENTS

This chapter was supported by the Swedish Medical Research Council No. 8319, the Söderström-König Foundation, the Kock Foundation and the Sjöbring Foundation.

REFERENCES

Adler, N. and Matthews, K.A. (1994) Health and psychology: why do some people get sick and some stay well? *Annual Review of Psychology*, **45**, 229–259.

Ahrens, B. and Linden, M. (1996) Is there a suicidality syndrome independent of specific major psychiatric disorders? Results from a split half multiple regression analysis. *Acta Psychiatrica Scandinavica*, **94**: 79–86.

Apter, A., Van Praag, H.M., Plutchik, R., Sevy, S., Korn, M. and Brown, S-L. (1990) Interrelationships among anxiety, aggression, impulsivity, and mood: a serotonergically linked cluster? *Psychiatry Research*, **32**: 191–199.

Arango, V., Underwood, M.D.and Mann, J.J. (1997) Postmortem findings in suicide victims: Implications for in vivo imaging studies. *Annals of the New York Academy of Science*, **836**: 269–287.

Arató, M., Banki, C.M., Bissette, G. and Nemeroff, C.B. (1989) Elevated CSF CRF in suicide victims. *Biological Psychiatry*, **25**: 355–359.

Bayard-Burfield, L., Sundquist, J., Johansson, S.-E. and Träskman-Bendz, L. (1999) Attempted suicide among foreign-born migrants. *Archives of Suicide Research*, **5**: 43–45.

Beck, A.T., Weissman, A., Lester, D. and Trexler, L. (1974) The measurement of pessimism: the Hopelessness scale. *Journal of Consulting and Clinical Psychology*, **42**: 861–865.

Benkelfat, C., Ellenbogen, M.A., Dean, P., Palmour, R.M. and Young, S.N. (1994) Mood-lowering effect of tryptophan depletion. Enhanced susceptibility in young men at genetic risk for major affective disorders. *Archives of General Psychiatry*, **51**: 687–697.

Berglund, M. (1984) Suicide in alcoholism. *Archives of General Psychiatry*, **41**: 888–891.

Bjork, J.M., Dougherty, D.M., Moeller, F.G., Cherek, D.R. and Swann, A.C. (1999)

The effects of tryptophan depletion and loading on laboratory aggression in men: time course and food-restricted control. *Psychopharmacology*, **142**: 24–30.

Brent, D.A., Bridge, J., Honson, B.A. and Connolly, J. (1996) Suicidal behavior runs in families. *Archives of General Psychiatry*, **53**: 1145–1152.

Coccaro, E.F., Siever, L.J., Klar, H.M., Maurer, G., Cochrane, K., Cooper, T.B., Mohs, R.C. and Davis, K.L. (1989) Serotonergic studies in patients with affective and personality disorders. Correlates with suicidal and impulsive aggressive behavior. *Archives of General Psychiatry*, **46**: 587–599.

Coccaro, E.F. and Astill, J.L. (1990) Central serotonin function in parasuicide. *Progress in Neuropsychopharmacology and Biological Psychiatry*, **14**: 663–674.

Cross, C.K. and Hirschfeld, M.A. (1986) Psychosocial factors and suicidal behavior. *Annals of the New York Academy of Science*, **487**: 77–89.

Deakin, J.F.W. (1998) The role of serotonin in depression and anxiety. *European Psychiatry*, **13**: 57–63.

Dumser, T., Barocka, A. and Schubert, E. (1998) Weight of adrenal glands may be increased in persons who commit suicide. *American Journal of Forensic Medical Pathology*, **19**: 72–76.

Ekman, R., Juhasz, P., Heilig, M., Agren, H. and Costello, C.E. (1996) Novel neuropeptide Y processing in human cerebrospinal fluid from depressed patients. *Peptides*, **17**: 1107–1111.

Engström, G., Alling, C., Oreland, L. and Träskman-Bendz, L. (1996) The Marke-Nyman Temperament (MNT) scale in relationship with monoamine metabolism and corticosteroid measures in suicide attempters. *Archives of Suicide Research*, **2**: 145–159.

Engström, G., Alling, C., Gustavsson, P., Oreland, L. and Träskman-Bendz, L. (1997) Clinical characteristics and biological parameters in temperamental clusters of suicide attempters. *Journal of Affective Disorders*, **44**: 45–55.

Engström, G., Alling, C., Blennow, K., Regnéll, G. and Träskman-Bendz, L. (1999) Reduced cerebrospinal HVA concentrations and HVA/5-HIAA ratios in suicide attempters. *European Neuropsychopharmacology*, **9**: 399–405.

Engström, G., Persson, B. and Levander, S. (1999) Temperament traits in suicide attempters and violent offenders. *European Psychiatry*, **14**: 278–283.

Fauci, A.S. (1978) Mechanisms of the immunosuppressive and anti-inflammatory effects of glucocorticoids. *Journal of Immunopharmacology*, **1**: 1–25.

Fawcett, J., Busch, K.A., Jacobs, D., Kravitz, H.M. and Fogg, L. (1997) Suicide: a four-pathway clinical-biochemical model. *Annals of the New York Academy of Science*, **836**: 288–301.

Funkenstein, D., King, S. and Drolette, M. (1954) The direction of anger during a laboratory stress-inducing situation. *Psychosomatic Medicine*, **16**: 404–413.

Furlong, R.A., Ho, L., Rubinsztein, J.S., Walsh, C., Paykel, E.S. and Rubinsztein, D.C. (1998) No association of the tryptophan hydroxylase gene with bipolar affective disorder, unipolar affective disorder, or suicidal behaviour in major affective disorder. *American Journal of Medical Genetics*, **81**: 245–247.

Geracioti, T.D., Loosen, P.T., Ekhator, N.N., Schmidt, D., Chambliss, B., Baker, D.G., Kasckow, J.W., Richtand, N.M., Keck, P.E. and Ebert, M.H. (1997) Uncoupling of serotonergic and noradrenergic systems in depression: preliminary evidence from continuous cerebrospinal fluid sampling. *Depression and Anxiety*, **6**: 89–94.

Golomb, B.A. (1998) Cholesterol and violence: Is there a connection? *Annals of Internal Medicine*, **128**: 478–487.

Gurvits, T.V., Shenton, M.E., Hokama, H., Ohta, H., Lasko, N.B., Gilbertson, M.W., Orr, S.P., Kikinis, R., Jolesz, F.A., McCarley, R.W. and Pitman, R.K. (1996)

Magnetic resonance imaging study of hippocampal volume in chronic combat-related post-traumatic stress disorder. *Biological Psychiatry*, **40**: 1091–1099.

Gustavsson, J.P., Pedersen, N.L., Åsberg, M. and Schalling, D. (1996a) Origins of individual differences in anxiety proneness: a twin/adoption study of the anxiety-related scales from the Karolinska Scales of Personality (KSP). *Acta Psychiatrica Scandinavica*, **93**: 460–469.

Gustavsson, J.P., Pedersen, N.L., Åsberg, M. and Schalling, D. (1996b) Exploration into the sources of individual differences in aggression-, hostility-and anger-related (AHA) personality traits. *Personal and Individual Differences*, **21**: 1067–1071.

Harro, J. and Oreland, L. (1996) Depression as a spreading neuronal adjustment disorder. *European Neuropsychopharmacology*, **6**: 207–223.

Heilig, M. and Widerlöv, E. (1990) Neuropeptide Y: an overview of central distribution, functional aspects, and possible involvement in neuropsychiatric illnesses. *Acta Psychiatrica Scandinavica*, **82**: 95–114.

Hibbeln, J.R. and Salem, N. (1995) Dietary poly-unsaturated fatty acids and depression: when cholesterol does not satisfy. *American Journal of Clinical Nutrition*, **62**: 1–9.

Hibbeln, J.R., Umhau, J.C., Linnoila, M., George, D.T., Ragan, P.W., Shoaf, S.E., Vaughan, M.R., Rawlings, R. and Salem, N. (1998) A replication study of violent and nonviolent subjects: cerebrospinal fluid metabolites of serotonin and dopamine are predicted by plasma essential fatty acids. *Biological Psychiatry*, **44**: 243–249.

Higley, D.J., Thompson, W.W., Champoux, M., Goldman, D., Hasert, M.F., Kaeremer, G.W., Scanlan, J.M., Suomi, S.J. and Linnoila, M. (1993) Paternal and maternal genetic and environmental contributions to cerebrospinal fluid monoamine metabolites in rhesus monkeys (Macaca mulatta). *Archives of General Psychiatry*, **50**: 615–623.

Holsboer, F. (1999) The rationale for corticotropin-releasing hormone receptor (CRH-R) antagonist to treat depression and anxiety. *Journal of Psychiatric Research*, **33**: 181–214.

Hucks, D., Lowther, S., Crompton, M.R., Katona, C.L. and Horton, R.W. (1997) Corticotropin-releasing factor binding sites in cortex of depressed suicides. *Psychopharmacology*, **134**: 174–178.

Irwin, M.R., Hauger, R.L., Brown, M.R. and Britton, K.T. (1988) CRF activates autonomic nervous system and reduces natural killer cytotoxicity. *American Journal of Physiology*, **255**: R744–R747.

Johansson, L.M. (1997) Migration, mental health and suicide. An epidemiological, psychiatric and cross-cultural study. Unpublished thesis, Karolinska Institute, Stockholm, Sweden.

Kaplan, J.R., Muldoon, M.F., Manuck, S.B. and Mann, J.J. (1997) Assessing the observed relationship between low cholesterol and violence-related mortality. *Annals of the New York Academy of Science*, **836**: 57–80.

Kaplan, H.B. (Ed.) (1996) *Psychosocial Stress: Perspectives on Structure, Theory, Life-course, and Methods*. San Diego, Academic Press.

Kendler, K.S., Kessler, R.C., Heath, A.C., Neale, M. C. and Eaves, L. J. (1991) Coping: a genetic epidemiological investigation. *Psychol. Med.*, **21**(2): 337–346.

Kendler, K.S., Neale, M.C., Kessler, R.C., Heath, A.C. and Eaves, L.J. (1993). A longitudinal twin study of personality and major depression in women. *Arch. Gen. Psychiatry*, **50**(11): 853–862.

Kunugi, H., Takei, N., Aoki, H. and Nanko, S. (1997) Low serum cholesterol in suicide attempters. *Biological Psychiatry*, **41**: 196–200.

Kunugi, H., Ishida, S., Kato, T., Sakai, T., Tatsumi, M., Hirose, T. and Nanko, S. (1999) No evidence for an association of polymorphisms of the tryptophan hydroxylase gene with affective disorders or attempted suicide among Japanese patients. *American Journal of Psychiatry*, **156**: 774–776.

Lester, D. (1992) The dexamethasone suppression test as an indicator of suicide: a meta-analysis. *Pharmacopsychiatry*, **25**: 265–270.

Lester, D. (1995) The concentration of neurotransmitter metabolites in the cerebro-spinal fluid of suicidal individuals: a meta-analysis. *Pharmacopsychiatry*, **28**: 45–50.

López, J.F., Palkovits, M., Arató, M., Mansour, A., Akil, H. and Watson, S.J. (1992) Localization and quantification of pro-opiomelanocortin mRNA and glucocorticoid receptor mRNA in pituitaries of suicide victims. *Neuroendocrinology*, **56**: 491–501.

Linnoila, M., Virkkunen, M., Scheinin, M., Nuutila, A. and Rimon, R. (1983) Low cerebrospinal fluid 5-hydroxyindoleacetic acid concentration differentiates impulsive from non-impulsive violent behavior. *Life Science*, **33**: 2609–2614.

Magne-Ingvar, U., Öjehagen, A. and Träskman-Bendz, L. (1997) Suicide attempters with and without reported overconsumption of alcohol and tranquillizers. *Nordic Journal of Psychiatry*, **51**: 415–421.

Magne-Ingvar, U. (1999) Persons who attempt suicide – social characteristics, social network and significant others. Unpublished thesis, Lund University, Sweden.

Makela, P. (1996) Alcohol consumption and suicide mortality by age among Finnish men, 1950-1991. *Addiction*, **91**: 101–102.

Mann, J.J., Malone, K., Nielsen, D., Goldman, D., Erdos, J. and Gelernter, J. (1996) Possible association of a polymorphism of the tryptophan hydroxylase gene with suicidal behavior in depressed patients. *American Journal of Psychiatry*, **154**: 1451–1453.

Mann, J.J. and Malone, K.M. (1997) Cerebrospinal fluid amines and higher lethality suicide attempts in depressed inpatients. *Biological Psychiatry*, **41**: 162–171.

Mann, J.J., Waternaux, C., Haas, G.L. and Malone, K.M. (1999) Toward a clinical model of suicidal behavior in psychiatric patients. *American Journal of Psychiatry*, **156**: 181–189.

Malone, K.M., Haas, G.L., Sweeney, J.A. and Mann, J.J. (1995) Major depression and the risk of attempted suicide. *Journal of Affective Disorder*, **34**: 173–185.

Muldoon, M.F., Manuck, S.B. and Matthews, K.A. (1990) Lowering cholesterol concentrations and mortality: A quantitative review of primary prevention trials. *British Medical Journal*, **301**: 309–314.

Nemeroff, C.B., Owens, M.J., Bissette, G., Andorn, A.C. and Stanley, M. (1988) Reduced corticotropin releasing factor binding sites in the frontal cortex of suicide victims. *Archives of General Psychiatry*, **45**: 577–579

Nielsen, D., Goldman, D., Virkkunen, M., Tukola, R., Rawlings, R., Linnoila, M. (1994) Suicidality and 5-hydroxyindoleacetic acid concentration associated with a tryptophan hydroxylase polymorphism. *Archives of General Psychiatry*, **51**: 34–38.

Niméus, A., Träskman-Bendz, L. and Alsén, M. (1997) Hopelessness and suicidal behavior. *Journal of Affective Disorders*, **42**: 137–144.

Nordström, P., Schalling, D. and Åsberg, M. (1995) Temperal vulnerability in attempted suicide. *Acta Psychiatrica Scandinavica*, **92**: 155–160.

Nässberger, L. and Träskman-Bendz, L. (1993) Increased soluble interleukin-2 receptor concentrations in suicide attempters. *Acta Psychiatrica Scandinavica*, **88**: 48–52.

Ordway, G.A. (1997) Pathophysiology of the locus coeruleus in suicide. *Annals of the New York Academy of Science*, **836**: 233–252.

Ostroff, R., Giller, E., Bonese, K., Ebersole, E., Harkness, L. and Mason, J. (1982) Neuroendocrine risk factors of suicidal behavior. *American Journal of Psychiatry*, **139**: 1332–1325.

Pendse, B., Westrin, Å. and Engström, G. (1999) Temperament traits in seasonal affective disorder, suicide attempters with non-seasonal major depression and healthy controls. *Journal of Affective Disorders*, **54**: 55–65.

Persson, M.L., Wasserman, D., Geijer, T., Jonsson, E.G. and Terenius, L. (1997) Tyrosine hydroxylase allelic distribution in suicide attempters. *Psychiatry Research*, **72**: 73–80.

Plomin, R., Scheier, M.F., Bergeman, C.S., Pedersen, N.S., Nesselroade, J.R. and McClearn, G.E. (1992) Optimism, pessimism and mental health: a twin/adoption study. *Personality and Individual Differences*, **13**: 921–930.

Post, R.M. (1992) Transduction of psychosocial stress into the neurobiology of recurrent affective disorder. *American Journal of Psychiatry*, **149**: 999–1010.

Prasad, A.J. (1985) Neuroendocrine differences between violent and nonviolent parasuicides. *Neuropsychobiology*, **13**: 157–159.

Roy, A., Ågren, H., Pickar, D., Linnoila, M., Doran, A.R., Cutler, N.R. and Paul, S.M. (1986) Reduced CSF concentrations of HVA and HVA to 5-HIAA ratios in depressed patients: relationships to suicidal behavior and dexamethasone non-suppression. *American Journal of Psychiatry*, **143**: 1539–1545.

Roy, A., Nielsen, D., Rylander, G. and Sarchiapone, M. (2000) The genetics of suicidal behaviour. In Hawton, K. and Van Heeringen, K. (Eds), *The International Handbook of Suicide and Attempted Suicide*. Chichester, Wiley.

Shneidman, E.S. (1986) Some essentials of suicide and some implications for response. In Roy, A. (Ed.), *Suicide*. Baltimore, Williams and Wilkins.

Shalling, D., Edman, G., Åsberg, M. and Oreland, L. (1988) Platelet MAO activity associated with impulsivity and aggressivity. *Personality and Individual Differences*, **9**: 597–605.

Sheline, Y.I., Wang, P.W., Gado, M.H., Csernansky, J.G. and Vannier, M.W. (1996) Hippocampal atrophy in recurrent major depression. *Proceedings of the National Academy of Science*, **93**: 3908–3913.

Stein, E., McCrank, E., Schaefer, B. and Goyer, R. (1993) Adrenal gland weight and suicide. *Canadian Journal of Psychiatry*, **38**: 563–566.

Stanley, M. and Mann, J.J. (1983) Increased 5HT-2 binding sites in frontal cortex of suicide victims. *Lancet*, **1**: 214–216.

Stenager, E. and Stenager, E. (1998) *Disease, Pain and Suicidal Behavior*. Binghamton, Haworth Medical Press.

Stratakitis, C.A. and Chrousos, G.P. (1995) Neuroendocrinology and pathophysiology of the stress system. *Annals of the New York Academy of Science*, **771**: 1–18.

Szigethy, E., Conwell, Y., Forbes, N.T., Cox, C. and Caine, E.D. (1994) Adrenal weight and morphology in victims of completed suicide. *Biological Psychiatry* **36**: 374–380.

Träskman, L., Åsberg, M., Bertilsson, L. and Sjöstrand, L. (1981) Monoamine metabolites in CSF and suicidal behavior. *Archives of General Psychiatry*, **38**: 631–636.

Träskman-Bendz, L., Åsberg, M., Bertilsson, L. and Thorén, P. (1984) CSF monoamine metabolites of depressed pateints during illness and after recovery. *Acta Psychiatrica Scandinavica*, **69**: 333–342.

Träskman-Bendz, L., Ekman, R., Regnéll, G. and Öhman, R. (1992) HPA-related CSF neuropeptides in suicide attempters. *European Neuropsychopharmacology*, **2**: 99–106.

Van Bockstaele, E.J., Colago, E.E.O. and Valentino, R.J. (1996) Corticotropin-releasing factor-containing axon terminals synapse onto catecholamine dendrites and may presynaptically modulate other afferents in the rostral pole of the nucleus locus coeruleus in the rat brain. *Journal of Computational Neurology*, **364**: 523–534.

Van Praag, H.M. and Korf, J. (1971) Retarded depression and the dopamine metabolism. *Psychopharmacologia*, **19**: 199–203.

Van Praag, H.M. (1996) Faulty cortisol/serotonin interplay. Psychopathological and biological characterization of a new, hypothetical depression subtype (SeCa-depression). *Psychiatry Research*, **65**: 143–157.

Virkkunen, M., De Jong, J., Bartko, J. and Linnoila, M. (1989) Psychobiological concomitants of history of suicide attempts among violent offenders and impulsive fire setters. *Archives of General Psychiatry*, **46**: 604–606.

Wasserman, D., Hellström, C., Wasserman, J., Beck, O., Andersson, E. and Åsberg, M. (1997) Natural killer cell activity and CSF monoamine metabolites in suicide attempters. *Archives of Suicide Research*, **3**: 153–169.

Westrin, Å., Ekman, R. and Träskman-Bendz, L. (1999) Alterations of corticotropin releasing hormone (CRH) and neuropeptide Y (NPY) plasma levels in mood disorder patients with a recent suicide attempt. *European Neuropsychopharmacology*, **9**: 205–211.

Westrin, Å., Regnéll, G., Ekman, R. and Träskman-Bendz, L. (2001). A follow-up study in suicide attempters: Increase of CSF-somatostatin but no change in CSF-CRH. *European Neuropsychopharmacology*, **9**.

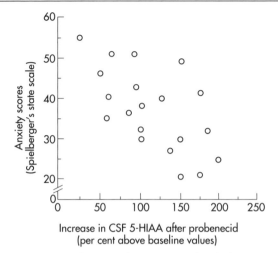

Figure 4.2   In patients with major depression, melancholic type, post-probenecid CSF 5-HIAA and trait anxiety are negatively correlated (Van Praag, 1988).

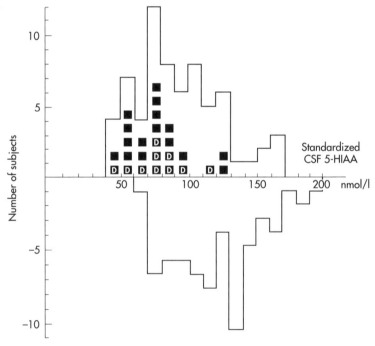

Figure 4.3   Standardized concentrations of CSF 5-HIAA in patients who have attempted suicide (*upward*) and healthy volunteer control subjects (*downward*). ■: Suicide attempts by a violent method (any method other than a drug overdose, taken by mouth, or a single wrist cut). **D**: A subject who subsequently died from suicide, in all cases but one within 1 year after the lumbar puncture (reproduced by permission of Åsberg et al, 1984).

Table 4.1 Low 5-HIAA depressives compared with normal 5-HIAA depressives present (Van Praag, 1988):

Finding	P
More suicide attempts	< 0.01
Greater number of contacts with police	< 0.05
Increased arguments with	
relatives	< 0.05
spouse	< 0.01
colleagues	< 0.05
friends	< 0.05
More hostility at interview	< 0.05
Impaired employment history (arguments)	< 0.05

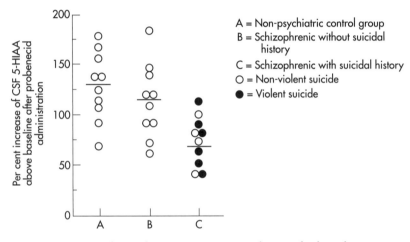

Figure 4.4 Post-probenecid CSF 5-HIAA in non-depressed schizophrenic patients with (C) and without (B) suicidal histories and in non-psychiatrically disturbed controls (A). The 5-HIAA levels in the suicidal group are significantly decreased. ○: Non-violent suicide; ●: violent suicide (Van Praag, 1983).

same appears to hold for outward-directed aggression, as a correlation between low-CSF 5-HIAA and increased levels of aggression was found in a variety of personality disorders (Figure 4.6; Brown et al, 1979; Coccaro et al, 1992). This association is particularly evident if the (auto-)aggressive behaviour is of an impulsive nature (Cremniter et al, 1999).

Another indication suggesting a relationship between 5-HT availability in the brain and the regulation of aggressive impulses is provided by the tryptophan-depletion method. This method leads to a rapid 5-HT depletion in the brain, and causes in healthy males an increase in

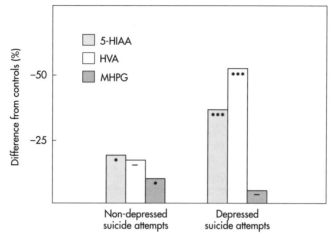

Figure 4.5 Differences in CSF monoamine levels (adjusted for age and height) between controls and depressed and non-depressed suicide "attempters". Symbols indicate significance levels of differences from mean of controls at following levels: minus sign, $p > 0.05$; asterisk, $p \leq 0.05$; and three asterisks, $p \leq 0.001$. 5-HIAA indicates 5-hydroxyindoleacetic acid; HVA, homovanillic acid; and MHPG, 3-methoxy-4-hydroxyphenyl glycol (reproduced by permission of Träskman et al, 1981).

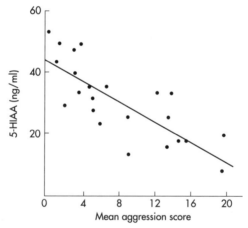

Figure 4.6 The relationship of aggression scores in young male subjects with personality disorders to CSF 5-HIAA (reproduced by permission of Brown et al, 1979).

objective and subjective aggression, in particular in those with high-trait aggression (Cleare and Bond, 1995).

Moreover, the level of 5-HIAA in the cerebrospinal fluid has predictive value, as suicidal probands with low-CSF 5-HIAA at the index admission showed an increased risk of repeated suicide attempts in the

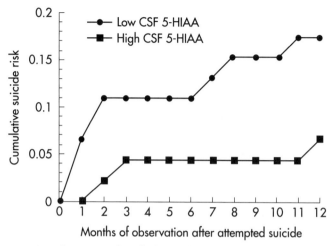

Figure 4.7 Cumulative suicide risk during first year after attempted suicide in patients with low versus high CSF concentrations of 5-HIAA. Filled circles indicate CSF 5-HIAA concentrations below the sample median and filled squares indicate concentrations above the sample median (reproduced by permission of Nordström et al, 1994).

Table 4.2 CSF 5-HIAA and risk of antisocial behaviour (Constantino et al, 1997)

	CSF 5-HIAA
Infants who had parents with antisocial personality disorder	735 pmol/ml (SD = 167)
Infants with negative family histories of antisocial personality disorder	827 pmol/ml (SD = 210)

following year (Figure 4.7; Nordström et al, 1994). A similar suggestion that CSF levels of 5-HIAA may have predictive value is provided by the finding of Constantino and colleagues (1997) who reported that the CSF concentration of 5-HIAA in newborns with a family history of antisocial behaviour was lower than that in newborns without such a history (Table 4.2).

In subhuman primates it has been shown that a global decrease in serotonergic functioning increases aggressive responding, while increasing serotonergic activity attenuates those responses (Higley et al, 1993; Mehlman et al, 1994).

The association between 5-HT disturbances and states of increased aggression, suicidality and anxiety is not surprising if one takes into account, first, that in humans these affective states are highly correlated across diagnoses (Apter et al, 1990), and, second, that both in animals and humans serotonergic circuits play an important role in the regulation of both anxiety and aggression (Cologer-Clifford et al, 1997; Saudou et al, 1994; Van Praag, 1996).

It can thus be concluded that disturbances in the serotonin metabolism, which were originally discovered in a subgroup of depression, appear to be nosologically non-specific, and correlate with violence, suicidality and anxiety. These affective states are psychopathological phenomena that are highly correlated and not specific for any particular diagnosis.

SEROTONIN RECEPTOR FUNCTION AND AFFECTIVE STATE

Not only the 5-HT metabolism was shown to be disturbed in a subgroup of depression. Dysfunctions of the 5-HT receptor have also been demonstrated, using challenge tests. Initially, presynaptic and thus indirectly acting 5-HT agonists were used. These are substances that do not bind to 5-HT receptors directly, and thus activate the 5-HT system as a whole. Fenfluramine, a 5-HT releaser and re-uptake inhibitor, is a good example of such a substance. Hormonal responses to this substance were repeatedly shown to be blunted in a subgroup of depressed patients, indicating a down-regulation of (parts of) the 5-HT-receptor system (Cowen and Wood, 1991; Deakin et al, 1990).

One of the 5-HT receptor subtypes involved in the down-regulation is the 5-HT_{1a} receptor, as was concluded from blunted hormonal responses to challenges with substances that bind specifically to these receptors and activate them, such as ipsaperone (Lesch et al, 1990). Some data suggest that the response to m-chlorophenylpiperazine, a 5-HT_{2c} receptor agonist, can be augmented in patients who suffer from (anxious) depression (Kahn et al, 1985). The latter phenomenon might be secondary to the down-regulation of 5-HT_{1a} receptors, since the two receptor systems are reciprocally linked, so that down-regulation of one system leads to up-regulation of the other (Krebs-Thomson and Goyer, 1998).

Are the 5-HT-receptor dysfunctions associated with depression, as such, or with a disturbed regulation of anxiety and aggression, irrespective of diagnosis, similar to metabolic-5-HT disturbances? Though the jury is still out on this issue, the available evidence suggests the latter. As shown in Figure 4.8, hormonal responses to

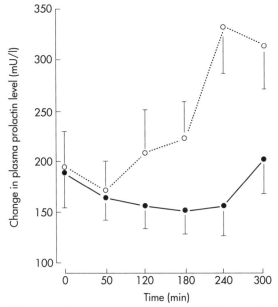

Figure 4.8   Plasma prolactin responses over time, following the administration of 30 mg d-fenfluramine, in nine patients with antisocial personality disorder (●−●) and nine healthy controls (○−○). Results are expressed as group means, with error bars showing SEM (reproduced by permission of O'Keane et al, 1992).

fenfluramine, for instance, are blunted not only in a subtype of depression, but also in personality-disturbed individuals with increased aggression (Manuck et al, 1998; Moss et al, 1990; O'Keane et al, 1992).

In addition, indications for an up-regulation of the 5-HT$_2$ receptor system have not only been found in depression, but also in states of increased anxiety, independently of psychiatric diagnosis (Figure 4.9; Kahn and Wetzler, 1991).

In summary then, in certain types of depression indications of a disturbed 5-HT-receptor function have been found, particularly of the 5-HT$_{1a}$ and 5-HT$_{2c}$ receptor systems. In animals, the 5-HT$_{1a}$ and the 5-HT$_{2c}$ receptor systems have been shown to play an important role in the regulation of aggression and anxiety. Furthermore, it can be concluded, though cautiously, that the same line of reasoning applies to the 5-HT-receptor disturbances as to the disturbances in 5-HT metabolism. The receptor disturbances apparently are functionally specific, and not categorically specific, indicating that they are associated with a dysfunction in psychological domains, particularly the regulation of anxiety and aggression, irrespective of psychiatric diagnosis.

An acquired or genetically determined defect of corticosteroid-receptor gene expression is conceivable in depression (Barden et al, 1995; Berrittini et al, 1995; Dinan, 1994; Murphy et al, 1991). This could lead to a marginal glucocorticoid feedback inhibition in normal conditions and early failure of this mechanism under stressful conditions. Affected individuals would thus be particularly vulnerable to the stress syndrome, and possibly to depression.

In support of this hypothesis, Barden and colleagues (1995) found that several types of antidepressants increase corticosteroid-receptor gene expression, increase the capacity of brain tissue to bind corticosteroids, and, finally, increase steroid-receptor immunoreactivity in the brain. In this way, feedback inhibition of HPA-axis activity by cortisol will be increased. The time course of the action of antidepressants on corticosteroid-receptor concentration follows that of clinical improvement (Reul et al, 1993, 1994). On these grounds it has been suggested that the therapeutic effect of antidepressants is related to normalization of HPA-axis activity (Barden et al, 1995).

On the other hand, one has to acknowledge that activation of the HPA axis is the core endocrine response to stress, irrespective of the development of depression. Cortisol-plasma levels have been found to correlate with anxious anticipation (Ceulemans et al, 1985) and negative affect (Buchanan et al, 1999). Dexamethasone non-suppression has been found in many psychiatric diagnoses, apart from depression (Coppen et al, 1983). Similarly, the reduced ACTH response to CRH is not diagnostically specific, as it has also been reported in panic disorder and anorexia nervosa (Checkley, 1992). Moreover, in anxiously depressed patients the blunting of the CRH–ACTH response is more pronounced than in those who suffer from non-anxious depression (Meller et al, 1995).

Thus, the HPA axis is activated in a subgroup of depression, leading to an overproduction of cortisol. It is unknown whether this phenomenon is specific for a particular type of depression, or whether it is part of the stress syndrome that precedes the depression and is subsequently sustained by the depression.

The interaction between serotonin and the HPA axis

Increased plasma concentrations of cortisol have a pronounced effect on the central serotonergic system, which is carried into effect via, at least, two mechanisms. First, sustained stress or sustained hypercortisolaemia reduces the metabolism of 5-HT (Weiss et al, 1981), possibly

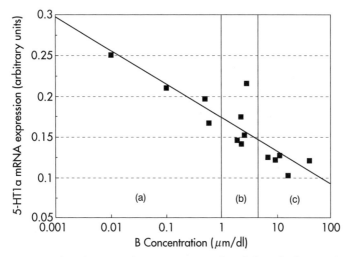

Figure 4.10   Adrenalectomized rats were treated with low, high, very high doses or no corticosterone replacement. The relationship between plasma corticosterone levels and 5-HT$_{1a}$ expression measured in the dentate gyrus. Hormone levels are on a logarithmic scale. $r^2 = 0.86$; (a) no corticosterone; (b) low corticosterone; (c) (very) high corticosterone (reproduced by permission of Meijer and De Kloet, 1994).

via activation of the enzyme tryptophan pyrrolase and the shunting of large amounts of tryptophan to the kinurenine pathway, leaving insufficient amounts of tryptophan for synthesis of 5-HT (Maes et al, 1990). A second mechanism is the reduced expression of 5-HT$_{1a}$ receptors caused by excess cortisol (Figure 4.10; Meijer and De Kloet, 1994).

As the two systems are reciprocally related, a reduced number or a reduced responsivity of the 5-HT$_{1a}$ receptor system leads secondarily to a hyperactivity of the 5-HT$_{2c}$ system.

Diminished activity in 5-HT$_{1a}$ circuits and increased activity in the 5-HT$_{2c}$ system will cause a destabilization in the regulation of anxiety and aggression (Van Praag, 1996), and thus lead to an increased risk of suicidal behaviour.

BIOLOGICAL VULNERABILITY FOR SUICIDAL BEHAVIOUR

Human existence is a journey along events, some of which are pleasurable and others may be traumatic. A majority of individuals are capable of coping with the latter; some, however, do not succeed in doing so and will show symptoms of depression, anxiety and/or suicidal behaviour.

Obviously not everyone resorts to suicide when pressures mount. Hence, one has to postulate a vulnerability to suicide. Generally speaking, increased propensity to resort to suicide is linked to personality make-up, to traits that hamper adequate mobilization of defence mechanisms (Nordström et al, 1995). As has been discussed, vulnerability to suicide can in addition be conceived of in biological terms. In order to provide the biological hypothesis of suicide with the substance of credibility, one has to make it plausible that the biological factors suggested to be involved (i.e. 5-HT disturbances and hyper-responsivity of the HPA axis) are chronically present and thus can be regarded as trait characteristics.

This has indeed been demonstrated. First, low-CSF 5-HIAA does not disappear after remission of the depression (Figure 4.11; Van Praag, 1988). Animal experiments have revealed that CSF 5-HIAA is a strongly genetically determined and stable characteristic (Higley et al, 1993; Oxenstierna et al, 1986). Moreover, as shown in Table 4.4, the prolactin response to fenfluramine does not normalize after remission in patients who showed a blunted response while being depressed (Flory et al, 1998). Thus, both the disturbances in 5-HT metabolism and those in the 5-HT-receptor function can be characterized as trait factors.

Initially, signs of HPA axis overactivity in a subgroup of depressed patients were thought to recede after remission of the depression. Thus it was concluded that disinhibition of the HPA axis was a state-related factor. Recent studies, however, have shed a different light on this subject. First, it was demonstrated that HPA-axis overactivity does not disappear completely. This was demonstrated with the dexamethasone–CRH test (Dex–CRH test), a refined variant of the dexamethasone suppression test (Holsboer-Trachsler et al, 1991; Von Bardeleben and Holsboer, 1991). Moreover, Modell and colleagues (1998) found an abnormal Dex–CRH test in healthy probands with a high genetic loading for affective disorders. The cortisol response fell between that of a control group and a group of depressed patients. Moreover, the outcome of the Dex–CRH test remained remarkably stable over time. This finding suggests that (mild) HPA-axis hyperactivity is a trait-related factor (Figure 4.12).

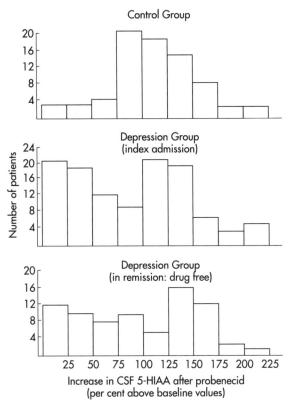

Figure 4.11 Increase in CSF 5-HIAA concentration after probenecid in patients suffering from major depression, melancholic type (endogenous depression; vital depression) and in a non-psychiatric control group. The columns indicate the number of patients. The increase in concentration is shown at the bottom of the column. As compared with the control group, there is significant increase in individuals with low CSF 5-HIAA in the depression group at the time of the index admission. After remission this value is still significantly increased (Van Praag, 1988).

A BIOLOGICAL SUSCEPTIBILITY TO SUICIDE AND ITS CONSEQUENCES FOR TREATMENT

Based on the data discussed above, I hypothesize that in a subgroup of the normal population the HPA axis is habitually slightly over-responsive.

The HPA system thus overreacts in times of stress, ultimately leading to excessive release of cortisol. The overproduction of cortisol causes a decline in synthesis of 5-HT, a down-regulation of the 5-HT_{1a} system and an up-regulation of the 5-HT_{2c} receptor system. Individuals in

Table 4.4　Plasma fenfluramine, norfenfluramine and prolactin levels in women and men with and without a past history of a major depressive episode (Flory et al, 1998).

	Depression history			
	Women		Men	
	+	−	+	−
Fenfluramine dose/weight (kg)	0.61 (0.08)[a]	0.64 (0.08)	0.63 (0.07)	0.64 (0.06)
Fenfluramine (ng/ml)	44.6 (14.0)	44.8 (11.5)	43.9 (12.6)	51.7 (17.6)
Norfenfluramine (ng/ml)	9.9 (4.1)	9.7 (4.5)	8.9 (2.5)	11.7 (4.3)
Baseline prolactin (ng/ml)	8.1 (6.8)	7.1 (3.2)	5.5 (1.7)	7.0 (3.4)
Max Δ prolactin (ng/ml)	3.2 (2.3)	6.3 (5.9)	2.6 (2.0)	3.4 (4.5)[b,c]

[a] Numbers presented are means and standard deviations.
[b] Depression history main effect, $p = 0.048$.
[c] Sex main effect, $p = 0.02$.

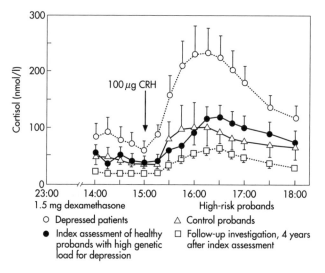

Figure 4.12　Plasma ACTH and cortisol concentrations (mean ± SEM) in dexamethasone-pretreated subjects before and after intravenous CRH injection (reproduced by permission of Modell et al, 1998).

whom the serotonin system already functions marginally are particularly prone to this effect.

As a result of the disturbances in the 5-HT_{1a} and 5-HT_{2c} receptor-regulated circuits the anxiety level increases and self-directed aggressiveness tend to rise above the still manageable level. Both factors increase the likelihood of suicidal behaviour.

From a therapeutic point of view, this hypothesis implies that rational biological suicide prevention is a conceivable concept. One can predict such an action from compounds that antagonize the actions of CRH and/or cortisol, and from serotonin agonists, particularly those that activate the 5-HT$_{1a}$ receptor system.

CRH and cortisol antagonist are presently studied with regard to their antidepressant potential, and the first reports appear to be promising (Arana et al, 1995; Missagh Ghadirian et al, 1995; O'Dwyer et al, 1995; Thakore and Dinan, 1995; Wolkowitz et al, 1993). Studies on their impact on suicidal behaviour per se are not yet available.

There is some emerging evidence that serotonin agonists decrease the strength of suicidal impulses. Montgomery and colleagues (1995) found that the selective serotonin re-uptake inhibitor paroxetine reduces suicidal thoughts more strongly than the reference tricyclic antidepressants and placebo. Verkes and colleagues (1998) showed a significant efficacy of paroxetine in patients with recurrent suicidal behaviour but no major depression.

Until recently no selective full post-synaptically acting 5-HT$_{1a}$ agonists were available. The buspirone group of compounds act as partial 5-HT$_{1a}$ receptor agonists in the hippocampus, but as 5-HT$_{1a}$ receptor antagonists in the frontal cortex. Borsini and colleagues (1994, 1998) recently developed the compound flibanserin that acts as a full agonist of 5-HT$_{1a}$ receptors, both in the hippocampus and in the frontal cortex. Based on the propounded hypothesis it can be predicted that this substance will exert anti-suicidal effects.

A caveat needs to be made here. Increased biological specificity of a psychopharmacological compound will probably lead to increased psychopathological specificity. In other words, the study of the effects of a biologically highly specific compound on psychopathological phenomena in depression, without further symptomatological or biological specification, is bound to weaken possible therapeutic signals. The study of drugs with high biological specificity requires precise syndromal and symptomatological definition of the study group and the introduction of biological diagnostic criteria, if available (Van Praag, 1995, 1992, 1997, 1998). I predict that flibanserin will exert an anti-suicidal effect in depressed and/or personality-disordered individuals with marked symptoms of anxiety and aggression and with signs of disturbed serotonergic functioning (i.e. a lowering of CSF 5-HIAA and blunted hormonal responses to flibanserin) and, in addition, signs of HPA-axis overactivity as indicated by the Dex–CRH test.

Chapter 5

PSYCHOLOGICAL ASPECTS OF THE SUICIDAL PROCESS

J. Mark G. Williams and Leslie R. Pollock

INTRODUCTION

Our aim in this chapter is to illustrate with some examples from our own and others' research what a psychological model can do to help our understanding of suicide and self-harm. In particular, we need to address the question of whether psychology can add anything to social or biological models. On the social side, there is overwhelming evidence that people who harm or kill themselves have experienced a large number of social stresses in their recent or remote past. Life events and difficulties—such as abuse, bullying, poverty, and social isolation—are undeniably linked to the increased risk of suicidal behaviour (e.g. see Van Egmond et al, 1993 and chapters 3 and 5 in Williams, 1997 for a review). When such evidence of external stresses exists, why search for psychological variables to explain suicidal behaviour? However, the fact that there are many more people with severe social problems who do not commit or attempt suicide encourages clinicians and researchers to look for psychological factors that may mediate the relationship between stressful events and suicidal responses.

On the other hand, of course, biological explanations for suicidal behaviour (see Chapters 3 and 4) appear to present a different sort of challenge for psychosocial models. Biological and genetic research is making good progress in determining who is vulnerable for the sort of violent and impulsive behaviour that characterizes much suicidal behaviour (Kety, 1990). Biological research has focused on examining the

Understanding Suicidal Behaviour. Edited by Kees van Heeringen
© 2001 John Wiley & Sons Ltd.

levels of the main serotonin metabolite 5-hydroxyindoleacetic acid (5-HIAA), which is a marker for serotonin. The relationship between suicidal behaviour and low cerebrospinal fluid (CSF) 5-HIAA first demonstrated in 1976 has now been found in over 20 studies (Åsberg, 1997). The evidence on the role and effects of the serotonergic system is reviewed in detail in Chapter 4.

What implication does this work have for psychosocial theories? If we can understand the long-term and short-term vulnerabilities in the neurotransmitter mechanisms that underlie suicide and suicidal behaviour, will this not dispose of the need for both social and psychological theory? We do not believe so. There is evidence that biological mechanisms are themselves triggered by events in the environment. Furthermore, the nature and intensity of the biological reaction to such events is determined by the person's learning history. For example, a person's biological stress responses to failure are governed by their previous experience of failures at school, in important relationships or at work. This previous experience includes both the actual experience, and the extent to which the person has come to believe that their reaction to the experience confirms they are "weak" or a total failure as a person.

However, it is not enough for psychologists to build their explanations in isolation. It is important to keep in mind how psychological explanations fit with social facts, on the one hand, and biological/genetic facts on the other. We are not engaged in a race in which either social, psychological or biological facts will win. Instead, we must look for how our different facts and theories can fit together. As psychologists, we need to keep in mind that psychological processes must fit with and illuminate life events and biological research. We start with an example of a striking phenomenon from the field of animal behaviour, since this field represents a place where biological, psychological and social theories can meet, as will be described in more detail in Chapter 7.

Consider the behaviour of birds establishing their territories. If birds meet within a single putative territory, they engage in aggressive displays. One wins, the other loses. The loser flies away to find another territory. It suffers little ill effects from its encounter. But if this meeting occurs in a limited territory, in a cage or other circumstance in which the defeated cannot escape, it is a different story. We quote from an early description of what happens then:

> Its behaviour becomes entirely changed. Deeply depressed in spirit, humbled, with drooping wings and head in the dust, it is overcome with paralysis, although one cannot detect any physical injury.

The bird's resistance now seems broken, and in some cases the effects of the psychological conditions are so strong that the bird sooner or later comes to grief.

(cited in Price and Sloman (1987) and discussed in Paul Gilbert's (1989) *Human Nature and Suffering*, to whom we are grateful for pointing out the analogy)

While it is dangerous to jump too readily from animal to human behaviour, there are still good reasons to allow such observations to help in generating *hypotheses* about what psychosocial and biological processes might underlie some human behaviour. In this chapter we wish to explore the possibility (a) that there exists an analogous reaction in humans, and (b) that this reaction is relevant to understanding suicidal behaviour.

Note certain things from the bird example. First, that the behaviour occurs in the absence of physical damage. Second, that the defeat itself is not sufficient to trigger the response. If the bird can escape to another territory, it shows no ill effect. It is the combination of *defeat* and the *lack of escape* that is needed for the reaction to occur (what Gilbert calls "arrested flight").

Third, Gilbert points out that research findings from the field of learned helplessness shows that, if animals that are showing these reactions are removed from the situation, they will recover, but it will take some time, perhaps up to 48 hours. This has suggested to many that what the defeat has done is to trigger an evolutionary primitive biological process, a biological process that then takes time to recover. So we have a third factor in the equation in addition to "defeat" and "no escape". We have the presence or *absence of rescue factors* that will determine how long-lasting the reaction is.

Turning now to the human parallel, we wish to explore the *Cry of Pain* hypothesis (Williams, 1997) that, in humans, similar biological scripts can be switched on by psychological representations. According to this model, suicidal behaviour represents the response (the "cry") to a situation that has these three components: defeat, no escape and no rescue (real or imagined). So if someone is exposed to (or is hypersensitive to) social signals that represent defeat, no escape and no rescue, they are likely to be vulnerable to the triggering of primitive "helplessness" biological processes (see Figure 5.1).

Figure 5.1 illustrates the role of internal and external stresses (especially those that signal defeat, reversal, loss or rejection). These need to be combined with an inability to see a way of escaping, or of being rescued to cause the biologically mediated "helplessness script" to be activated. The activation of this script is required to support the

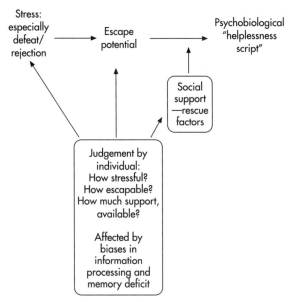

Figure 5.1 Internal and external stresses (especially those that signal defeat, reversal, loss or rejection) combined with differences in a person's ability to see a way of escaping or being rescued, causes the helplessness biological script to be activated. The strength of the activation of the script is moderated by information-processing biases that affect the perceived aversiveness and likelihood of escape and rescue.

impulse to escape by self-harm or by dying. At this point, whether someone acts on the impulse may depend on the availability of models to be imitated (see page 89) and the availability of methods. The effect of seeing no escape by any other means, and especially whether or not rescue is perceived to be likely, is moderated by the presence of social "closeness" or *perceived* social "closeness", the opportunities to both receive and give emotional and instrumental support. There are gender differences in the perception and use of such opportunities, men having (or taking) less opportunities (Murphy, 1998). Psychological processes intervene at important points in the causal pathway through biases in information processing, which distort a person's estimates of the aversiveness of defeat, its escapability and how much rescue via social support is available. Let us look at each of these psychological processes in turn to see if evidence exists to support the model.

SENSITIVITY TO SIGNALS OF DEFEAT

In looking for evidence of a psychological process that renders a person particularly sensitive to stimuli signalling possible or actual defeat or "loser status" we need to look at the literature on attention. Consider a patient TS, who is anxious and depressed. He is becoming preoccupied with his inability to work. He feels defeated, that he is a loser. He tells the therapist that "there are so many suicide stories in the newspapers". His wife is becoming more and more angry with him ruminating about these things. She says there are no more of such stories than usual. He is simply noticing them more. Experimental evidence suggests that she may well be right. There is a well-described phenomenon called "perceptual pop-out" in which a stimulus that is of great interest to a person (a current concern) appears to "jump out" at a person. This is closely related to one's ability to hear one's own name, even across a crowded room at a party (hence called the "cocktail party phenomenon"). As such it is a normal perceptual/attentional process, ensuring that one does not "miss" information that is important for one's well-being. It occurs when one is buying a new car (suddenly one sees many such types of car on the road) or buying a house (the salience of "For Sale" signs increases dramatically).

Research has found that the way in which such salient items "pop out" is almost completely involuntary (see chapters 4 and 5 in Williams et al, 1997 for a review). In Figure 5.2 we can imagine how the word "DEAD" might appear to "pop out" for the patient TS, even when effectively hidden within the other letters for other readers. Similarly, for someone who is sensitive (or has been made sensitive by their circumstances), their world will appear to have many more aspects which refer to defeat and rejection. At the point in their lives when they most need to have relief from stress and pressure, the attentional bias causes them instead to be bombarded with stimuli signalling that they are a loser. What might start as a voluntary rumination becomes more automatic and involuntary, out of the person's control.

The evidence that this process occurs in suicidal people comes from research on the emotional Stroop task (see Williams et al, 1996 for a review). In this task the person is shown a series of words that are

```
L A L F L T L W P A S T E C G F
T D K W B N D A O K F D Y H H
N G V L D E A D T H P S Y O D
D P C H A C I T H K K L D T V Y
J D A G C A R S K O H U W D T
```

Figure 5.2 An illustration of "perceptual pop-out". Someone who was overconcerned with dying may see the word "DEAD" sooner than other words in this array of letters.

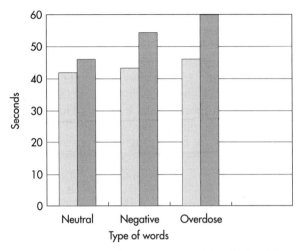

Figure 5.3   Emotional Stroop performance in suicidal (right-hand bars) and controls (left-hand bars). Suicidal individuals are slower to name the colours in which words are printed if their attention is captured by the meaning of the word (e.g. negative word such as *hopeless* or overdose word such as *drug*).

printed in coloured inks. The task is to call out the colours in which the words are printed, as fast as possible but making as few errors as possible. A large number of studies have shown that, if the meaning of the word is salient (i.e. tends to "pop out") there will be interference with the naming of the colour. Colour naming slows down on those words that are particularly salient for the patient because they are distracted by the word's meaning. Because the attentional pop-out is involuntary, it is difficult for the patient to avoid slowing down their colour naming on these words.

Figure 5.3 shows the results of an experiment in which patients who had recently taken an overdose were asked to name the colours of 50 words (actually five words repeated ten times, printed in five different colours) (Williams and Broadbent, 1986). The words were either neutral (e.g. folded, structure), generally negative (e.g. hopeless, lonely) or related to overdose (e.g. drug, fatal). The neutral words were included as controls for the negative words, and to check that the overdose patients were not merely slower on everything. The patients' time taken to colour name the 50 words was compared with the time taken by a control group of patients who were recruited from the same general-hospital wards.

The results showed clear evidence of attentional bias (perceptual pop-out). Overdose patients were slowed down in their colour naming of words signalling defeat and rejection, and, given their recent history, particularly slowed down by words concerning the overdose. Such involuntary hypersensitivity to stimuli signalling "loser" status increases the risk that the defeat response will be triggered. The clinical implication is that we need to work with patients in helping them to identify when such hypersensitivity may be occurring: noticing the tendency, even if only responding to it by marking a piece of paper. Their task is to begin to "notice the noticing". For only when they have started to see what is happening to their own attentional processes can they begin to distance themselves from its effects, and start to seek solutions. But as we know, finding solutions itself can be an immensely difficult process. This brings us to our second psychological process. Recall that we observed that the defeat (or signals of defeat) were not enough to trigger the full-blown reaction. There also needed to be the sense of "no escape", "entrapment", "arrested flight".

THE SENSE OF BEING TRAPPED

Numerous studies have pointed out the importance of problem-solving difficulties in suicidal patients (see Pollock and Williams, 1998 for a review). Our analysis suggests that problem-solving difficulties in themselves are not important. It is the fact that they indicate to the person "there is no escape" which makes them significant. If one cannot define a problem, if one cannot generate some ideas about how to solve it, if one cannot decide what to do, then the sense of being trapped is never likely to be far away. How do such problem-solving difficulties arise?

Our research suggests that a critical aspect of a person's ability to solve current problems is their ability to access past events from their lives. But not any type of memory will do. Quite by chance, some years ago, we discovered that people give different types of memory responses when asked about their past (see Williams, 1996 for a review). Imagine being asked to recall an event from your past that made you happy. It could come from the recent past, or from a long time ago. People normally have little difficulty in retrieving an example: "when I got top marks in Maths"; "when my daughter brought me a bunch of flowers in from the garden"; "the day we collected our new puppy".

We found that suicidal patients tend to give a type of response, which, though similar in some ways, differs in one important respect. Take, for example, the following responses: "when people give me presents", "getting good marks at school", "taking the dog for a walk every Sunday when we used to live near the beach". Notice that these do not mention a specific event. Instead they are summaries of a number of events. It is as if these patients have "stopped short" of retrieving the specific event, even though the event they were searching for was unlikely to be traumatic. It is possible that such patients suffer from a large number of intrusive memories from the past, and have adopted a strategy of overgeneral memory to regulate their emotion. They stop short of recalling specifics lest it brings up an event that might remind them of a difficulty or a trauma. This occurs for positive as well as negative recall.

There have now been several studies, in both suicidal patients (Evans et al, 1992; Sidley et al, 1997; Pollock and Williams, in press) and in patients suffering from depression (Goddard et al, 1996), showing that these types of vague, summary memories reduce a person's ability to solve interpersonal problems. To generate potential solutions to problems, a person needs to have access to the past in some detail. The past is their "database" from which to seek hints for how to deal with current problems. Overgeneral memories prevent a person from efficient use of their own "database". It is as if a person was trying to look something up in an encyclopaedia, but got stuck at the Index. An index is a useful tool for navigating around a large dataset, but it is no substitute for the data itself.

For example, if a person feels defeated or rejected, it would be helpful for them to have efficient access to specific times in the past when they have felt successful, loved or respected. An overgeneral memory that summarizes a number of occasions (e.g. I used to go for walks with friends) is less useful than even one specific occasion (e.g. I was out for a walk last month when I met Tim and we went back for a drink). The specific event contains within it more "hints" for ways to solve current problems (there is "the walk", "Tim", "the drink", and the possibility that these items would also cue other aspects, such as the topics they talked about). So the specific memory contains within it several cues to help generate ideas about what action might be taken to escape from the feeling of defeat and rejection.

The clinical implications of these findings are that, should therapist and patient become stuck during therapy (e.g. when attempting to generate alternative approaches to problems), it may help the patient to know the possible reasons why they may be having difficulty, and to practice detailed recollection of past events (e.g. starting by recalling relatively neutral events from the past week). It is interesting to note how Dialectical Behaviour Therapy (DBT; Linehan, 1993a), includes very detailed rehearsal of each component of what led to any and all occasions between and within sessions where suicidal urges or behaviour occurred. Further, DBT-skills training for such borderline patients include a mindfulness component. This component aims to help patients focus on moment-by-moment experience in a non-judgemental way. As a result, it is likely that patients learn to *encode* events in a more specific, and less schematic way. So, if a friend passed the patient in the street without seeing them, the patient might normally have come rapidly to the conclusion that this was just one more (typical) occasion when someone rejected them. Following mindfulness training, they would be more likely to notice some other details about the event: that the traffic was busy, or that their friend was not wearing their glasses, information that might suggest alternative explanations. In fact, a recent study examining the impact of mindfulness training in preventing relapse in depression shows that such training can reduce the tendency to be overgeneral in memory (Williams et al, 2000).

We have suggested that if patients can adopt a more specific retrieval style, this will give them a better database for solving their current problems. This, in turn, will reduce the sense that there is "no escape", the feeling of being trapped. We should sound a note of caution, however. We have assumed, on the basis of the evidence linking overgeneral memory with the occurrence of trauma, that such a retrieval style is adaptive for them, perhaps as an affect regulation strategy. If this is true, then moving to a more specific style of encoding and retrieval will not be a trivial change. At first, it may be seen as too dangerous a strategy, and result in increased mood disturbance (Williams et al, 1999). Such increases in disturbance, especially if they are felt to be uncontrollable, may exacerbate, rather than decrease, a sense of helplessness. These risks may need to be explored with the patient as part of therapy. In this regard, it is worth noting that while problem-solving approaches focus on skills designed to help with interpersonal and other "external" problems, there will be an increasing need to focus on appropriate ways to deal with emotion and its regulation (e.g. as the skills training in DBT does explicitly; Linehan, 1993b).

RESCUE FACTORS

We have seen how attentional and memory processes may combine to affect the risk of suicidal feelings and behaviour. However, we also noted in the "defeated bird" analogy that the longer term prospects for the defeated animal depended upon whether they were rescued, removed to a place of safety where recovery could take place. This generates the hypothesis that there may be a third psychological process: the judgement by an individual about whether "rescue" is possible. What processes determine whether people believe that they themselves, or other people or circumstances, will change for the better? How do people estimate the likelihood that something positive may happen involving their relationships, their job, their financial situation and so on? To examine this more closely we need to look at the research on the psychology of judgement and in particular the new domain of "prospective cognition". Although a comprehensive review of this topic is beyond the scope of this chapter, such a review can be found in MacLeod (1999; see also Williams et al, 1996 and MacLeod et al, 1997).

Research on prospective cognition examines, for example, judgements about the risks of negative events (such as getting cancer or getting burgled) and about the chance of positive events (such as getting promotion or winning the lottery). One conclusion of this research is that judgement about the future is partly made on the basis of how fluently one is able to generate images of the scenario in question. In the case of suicidal people, it is unclear whether they are too fluent in thinking of negative future events that might happen, or not fluent enough in thinking of positive events.

A study to examine this particular issue was conducted by MacLeod and co-workers (1993). Overdose patients were matched (for age and educational level) with non-depressed control groups taken from the same hospital wards as the suicidal patients and from a community sample. Since we intended to study fluency, all participants were tested with a neutral fluency test (the FAS test, in which participants generate as many words as they can, starting with the letters F, then A then S, each for 30 seconds in this study). No difference between the groups on this control task was found.

The fluency task of main interest required participants to generate as many events (even trivial events) that were likely to happen over the next period of (a) a day, (b) a week, (c) a month, (d) a year and (e) 10 years. For each period, participants were given 30 seconds to come up with as many events as possible. The task was run through three times. On the first trial, participants were not given any instructions about whether the events to be generated were to be positive or negative. But on the second and third runs through (and in counterbalanced order across participants), they were told to generate positive events that might occur ("things you are looking forward to") or negative events that might occur ("things you are not looking forward to").

The results showed that suicidal patients were no more fluent in generating future negative events than the control groups. However, the suicidal patients were less fluent in coming up with positive events that might happen in the future. This suggests that the important difference between the suicidal and non-suicidal participants was the relative lack of positive rescue factors for the suicidal group, rather than the excessive anticipation of negative things in the future. Further confirmation of this was provided by the pattern of correlations. There was no correlation between the fluency of generating negative future possibilities and level of hopelessness, measured using the Beck Hopelessness Scale ($r = 0.06$, n.s.). By contrast, there was a correlation between the fluency of generating positive future events and level of hopelessness: the less fluent participants were in generating future positive possibilities, the more hopeless they were ($r = 0.48$, $p < 0.05$). This suggests that hopelessness does not consist of the anticipation of an excess of negative events. Hopelessness is more the failure to generate sufficient positive factors, the failure to generate things that might happen in the future to "rescue" the situation.

One aspect of these results was particularly interesting for clinical approaches to hopelessness. Because the study required people to generate possible future events over several time periods (from 1 day to 10 years) it was possible to examine whether hopelessness mainly affected a person's long-term view of their future or mainly affected a short-term view. The results showed that time interval made no difference. Those who had most difficulty constructing a positive long-term future for themselves were equally unlikely to be able to come up with something positive that might occur within the next 24 hours. When a client is very hopeless the feeling can seem to come from a sense that his or her whole life holds no promise, stretching into the far distance. One possible implication of this study is that it would be wise for therapists to encourage clients to practise generating positive (rescue) events focusing on the next few days, rather than be drawn into discussing the next few years. This can be followed up with homework experiments to test out their ideas about what factors might provide a sense of rescue, a sense that things might change.

What other psychological factors might affect the sensitivity of individuals to the stimuli we have outlined? A major possibility is that temperament and personality may affect these sensitivities, and so it is to these that we now turn.

PERSONALITY VARIABLES

The personality variables that have been studied by different research groups over the years have very much reflected their different theoretical interests. Eyman and Eyman (1992) reviewed three personality-assessment methods—the Rorschach, the Thematic Apperception Test and the Minnesota Multiphasic Personality Inventory (MMPI). In each case, studies in the 1950s and 60s that appeared to show some promise could not be replicated. It is possible that such difficulties arise from a failure to discriminate different subgroups within those who show suicidal behaviour. For example, in one early study of parasuicide by Williams and Hassanyeh (1983), extreme scores on Eysenck's personality questionnaire (EPQ; Eysenck and Eysenck, 1975) were shown in those who had cut themselves, but not in patients who had harmed themselves by taking an overdose.

Lolas and colleagues (1991), Nordström and co-workers (1995), and Pallis and Jenkins (1977) have found that suicide attempters scored more highly than controls on neuroticism, psychoticism, interpersonal aversion, non-conformity, hopelessness, indirect aggression and lower on socialization. Later studies have focused more on the personality variables of impulsivity (Apter et al, 1993; Evans et al, 1996) and anger or hostility (Maiuro et al, 1989). The evidence on the association between these characteristics and an increased suicide risk is reviewed in Chapter 6.

More recently, interest has turned to the attempt to examine the connection between biological factors and personality in more detail. For this purpose Cloninger developed a psychobiological model of personality that distinguishes temperament from character (Cloninger et al, 1993, 1994). We shall describe the model in some detail, since it appears to us to offer the best chance of relating these two important fields of enquiry. According to the theory, four dimensions of *temperament* are distinguishable, each with a heritability component suggesting genetic mediation. The four dimensions are:

(a) Novelty seeking, describing the bias in responding to novelty and cues for reward. Persons who score high on this dimension are excitable rather than rigid, impulsive rather than reflective, extravagant rather than reserved and disorderly rather than regimented. Novelty seeking is hypothesized to be mediated by variation in basal dopaminergic activity, a behavioural-activation system. There is evidence that it is genetically homogeneous (Benjamin et al, 1996; Ebstein et al, 1996).

(b) Harm avoidance, referring to the extent to which a person responds to aversive stimuli. A person with a high score on this dimension is worried about the future rather than optimistic, fears uncertainty rather than being confident, is shy rather than gregarious and easily fatigued rather than energetic. Harm avoidance is hypothesized to be mediated by variation in serotonergic activity, a behavioural-inhibition system.

(c) Reward dependence, describing the bias in reacting to actual rewards and thereafter in maintaining behaviour previously associated with rewards. A person scoring high on this dimension finds him/herself attached to people, places or objects, is sentimental about things and dependent on others rather than independent. Reward dependence is hypothesized to be mediated by variation in basal noradrenergic activity, a behavioural-maintenance system.

(d) Persistence, describing persistence despite only intermittent reward. High persistence is associated with being resolute and persisting despite frustration and fatigue. Originally conceived as part of the reward-dependence factor, empirical studies showed it to be independent, though its biological mediators are not yet clear.

These four dimensions of temperament are said to relate to individual differences in implicit or perceptual memory systems, the habit-formation systems of associative learning and memory. In addition, however, Cloninger's theory also includes three dimensions of *character*, or self-concepts, describing the way individuals acquire, to varying degrees, a coherent sense of who they are (self-directedness), how they relate to others (cooperativeness) and how they relate to the universe (self-transcendence). Unlike the four temperament dimensions, the character dimensions are hypothesized to relate to individual differences in concept-driven, declarative memory systems (for further description of differences in these memory systems and their relationship to emotion see Williams et al, 1997). Although character development may have a genetic component, the theory implies that there is a greater role for cultural influences and social learning.

There are a number of reasons for believing that Cloninger's model might have greater prospects of being useful in suicide research. First, it has been shown to be at least as comprehensive in the way it accounts for individual differences in behaviour as other personality models such as that of H.J. Eysenck or J.A. Gray (see Stallings et al, 1996). Second, it distinguishes between basic temperament, with its large heritable component, and more changeable 'character', with its prominent learning and developmental component. Third, it maps onto important distinctions in cognitive psychology, between implicit (procedural/behavioural) memory and explicit (declarative, concept-driven) memory. Finally, it suggests specific ways in which the different dimensions are mediated by different biological subsystems, leading to testable hypotheses regarding the origins of psychopathology.

Van Heeringen and co-workers have studied this model in several samples of attempted-suicide patients. The results of these studies are reviewed in detail in Chapter 8. In general, the findings indicated the involvement of temperamental characteristics in the development of suicidal behaviour at two levels. Moreover, the findings provided additional support for the hypothetical biological underpinnings of these dimensions. First, attempted-suicide patients were characterized by comparatively lower scores on reward dependence, which correlated significantly but negatively with cortisol production. As was described in Chapter 3, cortisol production can be regarded as a marker of the stress-response syndrome. Reward dependence may thus be involved in the development of suicidal behaviour by reflecting the sensitivity to social signals, which is one of the major psychological characteristics associated with suicidal behaviour, as described earlier in this chapter. Second, harm-avoidance scores were found to be increased among attempted suicide patients when compared with normal controls, indicating a tendency towards behavioural inhibition when confronted with particular stressors, which may correspond with the "arrested flight" concept as described earlier in this chapter. Noteworthy were the significant positive correlations between scores on harm avoidance, levels of hopelessness and the binding potential of prefrontal serotonin 5-HT$_{2a}$ receptors. The latter finding thus suggests an association between perceived arrested flight and the development of feelings of hopelessness, which is mediated by the serotonergic-neurotransmission system.

MODELLING OF SUICIDAL BEHAVIOUR

We saw at the outset that there were a number of variables that might affect whether people are likely to act on the impulse to harm or kill themselves. One of these is the availability of methods, discussion of which is beyond the scope of this chapter, though for which there is increasingly compelling evidence (Kelly and Bunting, 1998). The other is the modelling of suicidal behaviour. It is likely that imitation is relevant for understanding at least some forms of suicidal behaviour (e.g. both cluster suicides and anniversary suicides can be explained in terms of modelling and imitation). A suicide cluster refers to an excessive number of suicides occurring in close temporal and/or geographical proximity, whereas imitation is the process by which one suicide becomes a compelling model for successive suicides (Gould, 1990).

Gould (1990) and Williams (1997) have reviewed evidence from a wide range of such studies, and concluded that there is evidence for imitative suicidal behaviour. For example, Phillips (1974) examined the monthly suicide rates in the USA for the years 1947–1968 and found that the suicide rates were heavier after a widely publicised suicide story. Schmidtke and Häfner (1988) found convincing evidence for a media effect on completed suicides. Following a television series, which included the fictional portrayal of a young male student's suicide on a railway line, broadcast in 1981 and again in 1982, there was a significant increase in railway suicides after each time the programme was shown. Hawton and colleagues (1999) found an increase in self-poisoning in the 2 weeks after a paracetamol overdose had been shown on a popular TV series *Casualty*, in the UK. A total of 49 accident-and-emergency departments and psychiatric services in the UK took part, and data on 4403 patients from 3 weeks before to 3 weeks after the broadcast were available. Results showed that presentations for self-poisoning rose by 17 per cent in the week after the event, and was also 9 per cent higher in the second week. The third week saw a return to baseline levels. Questionnaire responses from 1047 patients (from 25 of the participating hospitals) was used to determine the specific impact of viewing the programme, and thereby to estimate the extent to which a direct modelling effect had taken place. Interest focused particularly on which drug had been used in the suicide attempts by those who had seen the programme. Results showed that the use of paracetamol doubled in those who had viewed the particular *Casualty* programme compared with viewers of previous episodes of *Casualty* who had been questioned in the 3 weeks before the programme. There was little evidence of such a change in choice of drug among non-viewers of the programme. This study is particularly valuable in having obtained information from the hospitals and psychiatric services, and questionnaire data from overdose patients, in the weeks prior to the showing of the critical programme. Its conclusion was that, although the effect of media presentation is complex, the fact that it does have an effect is beyond doubt.

CONCLUDING REMARKS

In this chapter, we have explored one way in which social, biological and psychological facts may fit together. We have suggested that there may exist evolutionary primitive biological scripts, which are triggered by actual or imagined defeat/loss/reversal, but that the full-blown script may require both defeat and the inability to escape. The final (and perhaps most lethal) component is the feeling of hopelessness, that no rescue is possible, that nothing about other people or circumstances or the self is likely to change. The "defeat", "no escape" and "no rescue" components can be triggered psychologically, so for psychological intervention to succeed we suggested that we needed to see what psychological mechanisms contribute to each of these triggers.

We have seen that the psychological mechanisms are those that involve attention, memory and judgement. First, attention is biased: suicidal individuals are hypersensitive to stimuli signalling defeat and rejection. Second, suicidal individuals have overgeneral memories that prevent adequate definition of and solutions for current problems, giving rise to a feeling of being trapped, of there being no escape. Third, lack of fluency in generating positive events that may occur in the future (reduced anticipation of rescue) leads to hopelessness.

It is important that we realize that talk of psychological mechanisms and information-processing biases do not undermine the observations that actual social factors are important. Clearly the defeat and arrested flight observed in birds, with which we started this discussion, has its more direct parallels in humans too. A violent partner both defeats and prevents escape, as does the bully in prison or in school. These will produce biological changes, and some people will be more susceptible to these changes than others, with differences in personality (as assessed in Cloninger's model) likely to be important. Our point is not that these real factors do not exist. Rather it is to suggest that there is no situation that is so bad that it cannot be made worse by biased cognitive processing, with devastating consequences.

REFERENCES

Apter, A., Plutchick, R. and Van Praag, H.M. (1993) Anxiety, impulsivity and depressed mood in relation to suicidal and violent behavior. *Acta Psychiatrica Scandinavica*, **87**: 1–5.

Åsberg, M. (1997) Neurotransmitters and suicidal behaviour: the evidence from cerebrospinal fluid studies. In D.M. Stoff and J.J. Mann (Eds), *The Neurobiology of Suicide: From the Bench to the Clinic*. New York: Annals of the New York Academy of Sciences.

Benjamin, J.B., Li, L., Greenberg, B.D., Murphy, D.L. and Hamer, D.H. (1996) Population and familial association between the D4 dopamine receptor gene and measures of novelty seeking. *Nature Genetics*, **12**: 81–84.

Cloninger, C.R., Przybeck, T.R., Svrakic, D.M. and Wetzel, R.D. (1994) *The Temperament and Character Inventory (TCI): A Guide to its Development and Use*. St Louis, Missouri, USA, Center for Psychobiology of Personality.

Cloninger, C.R., Svrakic, D.M. and Przybeck, T.R. (1993) A psychobiological model of temperament and character. *Archives of General Psychiatry*, **30**: 975–990.

Ebstein, R.P. Novick, O., Umansky, R. et al. (1996) Dopamine D4 receptor exon III polymorphism associated with the human personality trait of novelty seeking. *Nature Genetics*, **12**: 78–80.

Evans, J., Platts, H. and Liebenau, A. (1996) Impulsiveness and deliberate self-harm: A comparison of "first-timers" and "repeaters". *Acta Psychiatrica Scandinavica*, **93**: 378–380.

Evans, J., Williams, J.M.G., O'Loughlin, S. and Howells, K. (1992) Autobiographical memory and problem-solving strategies of parasuicide patients. *Psychological Medicine*, **22**: 399–405.

Eyman, J.R. and Eyman, S.K. (1992). Personality assessment in suicide prediction. In R.W. Maris; A.L. Berman; J.T. Maltsberger and R.I. Yufit (Eds), *Assessment and Prediction of Suicide*. New York, Guilford.

Eysenck, H.J. and Eysenck, S.B.G. (1975) *Manual of the Eysenck Personality Questionnaire*. London, Hodder and Stoughton.

Gilbert, P. (1989) *Human Nature and Suffering*. Hove and London, Lawrence Erlbaum Associates.

Goddard, L., Dritschel, B. and Burton, A. (1996) Role of autobiographical memory in social problem solving and depression. *Journal of Abnormal Psychology*, **105**: 609–616.

Gould, M. (1990) Suicide clusters and media exposure. In S. Blumenthal and D. Kupfer, (Eds), *Suicide over the Life Span*. Washington DC, American Psychiatric Press.

Hawton, K., Simkin, S., Deeks, J.J., O'Connor, S., Keen, A., Altman, D.G., Philo, G. and Bulstrode, C. (1999) Effects of drug overdose in a television drama on presentations to hospital for self poisoning:time series and questionnaire study. *British Medical Journal*, **318**: 972–977.

Kelly, S. and Bunting, J. (1998) Trends in Suicide in England and Wales, 1982–96. *Population Trends*, **92**: 29–41.

Kety, S. (1990) Genetic factors in suicide. In S. Blumenthal and D. Kupfer, (Eds) *Suicide over the Life Cycle: Risk Factors, Assessment and Treatment of Suicidal Patients*. Washington DC, American Psychiatric Press.

Linehan, M.M. (1993a) *Cognitive Behavioural Treatment for Borderline Personality Disorder*. New York, Guilford Press.

Linehan, M.M. (1993b) *Skills Training for Borderline Personality Disorder*. New York, Guilford Press.

Lolas, F., Gomez, A. and Suarez, L. (1991) EPQ-R and suicide attempt: The relevance of psychoticism. *Personality and Individual Differences*, **12**: 899–902.

MacLeod, A.K. (1999) Prospective cognition. In M. Power and T. Dalgleish (Eds), *Handbook of Cognition and Emotion*, Chichester, Wiley.

MacLeod, A.K., Rose, G.S. and Williams, J.M.G. (1993) Components of hopelessness about the future in parasuicide. *Cognitive Therapy and Research*, **17**: 441–455.

MacLeod, A.K., Pankhania, B., Lee, M. and Mitchell, D. (1997) Parasuicide, depression and the anticipation of positive and negative future experiences. *Psychological Medicine*, **27**: 973–977.

Maiuro, R.D., O'Sullivan, M.J., Michael, M.C. and Vitaliano, P.P. (1989) Anger, hostility and depression in assaultive vs. suicide-attempting males. *Journal of Clinical Psychology*, **45**: 532–541.

Murphy, G.E. (1998) Why women are less likely than men to commit suicide. *Comprehensive Psychiatry*, **39**: 165–175.

Nordström, P., Schalling, M. and Åsberg, M. (1995). Temperamental vulnerability in attempted suicide. *Acta Psychiatrica Scandinavica*, **92**: 155–160.

Pallis, D.J. and Jenkins, J.S. (1977) Extraversion, neuroticism and intent in attempted suicides. *Psychological Reports*, **41**, 19–22.

Phillips, D.P. (1974) The influence of suggestion on suicide: substantive and theoretical implications of the Werther effect. *American Sociological Review*, **39**: 340–354.

Pollock, L.R. and Williams, J.M.G. (1998) Problem solving and suicidal behavior. *Suicide and Life-Threatening Behavior*, **28**: 375–387.

Pollock, L.R. and Williams, J.M.G. (in press) Effective problem solving depends on specific autobiographical recall. *Suicide and Life-Threatening Behavior*, in press.

Price, J.S. and Sloman, L. (1987) Depression as yielding behaviour: an animal model based on Schjelerup-Ebb's pecking order. *Ethology and Sociobiology*, **8**: 85–98.

Schmidtke, A. and Häfner, H. (1988) The Werther effect after television films: new evidence for an old hypothesis. *Psychological Medicine*, **18**: 665–676.

Sidley, G.L., Whitaker, K., Calam, R.M. and Wells, A. (1997) The relationship between problem-solving and autobiographical memory in parasuicide patients. *Behavioural and Cognitive Psychotherapy*, **25**: 195–202.

Stallings, M.C., Hewitt, J.K. Cloninger, R.C., Heath, A.C. and Eaves, L.J. (1996) Genetic and environmental structure of the Tridimensional Personality Questionnaire: three or four temperament dimensions? *Journal of Personality and Social Psychology*, **70**: 127–140.

Van Egmond, M. Garnefski, N., Jonker, D. and Kerkhof, A. (1993) The relationship between sexual abuse and female suicidal behavior. *Crisis*, **14**, 129–139.

Williams, J.M.G. (1996) Depression and the specificity of autobiographical memory. In D.C. Rubin (Ed.), *Remembering Our Past – Studies in Autobiographical Memory*, Cambridge, Cambridge University Press.

Williams, J.M.G. (1997) *Cry of Pain: Understanding Suicide and Self-harm*. London, Penguin.

Williams, J.M.G. and Broadbent, K. (1986) Distraction by Emotional Stimuli: use of a Stroop task with suicide attempters. *British Journal of Clinical Psychology*, **25**: 101–110.

Williams, J.M.G., Ellis, N., Tyers, C., Healy, H., Rose, G. and Macleod, A.K. (1996) The specificity of autobiographical memory and imageability of the future. *Memory & Cognition*, **24**: 116–125

Williams, J.M.G. and Hassanyeh, F. (1983) Deliberate self-harm, clinical history, and extreme scoring on the EPQ. *Personality and individual differences*, **4**: 347–350.

Williams, J.M.G., Mathews, A. and MacLeod, C. (1996) The emotional Stroop task and psychopathology. *Psychological Bulletin*, **120**: 3–24.

Williams, J.M.G., Stiles, W.B. and Shapiro, D.A. (1999) Cognitive mechanisms in the avoidance of painful and dangerous thoughts: elaborating the assimilation model. *Cognitive Therapy and Research*, **23**: 285–306.

Williams, J.M.G., Teasdale, J.D., Segal, Z.V. and Soulsby, J. (2000) Mindfulness-based cognitive therapy increases the specificity of autobiographical memory. *Journal of Abnormal Psychology*, **109**: 150–155.

Williams, J.M.G., Watts, F.N., Macleod, C. and Mathews, A. (1997) *Cognitive Psychology and Emotional Disorders* (Second Edition). Chichester, Wiley.

Chapter 6

PERSONALITY CONSTELLATIONS AND SUICIDAL BEHAVIOUR

Alan Apter and Hadas Ofek

INTRODUCTION

There has been considerable progress in the identification of psychiatric risk factors for suicidal behaviour. Up to 90 per cent of suicides and suicide attempts are associated with an Axis-I disorder, which is most commonly a depression, but often complicated by co-morbid conditions (Brent et al, 1987; Brent et al, 1990; Apter et al, 1991; Brent et al, 1993a; Brent et al, 1993b; Brent et al, 1993c). However, these diagnostic categories have low specificity in the prediction of suicidal behaviour, and do not shed light on its aetiology.

Since the majority of patients with a psychiatric disorder do not commit or even attempt suicide (Brent et al, 1993d), psychiatric disorder may well be a necessary but not a sufficient condition for suicide. Therefore, one of the most pressing clinical research questions in the area of suicide is to determine which factors beyond psychiatric disorder predispose to suicide.

There are many different ways to conceptualize such factors. For instance, as discussed in Chapter 11, there is substantial evidence showing that the course of the suicidal process is influenced by sociological factors, and that many of the risk factors are social in nature. Thus unemployment, poverty, availability of guns and even "national character" are important risk factors for suicidal behaviour. In addition,

Understanding Suicidal Behaviour. Edited by Kees van Heeringen
© 2001 John Wiley & Sons Ltd.

as described in Chapters 3 and 4, biological factors underlie at least some forms of suicidal behaviour, and must be taken into account in any explanation of suicidal behaviour.

This chapter will focus on a third group of factors, which may be associated with suicidal behaviour beyond psychiatric disorders (i.e. personality-related characteristics). Based on current knowledge, hypotheses about their role in the development of suicidal behaviour will be discussed. These hypotheses are based on the authors' work with suicidal adolescents in an adolescent psychiatric in-patient unit and in the emergency room of a large general hospital, as part of an epidemiological study of attempted suicide. Additional information was provided by psychological post-mortem studies of adolescents aged 18 to 21 years, who killed themselves while doing their compulsory military service in the Israel Defence Force.

This chapter will provide an overview of the evidence supporting the role of three sets of personality constellations in the development of the suicidal process. These constellations include, first, narcissism, perfectionism and the inability to tolerate failure and imperfection, in combination with an underlying schizoid-personality structure that does not allow the individual to ask for help and deny him the comforts of intimacy. The second constellation consists of impulsive and aggressive characteristics in combination with an over-sensitivity to apparently minor life events. This sensitivity often leads to angry and anxious reactions, potentially resulting in a secondary depression. Individuals suffering from this constellation of characteristics tend to use defences such as regression, splitting, dissociation and displacement, and commonly have experienced childhood physical and sexual abuse. There is often a history of alcohol or substance abuse, and there appears to be a connection with an underlying disturbance of serotonin metabolism, which might be genetic in origin. In Chapter 4 Van Praag describes this association between psychotraumatic experiences and biological disturbances in detail. Third, there are persons whose suicidal behaviour is driven by a hopelessness that is commonly related to an underlying depression. This hopelessness and depression usually result from mental illnesses such as affective disorder, schizophrenia, anxiety disorder or anorexia nervosa.

THE NARCISSISTIC–PERFECTIONIST CONSTELLATION

The evidence in support of this concept was provided principally by the psychological post-mortem studies that we have conducted in the Israel Defence Force. Many of these suicides seemed to be very different from the patients seen on the adolescent unit or in the emergency room; in fact, the vast majority had never been in contact with mental-health care. However, further study of this maladaptive personality style showed some similarities with that of adolescent patients, especially those who made serious suicide attempts.

Case Study 1

1. David told us that, since he was 8 years old, he had been concerned by thoughts of death. At the age of 11 he had told his friends that he would kill himself on the day of his bar mitzvah at age 13. One week before this celebration he had stolen a rope from the headquarters of the scout group to which he belonged. He wrote an elaborate suicide note to his parents in which he stated that he did not believe in the hereafter and that he would just "cease to exist". The day after his party he stayed home from school and hanged himself. Only by a curious twist of chance was he found by his mother who cut the rope. He was unconscious for 14 days before he recovered. It became apparent that there had been no obvious signs of depression or mental anguish, and nobody suspected that he was mentally disturbed before attempting suicide. His friends had not taken him seriously as they thought he was just boasting, and they had long forgotten his promise. During therapy with the patient and his family it appeared that David was a very intelligent boy who suffered, however, from a mild reading disability. This had made it very difficult to live up to the expectations of his high-achieving family, especially when compared with an older brother who was exceptionally brilliant. Although David was a popular boy in school, it soon became clear that he had no intimate friends and felt very lonely. After 1 year of therapy, extensive psychological testing and observation no major axis-I psychiatric disorder could be diagnosed.

2. Jonathan was a 20-year-old officer when he killed himself. His father was a well-known person in the Israeli educational system, while his mother ran a small business. The family, which included two brothers, was oriented towards achievement and had high moral standards. They believed in being honest and industrious, in helping one's neighbour and in public service. Emotional control and living up to high standards were stressed as personal ideals. The father was respected and regarded as a role model by his family. Any conflict in the home was seen as a threat to the father's authority and was thus suppressed. Mother was subservient to her husband in most matters. All who knew Jonathan described his early development as "excellent". He was an intelligent, curious, industrious and persistent child, a natural leader and popular with his teachers and peers. He was described as "slightly arrogant" but always ready to help a weaker child. He became a senior leader in the scouts' movement and a camp councillor. Despite his popularity, however, Jonathan

seems not to have had any close friends in whom he confided, suggesting difficulty with intimacy. In the army, Jonathan did very well and he was chosen for an officers' training course which he completed with flying colours. He was selected as an instructor for new recruits. During advanced training he performed very well apart from one slip-up for which he was reprimanded. He took this in his stride and finished the course. His superior commended him for his ability to perform under stress. Jonathan was thrilled by his appointment as an instructor and told his father that he was determined to become the best instructor on the base. He became totally involved in his new duties, despite some difficulties as a teacher as a result of being pedantic and somewhat naive. His platoon of trainees did rather well, although the rating of their overall performance was only average. Following the ceremony in which the new recruits received their berets and rifles Jonathan went to his room and shot himself.

Psychological post-mortem studies of soldiers in the Israeli Defence Force have shown some features that differ from those found in similar studies conducted in Europe and the USA (Apter et al, 1993; King and Apter, 1997). Strong narcissistic and perfectionist patterns were a characteristic of about a quarter of the suicides, while in 40 per cent their personalities showed schizoid and avoidant traits. The Defence Force is for many Israeli youngsters a chance to prove their worth, much like a prestigious college or university career for European or American students. For many the military is a second chance to redeem earlier shortcomings or to confirm a sense of competent identity. Among the young men who committed suicide these high self-expectations and hopes may also have made it difficult to acknowledge or bear even marginal difficulties or personal limitations that emerged during their subsequent active duty, and any shortcoming was perceived as devastating. These features were often complicated by strong isolative traits, which seemed to be common in many suicide victims. In a majority of cases these characteristics appeared to reflect lifelong personality patterns that were not related to stress or periods of depression. Their parents, teachers and friends remembered them as being very isolated children. Their superior officers often termed them as being very private.

This combination of traits had several very dangerous consequences. Many of these young people seemed to have felt an overwhelming need to make a good impression at the occasion of their pre-induction assessments, which are made in all Israeli teenagers at the age of 16. A good score during this assessment means the opportunity to be assigned to a prestigious battle unit, which is to be regarded as a highly prestigious attainment in the Israeli society.

This is exemplified by another finding, which is not reported in previous studies of suicide. The suicide victims in our study had much higher physical-fitness ratings than the average Israeli soldier, probably reflecting their tendency to minimize non-specific and subjective physical symptoms, such as backache and flat feet, and/or to train intensively in order to reach high levels of fitness before conscription. Once these young men were confronted with perceived difficulties, shame related to their unrealistically high standards combined in many cases with an isolative style, prevented them from turning to peers, officers or clinicians for help or support.

Consequently, even setbacks, which may appear minor to the external observer, could rapidly spiral into disaster. Burgeoning anxious preoccupation, depressive rumination and withdrawal further interfered with the recruit's ability to perform at the high levels he demanded of himself or to reach out to others, triggering a vicious cycle of isolative decompensation, with suicide as the only way out (King and Apter, 1997). This is exemplified by the motto of the Israeli Defence Force Northern Command: "better death than shame". Recruits who used achievement as a kind of pseudo-mastery (Zetzel, 1970) to substitute for a lack of real interpersonal closeness appeared to be particularly vulnerable to this kind of catastrophic decompensation.

We have also studied this issue in adolescent patients who were hospitalized in a psychiatric unit following a suicide attempt. Following Blatt et al (1993) we hypothesized that there are two pathways to mental disorder in general and depression in particular. Blatt and Zuroff (1992) developed an instrument to measure depression, which is called the Depressive Experience Questionnaire (DEQ). Although similar to and strongly correlating with the more familiar Beck Depression Inventory (BDI), this scale divides depression into two major types (i.e. the interpersonal ("anaclitic") and self-critical types). The difference between these two types of depression parallels the difference between two pathways of development of personality profiles (i.e. the "interpersonal" and the "personal" profile, respectively). We were able to show that the hospitalized adolescents could be divided in two groups using a partial-order scalogram analysis. A first group was characterized by: high scores on self-oriented perfectionism, as measured by means of the Child and Adolescent Perfectionism Scale (Flett et al, 1993); high scores on self-critical depression, as measured by the DEQ; and high scores on a measure of narcissism (i.e. the Narcissistic Personality Inventory, Raskin and Perry, 1988). The personality characteristics of these adolescents appeared to be in many ways similar to those of the Israeli Defence Force suicide victims as described above. In contrast, the second group of patients showed a personality profile which was characterized by high scores on socially prescribed perfectionism and anaclitic depression and low scores on self-critical depression and narcissism. Youngsters in the latter group appeared to suffer more commonly from borderline or classical affective disorders. Interestingly, adolescents showing a narcissistic and more pronounced "personal profile" scored higher on measures of the risk of suicidality, and more commonly had a history of more serious attempts with higher lethality than the "interpersonal group".

Based on our experience in the Israeli Defence Force we have also tried to test the hypothesis that schizoid or isolative traits are an important risk factor for serious suicidal behaviour. More specifically, the clinical and research impressions as described above brought us to postulate that communication styles may differentiate between the low-risk attempter who uses his suicidal behaviour to communicate his distress, and the suicidal individual who is at high risk of suicide, since he is unable to or chooses not to communicate his distress, either verbally or by his behaviour.

Stengel (1958) and Kreitman (1977) have suggested that non-fatal suicidal behaviour may be a form of communication. Kreitman hypothesized that this kind of behaviour might represent a way of communicating distress that could bring about changes in the individual's social network.

Revealing intimate information to others and ways in which this information is perceived can be considered as parts of "disclosure processes". The fundamental assumption of the study of disclosure processes is that a person's verbal and non-verbal communications may vary dimensionally from very personal or intimate to very superficial.

The lack of ability to communicate personal feelings has been operationalized by Jourard and Lasakow (1958) in the "self-disclosure" concept. Jourard and Lasakow (1958) regards this characteristic as the ability to share intimate feelings with others, and thus as an essential part of mental health and well-being (Kaplan, 1967; Axtell and Cole, 1971; Altman and Taylor, 1973). Many people experience that their lack of this ability is responsible for feeling lonely and distressed (Cozby, 1973; Goldstein and Reinelcker, 1974; Carpenter and Freeze, 1979; Horowitz and French, 1979; McAdams, 1980; Jones et al., 1981; Solano et al, 1982). Discussions of the nature of "self-disclosure" are reminiscent of the interpersonal psychoanalytical theories of Sullivan (1953). Lack of the ability for self-disclosure has been associated with psychiatric illness (Jourard, 1964; Taylor, 1968; Jourard, 1971; Chaikin and Darlega, 1974), neuroticism (Mayo, 1968), anxiety (Archer, 1979) and aggression (Archer et al, 1982).

In a study of 100 patients suffering from affective disorder we found that self-disclosure was comparatively limited in subjects with more severe suicidal behaviour. In addition, self-disclosure appeared to be independent of levels of depression or anxiety and hopelessness. Thus it may be that limited self-disclosure acts as a mediating risk factor, which facilitates serious suicidal behaviour when other risk factors such as psychopathology, anxiety/depression and hopelessness are present (Grafi, 1997). Limited self-disclosure may affect suicidal individuals in different ways. If related to intent, it diminishes the likelihood that suicidal impulses will be detected. Individuals who disclose easily and early would possibly be more prone to engage in non-fatal suicidal behaviour. As might be expected from the notions of Stengel and Cook (1958) and Kreitman (1977), the ability of self-disclosure is as high among patients at limited risk of suicide as among healthy controls. Bearing in mind that these subjects were suffering from affective illness, it seems that they were able to signal their pain in a way that is less life threatening and to get attention from the people around them. Patients who made more serious suicide attempts were those who lacked the ability of self-disclosure, and thus had to take more desperate measures to end their pain.

Impaired ability of self-disclosure may also increase isolation, loneliness and suffering. An association between loneliness and a lack of self-disclosure has been demonstrated (Horowitz and French, 1979; Solano et al, 1982). Although the relation between lack of ability of self-disclosure and suicide has not been studied, there is an extensive literature on the relationship between loneliness and severe suicidal behaviour (Maris, 1992a). For example, the loss of social support may be associated with a fatal outcome (Maris, 1992a), and the association between living alone and suicide has been described (Clayton, 1985). However, the lack of the possibility to share feelings and thoughts with others may lead to loneliness, which in certain circumstances may lead to suicide. Similarly, when an individual has at least one person with whom he can feel intimacy, he may not feel lonely even when socially isolated (Solano et al, 1982). An intimate partner may also be important for the correction of negative perceptions of oneself or the environment. These perceptions may lead to the attenuation of negative emotions such as depression, anxiety and anger, which are important facilitators of suicidal behaviour (Maris, 1992b).

THE IMPULSIVE–AGGRESSIVE CONSTELLATION

Case study 2

1. Deborah had a history of multiple admissions to the adolescent unit, most commonly because of suicidal thoughts and behaviour, including severe ideation, threats, gestures and some serious attempts, which made hospitalization in the intensive-care unit necessary. Since being a child she had always been impulsive and oppositional. At about the age of 11 she developed anorexia nervosa, probably or at least partly as a result of her being an accomplished dancer in a ballet troupe. With the onset of adolescence she developed very severe bulimia that was complicated by severe disturbances in potassium metabolism. She was admitted to a psychiatric unit a first time after writing a suicide note to her teacher at school. On the unit she was "an impossible patient". She was impulsive, dramatic and violent. She would smash plates and glasses, and use the fragments to attack staff members and to cut herself. To revenge herself on the ward personnel she would vomit in the air conditioners or while being in the nurses' station. By the time she was 22 she had made more than 100 suicide attempts. She also abused alcohol and indulged in shoplifting. She received all kinds of psychosocial and biological therapies but to no avail, although there was some tempering of her emotional instability with getting older.

2. Amit, an 18-year-old soldier, killed himself a few months after induction in the army. He had grown up under conditions of economic deprivation. His parents were uneducated: his mother was a housewife and his father a blue-collar worker. The father was a "weak" and closed person who avoided confrontation, while the mother was a warm, very emotional woman who found it difficult to cope with running the household and the education of her children. The atmosphere in the house was characterized by angry accusations from the mother and passive silence from the father. Amit was described as "difficult" since his birth. He did poorly in elementary school, experienced problems in concentrating, caused disturbances in the class, and was often involved in fights. He did not drop out of school, however, and managed to complete a vocational high school with fairly good grades. During high school his behaviour changed and he became more compliant and eager to please. Neither his teachers nor his parents ever thought of referring him for counselling. He was described as being very close to his mother and easily hurt by insults such as being called "childish" or "mummy's boy". Amit looked forward to his army service, feeling that it would make a man out of him, and he asked to be sent to a front-line unit. During the psychological evaluation at induction, he denied the existence of any emotional and social difficulties. The psychological interviewer considered that he was likely to do well under battle conditions. He was a highly motivated and generally well-behaved recruit

who, however, tended to become flustered under stress and to have angry outbursts towards his friends and even sometimes towards the officers. One day he returned late from a home pass saying that there were problems at home, as a consequence of which he was told that his next leave was cancelled. He became irritable and angry, and his performance began to suffer. He also began to complain of multiple somatic symptoms. The teaching staff on the base broached the possibility of his being unsuitable for a front-line unit, but he became upset and insisted on continuing. While he was resting after a training exercise one of the other recruits began taunting him. Amit lost his temper and attacked his tormenter. After friends separated them, he ran to his tent and shot himself with his gun.

As described in more detail in Chapter 4, Van Praag (1997) has conceptualized a constellation that is very relevant to suicide, especially in young people. He has termed this constellation "serotonin-related, anxiety/aggression driven, stressor-precipitated depression". This concept implies that certain individuals, when faced with relatively minor life stressors, will react with anger and anxiety, and then develop a secondary depression, which is often accompanied by suicidal behaviour. Although the description of this constellation refers to a depressive condition it implies the existence of particular personality characteristics, which include a vulnerability for specific stressors and a tendency to react impulsively in an anxious and/or aggressive way. Van Praag argues that serotonin abnormalities underlie many of the psychological dimensions, which are correlated with suicidal behaviour such as depression, anger, violence, anxiety and impulsivity.

Evidence for this hypothetical constellation has been found in a number of studies. For example, using symptom-scale scores from a semi-structured interview—the children's version of the Schedule for Affective Disorders and Schizophrenia (the K-SADS)—we found significant positive correlations between depression (both "endogenous" and "associated"), suicidality and aggressive conduct in a study of adolescent inpatients (Apter et al, 1995). We also found that conduct symptoms and suicidality were highly correlated even when depression was controlled. In a similar study, we found significant and positive correlations between suicidality, violence, impulsivity, depression and anxiety (Apter et al, 1993).

These considerations have led some investigators to state that a tendency towards impulsive *aggression*, defined as a tendency to respond to provocation or frustration with anger or aggression without forethought, may predispose to suicidal behaviour independently from, or interactively with, psychiatric disorder. In fact, the risk for suicide is supposed to be substantially increased when psychiatric disorder and impulsive aggressive personality traits co-occur (Brent et al, 1993e; Brent et al, 1993f; Brent et al, 1993g; Brent et al, 1993h). Demonstrated associations between aggression, cluster-B personality disorder, impulsivity and completed (Brent et al, 1993c; Beautrais et al, 1996) as well as attempted suicide (Beck et al, 1961; Barrat, 1965; Barraclough et al, 1974; Beck et al, 1974; Åsberg et al, 1986; Brent et al, 1988; Apter et al, 1991; Brent et al, 1994) support this viewpoint. Furthermore, there is evidence for both independent and interactive contributions of aggression and impulsivity to the risk of suicidal behaviour (Barrat, 1965; Brown et al, 1979; Apter et al, 1993; Brent et al, 1993c; Beautrais et al, 1996). Therefore, in order to determine personality traits predisposing to suicidal behaviour, it is essential to assess aggression, impulsivity and their confluence (i.e. the impulsive–aggressive constellation). Psychoanalysts have recognized the relationship between suicide, attempted suicide and aggression. For example, Menninger (1933) proposed that a dynamic triad underlies all aggressive behaviour, whether directed inward or outward, consisting of the wish to die, the wish to kill and the wish to be killed. These are all considered as derivatives of Freud's concept of "Thanatos" or the death instinct.

There are many reports of murderers who commit suicide in the daily press. Approximately every fourth patient with a history of violent behaviour also has a history of attempted suicide (Skodal and Karasu, 1978; Tardiff and Sweillam, 1980a). Inmadar and colleagues (1982) studied the prevalence of violent and suicidal behaviour in a sample of 51 hospitalized adolescents, and found that 66.7 per cent had been violent, 43.1 per cent had been suicidal and 27.5 per cent had been both. According to various authors, between 7 and 48 per cent of patients with a history of violent behaviour have also made suicide attempts in the past. This has been reported in adults (Skodal and Karasu, 1978), prepubertal children (Pfeffer et al, 1983), and prisoners (Climent et al, 1977).

Looking at the issue in terms of patients who are predominantly suicidal, Tardiff and Sweillam (1980b) found among a large group of suicidal patients admitted to mental hospitals that 14 per cent of males and 7 per cent of females were assaultive at the time of or just prior to admission. Similarly, on the basis of detailed studies of psychotic patients, Kermani (1981) identified what he calls the "violent depressive type" of patient, who has a long history of suicide attempts as well as a history of violence. It has likewise been reported that female suicide attempters show more hostility and engage in more arguments and friction with friends and relatives than a comparable group of non-suicidal depressed women. Hospitalized depressed patients with a history of self-destructive acts have been found to have comparatively high levels of hostility and violence as measured by their need for seclusion and restraint (Weissman et al, 1973).

In a large group of psychiatric in-patients with mixed diagnoses, about 40 per cent had a history of attempted suicide, 42 per cent had engaged in violent behaviour in the past and 23 per cent had histories of both types of behaviour (Plutchik et al, 1985). Almost all of the 30 variables measured in these patients turned out to be significant risk factors for both suicide and violence. These results strongly support the hypothetical close link between suicide risk and violence risk regardless of diagnosis.

Shaffer and Fisher (1981) reported another important finding in this regard. They found that a combination of depressive symptoms and antisocial behaviour was the most common antecedent of teenage suicide. Assaultiveness (Pfeffer et al, 1983) and instability of affect as reflected in borderline personality disorder may also be important correlates of adolescent suicidal behaviour, especially in combination with depression. Aggressive or violent behaviour is highly correlated with suicidal behaviour on psychiatric wards (Plutchik and Van Praag, 1986), in the histories of psychiatric patients with all kinds of diagnoses (Skodal and Karasu, 1978; Tardiff and Sweillam, 1980b; Inmadar et al, 1982) and in all age groups (Pfeffer et al, 1983). A study by Plutchik and Van Praag (1986) showed that psychometric measures of violence risk were highly correlated with measures of suicide risk.

There is now substantial evidence showing that suicide in younger people differs from suicide among adults with regard to certain aspects. Specifically, there is a comparatively more prominent role of impulsivity, substance abuse and antisocial and other personality disorders in younger completed suicides (Centers for Disease Control, 1994, 1998). Impulsivity and aggression are likely to be involved in the genetics of suicidal behaviour, as will be described on page 105.

A higher familial loading for suicidal behaviour was found in attempters and completers who made more medically dangerous attempts (Buss et al, 1957; Brunner et al, 1993) and who were more aggressive (Andrews et al, 1992). Remarkably, the rate of familial suicide attempts was found to be six times higher among individuals who committed suicide by means of aggressive methods than among those who use non-aggressive methods (Andrews et al, 1992) and three times higher in aggressive than in non-aggressive suicide attempters. This, along with the above-noted findings of Wender and colleagues (1986), suggest a relationship between the genetics of aggression and that of suicidal behaviour.

The association between altered serotonergic neurotransmission, suicidal behaviour and impulsive violence constitutes probably the most consistent finding in biological psychiatry. Numerous studies using neuroendocrine challenges or levels of monoamine metabolites in cerebrospinal fluid have shown altered central serotonergic neurotransmission in association with attempted suicide and with impulsive violence (Garfinkel et al, 1982; Garrison et al, 1991; Apter et al, 1993; Apter et al, 1996; Arango et al, 1993; Arango et al, 1995; Fergusson et al, 1995b). Similar correlation coefficients have been found in studies of the correlation between measures of serotonin and attempted suicide ($r = 0.42$–0.59), aggression ($r = 0.46$–0.78) and impulsive risk taking ($r = 0.42$–0.62). Post-mortem studies of suicide completers have shown area-specific alterations in numbers of serotonin receptors in the ventral area of the prefrontal cortex, an area known to be the key brain region in the exercise of restraint of impulsive activity, when compared with matched controls (Garrison et al, 1993). Hence, given the abundance of evidence, changes in serotonin-mediated neurotransmission apparently link suicidal behaviour with impulsive violence.

Impulsivity has indeed frequently been described as a risk factor for suicide and as a personality characteristic of adolescent suicide attempters (Crumley, 1981). Lack of impulse control has been found to distinguish between adolescent suicide attempters and adolescents with an acute illness without a history of suicidal behaviour (Slap et al, 1988). However, since group comparisons have demonstrated no difference between suicidal patients and non-suicidal controls on measures of cognitive impulsivity, impulsivity does not seem to characterize all suicide attempters (Spirito et al, 1989). Instead, impulsivity may be important in identifying high-risk subgroups. A 1-year follow-up of suicide attempters showed repeaters to be more impulsive than non-repeaters. Furthermore, it has been suggested that impulsive suicide attempters come from families where action supersedes verbal mediation and that male attempters are more impulsive than female attempters (Marks and Haller, 1977). Finally, impulsive suicide attempters have been found to be less depressed and less hopeless than non-impulsive attempters (Williams et al, 1980). In view of the frequent reference to teenage suicide attempts as impulsive, the limited number of studies on the relationship between impulsivity and teenage suicide is surprising. Moreover, the few existing studies suffer from methodological shortcomings, as the distinction between an impulsive cognitive style and impulsive attempts often is not made. Another problem is that the measures of impulsivity used in these studies often reflect angry and aggressive behaviour as much as behaviour that is not preceded by reflection or planning.

Several authors have indicated that *anger* as an emotional state commonly is associated with adolescent suicide attempts. However, there has been little empirical investigation of this association (Spirito et al, 1989). Pfeffer and colleagues (1985a) have described an angry assaultive subtype of childhood suicidal behaviour, and indicated that angry feelings are common in children referred for psychiatric consultation, including those who are not suicidal. Withers and Kaplan (1987) found that a substantial proportion of suicide attempters in an emergency room reported intense anger prior to the attempt. Moreover, adolescent suicide attempters often exhibit a wide range of aggressive behaviours (Garfinkel et al, 1982).

Anxiety has been identified as an important risk factor for suicidal behaviour in adults. A follow-up study of patients with major affective disorder showed that anxiety symptoms were strongly related to completed suicide within 1 year following the initial assessment (Fawcett et al, 1990). There have also been studies that indicate that anxiety disorders are associated with an increased risk of suicidal behaviour (Allgulander and Lavori, 1991; Mannuzza et al, 1992; Massion et al, 1993; Allgulander, 2000). Studies in adolescents have shown mixed results. Taylor and Stansfield (1984) found that, when compared with psychiatric outpatients, suicide attempters more commonly exhibited higher levels of anxiety (38 versus 22 per cent); the difference, however, not being significant. Another study demonstrated that depressed individuals who reported suicidal ideation (of whom 39 per cent had attempted suicide) showed high levels of anxiety (76.4 per cent), but these levels were not significantly different from those of depressed non-suicidal adolescents (Kosky et al, 1986). Interestingly, Bettes and Walker (1986) found in a large sample of disturbed in- and out-patient youngsters that male adolescents who expressed suicidal thoughts in the absence of behaviour were more likely to be rated as anxious when compared with suicide attempters. The authors interpreted this finding by suggesting that engaging in suicidal acts may serve to reduce symptoms, and this might account for the lower rate of anxiety among males who engage in such acts. Consistent with this finding, Andrews and Lewinsohn (1992) found a significant association between anxiety disorders and suicide attempts in males, but not in females in a large community sample of adolescents. Most research on anxiety as a risk factor for suicidal behaviour has focused on the measurement of state anxiety. This may not be a fruitful method if state anxiety is significantly reduced following a suicide attempt.

Ideally, risk factors used for predictive purposes should be stable (Hawton, 1987). As such, research on the relationship between anxiety and suicidal behaviour might benefit from measuring anxiety as a trait rather than a state. In fact, Apter and his colleagues (1990, 1993) found that adult psychiatric in-patient suicide attempters had significantly higher levels of trait anxiety than in-patient non-attempters, whereas state anxiety did not discriminate between the two groups. Moreover, trait anxiety was strongly associated with suicide risk as measured by means of a self-report scale. Another study found that adult depressed patients with suicidal ideation had significantly higher levels of state and trait anxiety than depressed patients with no suicidal ideation (Oei et al, 1990). A recent study of Dutch adolescents found that suicide attempters, half of them being psychiatric patients and half high-school students, exhibited significantly higher levels of state and trait anxiety than non-depressed non-attempters in the sub-sample of high-school students (de Wilde et al, 1993). However, the suicide attempters did not differ in levels of state and trait anxiety from the depressed non-attempters, one-third of them being psychiatric patients and the rest being high-school students. Furthermore, the attempters and the depressed non-attempters did not differ in levels of depression.

MENTAL ILLNESS–DEMORALIZATION–HOPELESSNESS CONSTELLATION

Case study 3

1. David came from a family with a distinguished military background. He was very shy in the interaction with his peers at school, but open with and dependent on his teachers. In retrospect, he appears to have suffered from a poor self-image during his school years, with intermittent periods of depression, insomnia and weight loss. His teachers recommended him to see a psychologist, but his parents refused. David looked forward to his army service with enthusiasm, hoping that success would redeem his low self-esteem. It is significant that he did not reveal any (previous) psychiatric problems or emotional difficulties or any of his history during his pre-induction screening. The psychological interviewer noted that David seemed "slightly strange" during the screening, but not to such an extent that further psychiatric evaluation was warranted. On the basis of his pre-induction evaluation David was found to be highly suitable for a combat unit. He applied to join an elite commando unit, but was turned down by the unit psychologist for unspecified reasons. In the army, according

to his officers, David did well in both basic and advanced combat training. Some of his comrades considered him "odd", but he was popular, as reflected by the routine sociometric ratings. Following his advanced training Davis was posted to a combat unit. He seemed to do well there, but complained to his parents of being depressed, losing weight and being unable to cope. His parents alerted the unit mental-health officer, who interviewed David. During the examination David minimized his symptoms and denied experiencing any depression or suicidal thoughts. However, he indicated that he could not continue to serve in a front-line unit. After consulting a more experienced senior psychiatrist, the mental-health officer diagnosed "adjustment reaction" and had Davis posted to a rear echelon. However, the prospect of reassignment made David feel like a "failure", and shortly after the examination, at the age of 18, he shot himself.

With the clarity of hindsight and as suggested by the detailed post-mortem accounts David appears to have suffered from a depression. The diagnosis was missed because of David's desperate denial of difficulties in the service, with its unrealistically high internal standards, and his fear of failure. Although he was not really up to the rigours of a combat unit, David strove desperately but unsuccessfully to over-function.

2. The second case is taken from the literature and consists of the famous "Case of Ellen West", reported by Binswanger and summarized by Hilda Bruch (1973, 1979). This woman was the daughter of wealthy Jewish parents to whom she remained closely attached and who maintained control over her. Her father interfered twice when she became engaged, and she finally married at the age of 28 with a cousin. At the age of 19 she developed the fear of becoming fat, and she developed a full-blown anorexia nervosa at the age of 21. Her diary was filled with recurrent passages like "the most horrible thing about my life is that it is filled with continuous fear. Fear of eating, but also fear of hunger and fear of fear itself. Only death can liberate me from this dread," and "since I am doing everything from the point of view whether it makes me thin or fat, all things lose their real value. My 'Fresslust' [German: obsession to eat] is my real obsession. It has fallen over me like a beast and I am helpless against it. It persecutes me continuously and I am helpless against it. It perse-cutes me continuously and drives me to despair ... This compulsion to think about food has become the curse of my life, it follows me when I am awake and when I am asleep. It stands next to me like an evil spirit and I feel as if I could never escape it." She was hospitalized, but this only increased her suicidal thoughts. She particularly reproached herself for having to lie to her physician by saying that she no longer took laxative tablets, although in fact she continued to do so. She was discharged from the sanatorium at the request of her family. On the third day after she had returned home, she appeared like a changed person, unusually quiet and relaxed. For the first time for 13 years she ate ordinary meals and enjoyed a walk with her husband. All depressive signs

and symptoms seemed to have fallen away from her. That evening she took a lethal dose of poison.

It appears that almost any chronic or severe mental illness can lead to feelings of demoralization, hopelessness and a secondary depression, and thus lead to suicidal thoughts and behaviour. Thus, almost all psychiatric illnesses are associated with increased rates of suicide, also among the young. Affective disorder in particular is a major risk factor for youth suicide, as it has been shown to be present in 25–75 per cent of youth suicides. However, personality disorder, in particular of the borderline type, is also commonly found, and rates of its presence in youth suicide vary between 25 and 40 per cent (Holinger et al, 1994).

There is a paucity of studies of serious suicide attempts in adolescents. The most robust scientific data come from the Canterbury study in New Zealand (Beautrais et al, 1996). The Canterbury Suicide Project is a case control study of 200 suicide cases, 302 medically serious suicide attempts and 1028 randomly selected control subjects. This study showed an elevated risk of suicide in association with mood disorder, substance abuse and conduct disorder. An excess mortality has also been shown among male adolescents with a history of psychiatric outpatient treatment. Pelkonen and colleagues (1996) studied a cohort of 156 male and 122 female Finnish adolescents 10 years after having received out-patient psychiatric care. They found that 16 male subjects but no female subjects had died. The mortality for any cause for males thus was 10.3 per cent, and mortality as a result of suicide was 7.1 per cent. Current suicidal ideation and suicide attempts, poor psychosocial functioning and a recommendation for psychiatric hospitalization during the index treatment were associated with mortality and suicide among the male adolescents. These findings are similar to those reported in earlier studies, which found that about 10 per cent of male adolescent psychiatric in-patients and about 1 per cent of female in-patients eventually killed themselves.

Psychiatric disorders are especially dangerous with regard to suicide in adolescents when they occur in conjunction with other risk factors for suicide, and when more than one illness is present. In our own clinical practice we have identified four co-morbid constellations which we believe to have particular significance for suicide in adolescent populations, and which require vigorous psychiatric intervention. The first is the combination of schizophrenia, depression and substance abuse. The second constellation consists of substance abuse, conduct disorder and depression. The third comprises affective disorder eating disorder and anxiety disorders, and the fourth consists of affective disorder, personality disorder (cluster A in *DSM* terminology*) and dissociate disorders. We recently surveyed admissions to our adolescent psychiatric unit over a period of 24 months (Stein et al, 1998). A total of 32 patients (20 per cent) had made one suicide attempt, 19 (11 per cent) had made multiple suicide attempts and 109 (69 per cent) had no history of suicidal behaviour. A majority of adolescents with such a history were suffering from affective and conduct disorder, but others had eating disorders or anxiety disorders. This survey was done before the recent upsurge of drug and alcohol abuse in Israel, which has led to an even higher incidence of attempted suicide patients in our ward.

Thus psychiatric disorders which may be associated with adolescent suicidal behaviour include affective disorders, schizophrenia, eating disorders and personality disorders. The role of *affective disorder* was demonstrated in a recent Swedish study (von Knorring et al, 1995). Among young people aged 16–17 years, 3.6 per cent of the boys and 8.8 per cent of the girls reported that they had attempted suicide at least once. A total of 60 per cent of the boys and 44 per cent of the girls who had attempted suicide were currently suffering from moderate or severe depression. The survey also showed that moderate or severe depression was present in only 2 per cent of the boys and 5 per cent of the girls who had not attempted suicide. The very common occurrence of depression among young people who have attempted suicide, as demonstrated in, among others, this study indicates the need for adequate diagnosis and treatment at an early stage. Recent studies have convincingly shown that depressive disturbances are more common among children and young people than was previously believed (Brent et al, 1993e).

Adolescents with bipolar disorder are at increased risk of completed suicide. Strober and colleagues (1995) found that 20 per cent of their adolescent subjects made at least one medically significant suicide attempt. The mean rate of completed suicide in adults suffering from bipolar disorder is estimated to be 19 percent (Lönnqvist, 2000). Patients who were male, or who were in the depressed phase of their illness, were at the highest risk of suicide.

Many patients suffering from *schizophrenia* are depressed and suicidal, especially when they are young and have not been ill for a long time. The differentiation between schizophrenia, psychotic depression or mania and schizoaffective disorder is not always easy in adolescence,

---

* American Psychiatric Association (1994) *Diagnostic and Statistical Manual of Mental Disorders* (Fourth Edition). Washington, DC, American Psychiatric Association.

and many conceptual and nosological issues remain to be decided. The co-morbid occurrence of depression and schizophrenia may be related to the fact that the young person feels that he is falling apart and becoming mentally ill, and there is indeed evidence that suicidality and depression in these patients is related to good premorbid function, better insight, higher intelligence and preservation of cognitive function (de Hert and Peuskens, 2000). Post-psychotic depression and neuroleptic medications may also have a role to play in this dangerous condition. About 10–15 per cent of patients suffering from schizophrenia eventually commit suicide, usually in the initial stages of their illness. Most schizophrenic suicide victims are unmarried men who have made previous suicide attempts. At least two-thirds of the suicides are related to depression and only a small minority to the psychotic symptoms such as command hallucinations. The suicide commonly occurs shortly after discharge, and thus may be related to a lack of social support.

Finally, many adolescents with schizophrenia also abuse drugs and alcohol, thus increasing their risk of suicide. The abuse may be an attempt at self-medication. Anti-cholinergic medications given for the relief of extra-pyramidal symptoms may give the patient a high to which he may become addicted. Patients may thus simulate extra-pyramidal symptoms in order to obtain these drugs. Childhood onset and adolescent schizophrenia are often preceded by difficulties in attention and learning for which stimulant medications may have been given. Again in the context of a developing schizophrenic illness there is a potential for abuse of these drugs and for drug-induced depression.

The increased risk of suicide in girls suffering from *eating disorders* has recently been recognized (Apter et al, 1995). The relationship between anorexia nervosa and depression is well documented. However, the suicide potential of these adolescents has been neglected in the literature, perhaps because these youngsters use denial to a large extent and because it was felt that starvation can be regarded as a suicidal equivalent, thus obviating the need for direct self-destructive behaviour in these patients. Recently, however, it has been pointed out that suicide is not rare in anorexia nervosa and that suicidal behaviour may be an important portent of a poor prognosis. Patton (1988) followed up 460 patients with eating disorders, and found that the increased standard mortality rate in anorectic patients was mostly due to suicide, with death occurring up to 8 years after the initial assessment. These findings were similar to those of the Copenhagen Anorexia Follow-up Study (Nielsen et al, 1998). Projective testing of anorectic patients has shown a preponderance of suicidal indicators. There also seems to be a group of late-onset anorexia patients in whom the loss of weight ultimately expresses a desire to die.

It is interesting to speculate on this association between depression, suicide and eating disorders. It is possible that for many girls weight loss is a form of self-medication for depression, since many healthy women indeed feel much better when they lose weight. Although this may be due to social approval, the release of endorphins from damaged muscle tissue or from vomiting may also play a role. In some cases we have seen depression resulting from weight gain, as if the patient was suffering from withdrawal symptoms from her addiction to thinness. However, weight loss may of itself induce quite severe depression and suicidal ideation, even in volunteers and in normal dieters. Another very dangerous form of depression occurs in treatment-resistant cases of anorexia nervosa, in which the constant battle against gaining weight, on the one hand, and the constant social pressure to gain weight, on the other, may become an intolerable burden. The diary of Ellen West, as described above, provides an excellent but dramatic example of this battle. An increased risk of suicidal behaviour has also been shown in adolescents suffering from bulimia nervosa. Suicidal behaviour can be part of an impulsive and unstable life style. Many of these patients show self-mutilation and cutting, but they often make serious suicide attempts with a potential fatal outcome. In our own series of former bulimic adolescent in-patients about 3.5 per cent died from suicide in a 15-year-long follow-up. This finding indicates that the risk of suicide in these patients may be approximately 300 times higher than the risk among other female adolescents with a history of in-patient psychiatric treatment. Recently, the term multi-impulsive bulimia has been coined to describe the increasingly more common association between bulimia, borderline or unstable personality disorder, substance abuse, depression and conduct disorder (Lacey, 1993). A majority of patients with this co-morbid constellation of disorders are women who are at high risk of repeated suicide attempts and suicide.

Non-fatal suicide attempts are a characteristic of *borderline personality disorder*, but there is increasing evidence that suicide is common in these patients as well (Linehan et al, 2000). Intentional self-damaging acts and suicide attempts are the "behavioural specialty" of these patients (Gunderson, 1984). Although affective instability is said to be one of the critical symptoms of this disorder, many patients suffering from borderline personality disorder appear to have a chronic underlying depression, and most of the adolescent borderline patients who require psychiatric help meet criteria for an affective disorder, most commonly major depression. In addition, many suffer from a chronic and stable depression characterized by hopelessness, worthlessness, guilt and helplessness. Another group of suicide-related symptoms is associated with anger. Many of these patients are very angry and even violent, while others are fearful of losing control over their anger and unable to express their aggressive feelings. Other frequent co-morbid conditions that increase the likelihood of suicide are conduct disorder, "multi-impulsive" bulimia, and substance abuse. An additional co-morbid condition of considerable interest is dissociative disorder, and this combination often seems to develop after incest or continuous non-injurious (in the physical sense) sexual abuse. Some authors report even seeing multiple personality disorder developing in these patients although our group has never seen such a case.

Although females have a lower rate of suicide than males, and approximately 75 per cent of patients suffering from borderline personality disorder are female (Linehan, 1993), approximately 9 per cent of patients with borderline personality disorder eventually kill themselves (Stone, 1989; Linehan et al, 2000). In a series of in-patients suffering from borderline personality disorder who were followed up for 10–23 years after discharge, patients exhibiting all eight DSM-III criteria for borderline personality disorder at the index admission had a suicide rate of 36 per cent, compared with 7 per cent of patients who met five to seven criteria.

CONCLUSIONS

Based on empirical evidence and clinical experience three constellations of psychopathological phenomena can be described which are associated with suicidal behaviour and in which personality characteristics play a major role. These constellations include the narcissistic–perfectionist, the impulsive–aggressive and the mental illness–demoralization–hopelessness constructs. These constellations refer to different vulnerabilities, which may share a common outcome (i.e. suicidal behaviour), and which describe different ways in which individuals perceive confrontations as adversities and act upon these perceptions. These reactions are multi-determined as they reflect influences from genetic factors and/or experiences in early life, which may be shaped by environmental constraints.

It can be expected that the recognition of personality characteristics like those described in this chapter will increase the specificity in predicting the occurrence of suicidal behaviour in association with psychiatric disorders. Moreover, their identification may lead to the development of novel interventions aimed at the prevention of suicide.

REFERENCES

Allgulander, C. (2000) Psychiatric aspects of suicidal behaviour: anxiety disorders. In K. Hawton and C. van Heeringen (Eds), *The International Handbook of Suicide and Attempted Suicide*. Chichester, Wiley.

Allgulander, C. and Lavori, P.W. (1991) Excess mortality among 3302 patients with "pure" anxiety neurosis. *Archives of General Psychiatry*, **48**: 599–602.

Altman, I. and Taylor, D. (1973) *Social Penetration: The Development of Interpersonal Relationship*. New York, Holt Reinhart and Winson.

Andrews, J.A. and Lewinsohn, P.M. (1992) Suicidal attempts among older adolescents: Prevalence and co-occurrence with psychiatric disorders. *Journal of the American Academy of Child and Adolescent Psychiatry*, **3**: 655–662.

Apter, A., Gothelf, D., Orbach, I., Weizman, R., Ratzoni, G., Har-Even, D. and Tyano, S. (1995) Correlation of suicide and violent behavior in different diagnostic categories in hospitalized adolescent patients. *Journal of the American Academy of Child and Adolescent Psychiatry*, **34**: 912–918.

Apter, A., Van Praag, H.M., Sevy, S., Korn, M. and Brown, S. (1990) Interrelationships among anxiety, aggression, impulsiveness and mood: a serotonergically linked cluster? *Psychiatry Research*, **32**: 191–199.

Apter, A., Bleich, A., Plutchik, R., Mendelsohn, S. and Tyano, S. (1998) Depression, suicidality and conduct disorder. *Journal of the American Academy of Child and Adolescent Psychiatry*, **27**: 669–696.

Apter, A., Fallon, T.J., King, R.A., Ratzoni, G., Zohar, A.H., Binder, M., Weizman, A, Leckman, J.F., Pauls, D.L., Kron, S. and Cohen, D.J. (1996) Obsessive-compulsive characteristics: From symptoms to syndrome. *Journal of the American Academy of Child and Adolescent Psychiatry*, **35**: 907–912.

Apter, A., Kotler, M., Sevy, S., Plutchik, R, Brown, S.L., Fotser, H., Hillbrand, M., Korn, M.L. and Van Praag, H.M. (1991) Correlates of risk of suicide in violent and non-violent psychiatric patients. *American Journal of Psychiatry*, **148**: 83–87.

Apter, A., Plutchik, R. and Van Praag, H.M. (1993) Anxiety, impulsivity and depressed mood in relation to suicide and violent behavior. *Acta Psychiatrica Scandinavica*, **87**: 1–5.

Arango, V., Ernsberger, P., Sved, A.F. and Mann, J.J. (1993) Quantitive autoradiography of a_1- and a_2- adrenergic receptors in the cerebral cortex of controls and suicide victims. *Brain Research*, **630**: 271–282.

Arango, V., Underwood, M.D., Gubbi, A.V. and Mann, J.J. (1995) Localized alterationsin pre- and postsynaptic serotonin binding sites in the ventrolateral prefrontal cortex of suicide victims. *Brain Research*, **688**: 121–133.

Archer, R.L. (1979) Role of personality in the social situation. In G.J. Chelune (Ed.), *Self Disclosure*. San Francisco, Jossey Bass.

Archer R.L., Hormuth S.E., and Berg J.H. (1982) Avoidance of self disclosure: An experiment under conditions of self awareness. *Personality and Social Psychology Bulletin*, **8**: 122–128.

Asberg, M., Nordström, P. and Träskman-Bendz, L. (1986) Cerebrospinal fluid studies in suicide: An overview. *Annals of the New York Academy of Science*, **487**: 243–255.

Axtell, B. and Cole, C.W. (1971) Repression sensitization response mode and verbal violence. *Journal of Personality and Social Psychology*, **18**: 133–137.

Barraclough, B.M. Bunch, J., Nelson, B. and Sainsbury, P. (1974) A hundred cases of suicide: Clinical aspects. *British Journal of Psychiatry*, **125**: 355–373.

Barrat, E.S. (1965) Factor analysis of some psychometric measures of impulsiveness and anxiety. *Psychology Reports*, **16**: 547–554.

Beautrais, A.L., Joyce, P.R. Mulder, R.T. Fergusson, D.M. Deavoll, B.J. and Nightingale, S. K. (1996) Prevalence and comorbidity of mental disorders in persons making serious suicide attempts: A case-controlled study. *American Journal of Psychiatry*, **153**: 1009–1014.

Beck, A.T., Schuyler, D. and Herman, I. (1974) Development of suicide intent scales. In A.T., Beck, D.J. Lettieri, and H.L.P. Resnick (Eds), *The Prediction of Suicide*. Maryland, Charles Press.

Beck, A.T., Ward, C.H. Mendelson, M., Mock, J. and Erbaugh, J. (1961) An inventory for measuring depression. *Archives of General Psychiatry*, **4**: 53–63.

Bettes, B.A. and Walker E. (1986) Symptoms associated with suicidal behavior in children and adolescents. *Journal of Abnormal Child Psychiatry*, **14**: 591–604.

Blatt, S.J. and Zuroff, D.C. (1992) Interpersonal relatedness and self-definition: Two prototypes for depression. *Clinical Psychology Review*, **12**: 527–562.

Blatt, S.J., Hart, B., Quinlan, D.M. and Leadbetter, B. (1993) Interpersonal and self-critical dysphoria and behavioural problems in adolescents. *Journal of Youth and Adolescence*, **22**: 253–269.

Brent, D.A., Perper, J.A. and Allman, C.J. (1987) Alcohol, firearms and suicide among youth : trends in Allegheny County, Pensylvania, 1960–1983. *Journal of the American medical Association*, **257**: 3369–3372.

Brent D.A., Perper, J.A., and Goldstein, C.E. (1988). Risk factors for adolescent suicide: A comparison of adolescent suicide victims with suicidal inpatients. *Archives of General Psychiatry*, **45**: 581–588.

Brent, D.A., Perper, J.A. and Moritz, G. (1993c) Psychiatric risk factors of adolescent suicide: a case control study. *Journal of the American Academy of Child and Adolescent Psychiatry*, **32**: 512–529.

Brent D.A., Perper, J.A., Moritz, G., Allman, C.J., Liotus, L., Schweers, J., Roth, C., Balach, L. and Conobbio, R. (1993h). Bereavement or depression? The impact of the loss of a friend to suicide. *Journal of the American Academy of Child and Adolescent Psychiatry*, **32**: 1189–1197.

Brent D.A., Perper, J.A., Moritz, G., Allman, C.J., Roth, C., Schweers, J. and Balach, L. (1993b) The validity of diagnoses obtained through the psychological autopsy procedure: use of family history. *Acta Psychiatrica Scandinavica*, **87**: 118–122.

Brent D.A., Perper, J.A., Moritz, G., Allman, C.J., Schweers, J., Roth, C., Balach, L., Condobio, R. and Liotus, L. (1993f) Psychiatric sequellae to the loss of an adolescent suicide. *Journal of the American Academy of Child and Adolescent Psychiatry*, **32**: 509–517.

Brent D.A., Perper, J.A., Moritz, G., Baugher, M. and Allman, C.J. (1993d) Suicide in adolescents with no apparent psychopathology. *Journal of the American Academy of Child and Adolescent Psychiatry*, **32**: 494–500.

Brent D.A., Perper, J.A., Moritz, G., Baugher, M., Schweers, J. and Roth, C. (1993a) Firearms and adolescent suicide: a community case-control study. *American Journal of Diseases of Children*, **147**: 1066–1071.

Brent D.A., Perper, J.A., Moritz, G., Liotus, L., Schweers, J., Roth, C., Balach, L. and Allman, C.J. (1993g). Psychiatric impact of the loss of an adolescent sibling to suicide. *Journal of Affective Disorders*, **28**: 249–256.

Brent, D.A. and Kolko, D.J. (1990) The assessment and treatment of children and adolescents at risk for suicide. In S.J. Blumenthal and D.J. Kupfer (Eds), *Suicide over the Life Circle: Risk Factors, Assessment and Treatment of Suicidal Patients*. Washington, DC, American Psychiatric Press.

Brent, D.A., Johnson, B., Bartle, S., Bridges, J. and Purpurce, J. (1993e) Personality disorder, tendency to impulsive violence and suicidal behavior in adolescents. *Journal of the American Academy of Child and Adolescent Psychiatry*, **32**: 69–75.

Brent, D.A., Johnson, B., Perper, J.A., Bartle, S., Rather, C. and Bridges, J. (1994) Personality disorder, personality traits, impulsive violence and completed suicide in adolescents. *Journal of the American Academy of Child and Adolescent Psychiatry*, **33**: 1080–1086.

Brown, G.L. Goodwin, F.K. Ballenger, J.C., Goyer, P.F. and Major, L.F. (1979) Aggression in humans correlates with cerebrospinal fluid amine metabolities. *Psychiatry Research*, **1**: 131–139.

Bruch, H. (1973) *Eating Disorders, Obesity, Anorexia Nervosa and the Person Within.* New York, Basic Books.

Bruch, H. (1979) The Golden Cage: The Enigma of Anorexia Nervosa. New York: Vintage.

Brunner, H.G., Nelen, M., Breakerfield, X.O., Ropers, H.H. and Van Oost, B.A. (1993) Abnormal behavior associated with a point mutation in the structural gene for monoamine oxidase A. *Science*, **262**: 578–580.

Buss, A. and Durkee, A. (1957) An inventory for assessing different kinds of hostility. *Journal of Consulting Psychology*, **21**: 343–349.

Carpenter, J.C. and Freeze, J. (1979) Three aspects of self disclosure as they relate to the quality of adjustment. *Journal of Personality Assessment*, **43**: 78–85.

Centers for Diseases Control (1994) Deaths resulting from firearms and motor vehicles related injuries, United States, 1968–1991. *Journal of the American Medical Association*, **27**: 495–496.

Centers for Diseases Control (1998) Suicide among black youths – United States, 1980–1995. *MMWR*, **47**: 193–196.

Chaikin, A.L. and Darlega, N.J. (1974) *Self Disclosure.* Morristown, General Learning Press.

Clayton, P.J. (1985) Suicide. *Psychiatric Clinics of North America*, **8**: 203–214.

Climent, C.E., Plutchik, R., Ervin, F.R. and Rollins, A. (1977) Parental loss, depression and violence III: Epidemiological studies of female prisoners. *Acta Psychiatrica Scandinavica*, **55**: 261–268.

Coccaro, E.F., Siever, L.J., Klar, H.M., Maurer, G. Cochrane, K., Cooper, T.B., Mohs, R.C. and Davis, K.L. (1989) Serotonergic studies in patients with affective and personality disorders. Correlates with suicidal and impulsive aggressive behavior. *Archives of General Psychiatry*, **46**: 587–599.

Cozby, P.C. (1973) Self disclosure: A literature review. *Psychological Bulletin*, **79**: 73–91.

Crumley, F.E. (1981) Adolescent suicide attempts and borderline personality disorder. *Southern Medical Journal*, **74**: 546–549.

De Hert, M. and Peuskens, J. (2000) Psychiatric aspects of suicidal behaviour: schizophrenia. In K. Hawton, and K. van Heeringen (Eds), *The International Handbook of Suicide and Attempted Suicide.* Chichester, Wiley.

De Wilde, E.J., Kienhorst, I.C., Diekstra, R.F. and Wolters, W.H. (1993) The specificity of psychological characteristics of adolescent suicide attempters. *Journal of the American Academy of Child and Adolescent Psychiatry*, **32**: 51–59.

Fawcett, J. Scheftner, W.A., Fogg, L., Clarck, D.C., Young, M.A., Hedeker, D. and Gibbons, R. (1990) Time-related predictors of suicide in major affective disorder. *American Journal of Psychiatry*, **147**: 1189–1194.

Fergusson, D.M. and Lynskey, M.T. (1995) Childhood circumstances, adolescent adjustment and suicide attempts in New Zealand birth cohort. *Journal of the American Academy of Child and Adolescent Psychiatry*, **34**: 1308–1317.

Flett, G.L., Hewitt, P.L., Boucher, D.J., Davidson, L.A. and Monro, Y. (1993) The

Child-Adolescent Perfectionism Scale: development, validation and association with adjustment. Manuscript under review. Under revision.

Garfinkel, B.D., Froese, A. and Hood, J. (1982) Suicide attempts in children and adolescents. *American Journal of Psychiatry*, **139**: 1257–1261.

Garrison, C.Z., Jackson, K.L., Addy, C.L., McKeown, R.E. and Waller, J.L. (1991) Suicidal behaviors in young adolescents. *American Journal of Epidemiology*, **133**: 1005–1014.

Garrison, C.Z., McKeown, R.E., Valois, R.F. and Vincent, M.L. (1993) Aggression, substance use, and suicidal behaviors in high school students. *American Journal of Public Health*, **83**: 179–184.

Goldstein, L.D. and Reinelcker, V.M. (1974) Factors affecting self disclosure: a review of the literature in Progress. In B.A. Mahler (Ed.), *Experimental Personality Research*, Vol 7. New York, New York Academic Press.

Graffi, H. (1997) Self Disclosure in Suicidal Patients. Unpublished MA thesis, Bar-Ilan University.

Gunderson, J.G. (1984) *Borderline Personality Disorder*. Washington, DC, American Psychiatry Press.

Holinger, P.C., Offer, D., Barter, J.T. and Bell, C.C. (1994) *Suicide and Homicide among Adolescents*. New York, Guilford Press.

Horowitz, L.M. and French, R. (1979) Interpersonal problems of people who describe themselves as lonely. *Journal of Consulting and Clinical Psychology*, **47**: 762–764.

Inmadar, S.E., Lewis, D.O. Siomopolous, G., Shanock S.S. and Lamella M. (1982) Violent and suicidal behavior in psychotic adolescents. *American Journal of Psychiatry*, **139**: 932–935.

Jones, W.H., Freeman, J.E. and Goswick, R.A. (1981) The persistence of loneliness: self and other determinants. *Journal of Personality*, **49**: 27–48.

Jourard, S.M. and Lasakow, P. (1958) Some factors in self disclosure. *Journal of Abnormal and Social Psychology*, **56**: 91–98.

Jourard, S.M. (1964) *The Transparent Self*. New York, D. Van Nostrand.

Jourard, S.M. (1971) *The Disclosure: An Experimental Analysis of the Transparent Self*. Chichester, Wiley.

Kaplan, M.F. (1967) Interview interaction of repressors and sensitizers. *Journal of Consulting Psychology*, **31**, 513–516.

Kermani, E.J.(1981) Violent psychiatric patients: A study. *American Journal of Psychotherapy*, **35**: 215–225.

King, R.A. and Apter, A. (1997) Psychoanalytic perspectives on adolescent suicide. *Psychoanalytic Study of the Child*, **51**: 491–505.

Kosky, R., Silburn, S. and Zubrick, S. (1986) Symptomatic depression and suicidal ideation: A comparative study with 628 children. *Journal of Nervous and Mental Disease*, **174**: 523–528.

Kreitman, N. (1977) *Parasuicide*. Chichester, Wiley.

Lacey, J.H. (1993) Self-damaging and addictive behaviour in bulimia nervosa. A catchment area study. *British Journal of Psychiatry*, **163**: 190–194.

Linehan, M.M., Rizvi, S.L., Welch, S.S. and Page, B. (2000). Psychiatric aspects of suicidal behaviour: personality disorders. In K. Hawton, and K. van Heeringen (Eds), *The International Handbook of Suicide and Attempted Suicide*. Chichester, Wiley.

Linehan, M.M., Heard, H.L. and Armstrong, H.E. (1993) Naturalistic follow-up of a behavioral treatment for chronically parasuicidal borderline patients. *Archives of General Psychiatry*, **50**: 971–974.

Lönnqvist, J. (2000) Psychiatric aspects of suicidal behaviour: depression. In K.

Hawton, and K. van Heeringen (Eds), *The International Handbook of Suicide and Attempted Suicide*. Chichester, Wiley.

Mannuzza, S., Aronowitz, B., Chapman, T., Klein, D.F. and Fger, A.J. (1992) Panic disorder and suicide attempts. *Journal of Anxiety Disorders*, **6**: 261–274.

Maris, R. (1992a) The relationship of non fatal attempts to completed suicides. In R.W. Maris, A.L. Berman, J.T. Maltsberger and R.L. Yuffit (Eds), *Assessment and Prediction of Suicide*. New York, Guiford Press.

Maris, R. (1992b) Overview of the study of suicide prediction and assessment. In R.W. Maris, A.L. Berman, J.T. Maltsberger and R.I. Yuffit (Eds), *Assessment and Prediction of Suicide*. New York, Guiford Press.

Marks, P.A. and Haller, D.L. (1977) Now I lay me down for keeps: A study of adolescent suicide attempts. *Journal of Clinical Psychology*, **33**: 390–400.

Massion, A.O., Warshaw, M.G. and Keller, M.B. (1993) Quality of life and psychiatric morbidity in panic disorder and generalized anxiety disorder. *American Journal of Psychiatry*, **150**: 600–607.

Mayo, P.R. (1968) Self disclosure and neurosis. *British Journal of Social and Clinical Psychology*, **7**: 140–148.

McAdams, D.P. (1980 A thematic coding for the intimacy motive. *Journal for Research in Personality*, **14**: 413–432.

Meninger, K. (1933) *Man Against Himself*. New York, Harcourt Brace.

Nielsen, S., Moller-Madsen, S., Isager, T., Jorgensen, J., Pagsberg, K. and Theander, S. (1998) Standardized mortality in eating disorders – a quantitative summary of previously published and new evidence. *Journal of Psychosomatic Research*, **44**: 413–434.

Oei, T.P., Evans, L. and Crook, G.M. (1990) Utility and validity of the STAI with anxiety disorder patients. *British Journal of Clinical Psychology*, **29**: 429–432.

Pelkonen, M., Marttunen, M., Pulkkinen, E., Koivisto, A.M. et al (1996). Excess mortality among former adolescent male out-patients. *Acta Psychiatrica Scandinavica*, **94**: 60–66.

Pfeffer, C.R. (1985a) Self-destructive behavior in children and adolescents. *Psychiatric Clinics of North America*, **8**: 215–226.

Pfeffer, C.R. (1985b) Variables that predict assaultiveness in child psychiatric inpatients. *Journal of the American Academy of Child Psychiatry*, **24**: 775–780.

Pfeffer, C.R., Plutchik, R. and Mizruchi, S. (1983) Suicidal and assaultive behavior in children, classification, measurement and interrelation. *American Journal of Psychiatry*, **140**: 154–157.

Plutchik, R. and Van Praag, H.M. (1986) The measurement of suicidality, aggressivity and impulsivity. Paper presented at the *International College of Neuropsychopharmacology*. New York, Neuropsychopharmacology Organization.

Plutchik, R., Van Praag, H.M. and Conte, H. (1985) Suicide and violence risk in psychiatric patients. In C. Shagass (Ed.) *Biological Psychiatry*. New York, Elsevier.

Raskin, R. and Perry, H. (1988) A principal component analysis of the Narcissistic Personality Inventory and further evidence of its construct validity. *Journal of Personality and Social Psychology*, **54**: 890–902.

Shaffer, D. and Fisher, P. (1981) The epidemiology of suicide in children and young adolescents. *Journal of the American Academy of Child Psychiatry*, **20**: 545–565.

Skodal, A.E., and Karasu, T.B. (1978) Emergency psychiatry and the assaultive patient. *American Journal of Psychiatry*, **135**: 202–205.

Slap, G., Vorters, D., Chawdhuri, S. and Sentor, R. (1988) Risk factors for attempted suicide during adolescence. Paper presented at *The American Society for Adolescent Medicine Meeting*. New York, The American Society for Adolescent Medicine Association.

Solano, C.M., Batten, P.G. and Parish, E.A. (1982) Loneliness and patterns of self disclosure. *Journal of Personality and Social Psychology*, **43**: 524–531.

Spirito, A., Brown, L., Overholser, J. and Fritz, G. (1989) Attempted suicide in adolescence: A review and critique of the literature. *Clinical Psychology Review*, **9**: 335–363.

Stein, D., Apter, A., Ratzoni, G., Har-Even, D and Anidan, G. (1998) Association between multiple suicide attempts and negative affects in adolescents. *Journal of the American Academy of Child and Adolescent Psychiatry*, **37**: 488–494.

Stengel, E. and Cook, N. (1958) *Suicide and Attempted Suicide*. London, Chapman and Hall.

Stone, M.H. (1989) Long-term follow-up of narcissistic/borderline patients. *Psychiatric Clinics of North America*, **12**: 621–641.

Strober, M., Schmidt, L.S., Freeman, R., Bower, S. et al (1995) Recovery and relapse in adolescents with bipolar affective illness: A five-year naturalistic, prospective follow-up. *Journal of the American Academy of Child and Adolescent Psychiatry*, **34**: 724–731.

Sullivan, H.S. (1953) *The Interpersonal Theory of Psychiatry*. New York, Norton.

Tardiff, K. and Sweillam, A. (1980a) Factors related to increased risk of assaultive behavior in suicidal patients. *Acta Psychiatrica Scandinavia*, **62**: 63–68.

Tardiff, K. and Sweillam, A. (1980b) Assault, suicide and mental illness. *Archives of General Psychiatry*, **37**: 164–169.

Taylor, D.A. (1968) The developmental of interpersonal relationships: Social penetration processes. *Journal of Social Psychology*, **75**: 79–90.

Taylor, E.A. and Stansfield, S.A. (1984) Children who poison themselves: I. A clinical comparison with psychiatric controls. *British Journal of Psychiatry*, **145**: 127–132.

Van Praag, H.M. (1997) Over the mainstream: diagnostic requirements for biological psychiatry. *Psychiatry Research*, **72**: 201–212.

Von Knorring, A.L. and Kristiansson, G. (1995) Depression och sjvlvmordsbeteende hos ungdomar (Depression and suicidal behavior in young people). In J. Beskoe (Ed.), Rvtt till livlust till liv. Om sjvlvmordsbeteende bland barn och ungdomar, Stockholm, *Forsningsruds-nvmnden, Rapport*, **95**(4): 35–43.

Weissman, M. and Klerman, G.L. (1993) *New Applications of Interpersonal Psychotherapy*. Washington, DC, American Psychiatric Press.

Weissman, M., Fox, K. and Klerman, G.L. (1973) Hostility and depression associated with suicide attempts. *American Journal of Psychiatry*, **130**: 450–455.

Wender, P.H., Kety, S.S., Rosenthal, D., Schulsinger, F., Ortmann, J. and Lunde, I. (1986) Psychiatric disorders in the biological and adoptive families of adopted indeviduals with affective disorders. *Archives of General Psychiatry*, **43**: 923–929.

Williams, C.L., Davidson, J.A. and Montgomery, I. (1980) Impulsive suicidal behavior. *Journal of Clinical Psychology*, **36**: 90–94.

Withers, L.E. and Kaplan, D.W. (1987) Adolescents who attempt suicide: A retrospective clinical chart review of hospitalized patients. Professional Psychology: *Research and Practice*, **18**: 391–393.

Zetzel, E.R. (1970) *The Capacity for Emotional Growth*. New York, International Universities Press.

Chapter 7

ETHOLOGY AND THE SUICIDAL PROCESS

Robert D. Goldney

INTRODUCTION

Ethology is the biological study of behaviour in natural settings. It was developed by Karl von Frisch, Konrad Lorenz and Nikko Tinbergen and some of its basic concepts have entered our language. These include "imprinting", a specific form of learning which occurs early in life, and which is only possible at a "critical period", a "fixed action pattern" which is a pre-determined behavioural pattern which is initiated by a specific "innate releasing mechanism", and "displacement activity", a form of behaviour which appears unrelated to other activity.

It may initially appear paradoxical to seek ethological analogies in regard to the suicidal process, as by implication ethology suggests an appropriate adaptation to external demands. However, that is not always the case, and biologists have used terminology to describe behaviour, which is, at the very least, self-injurious in a number of different species. For example, it has been recorded in macaques, marmosets, squirrel monkeys, leopards, lions, jackals, hyenas, rodents and opossums (Jones, 1982), as well as in dolphins, pink bollworm moths, butterflies, pea aphids, birds and some bacteria (Lester and Goldney, 1997). Indeed, it is not only in the last few decades that such observations have been made, as "The suicide of animals" was well documented by Westcott (1885) over a hundred years ago. Therefore there appears

Understanding Suicidal Behaviour. Edited by Kees van Heeringen
© 2001 John Wiley & Sons Ltd.

to be a sound basis for examining how an ethological approach could assist our understanding of the suicidal process.

THEORETICAL HYPOTHESES

Theoretical hypotheses applying ethological concepts to the suicidal process are by no means new. For example, Stengel and Cook (1958), in referring to the then relatively new discipline of ethology, suggested that "the suicidal attempt acts very much as a 'social releaser'", and Stengel (1962) wrote that "the suicidal attempt functions as an alarm system and an appeal for help. It does so almost with the regularity of an 'innate release mechanism'". It is also pertinent that these concepts are embodied well in the title of Farberow and Shneidman's (1961) influential book, *The Cry for Help*, where the suicide attempt results in care being provided, in a manner similar to that described by Henderson (1974), who referred to attempted suicide as "care-eliciting behaviour", and saw it as a developmentally primitive signal for care.

Although the application of ethological principles to humans must be pursued with caution, it is recognized increasingly that insights gained from such an approach to behaviour may be of clinical and theoretical relevance. Early examples included those of Bowlby (1958) who utilized such principles in his work on attachment theory and the consequences of maternal deprivation, and the work of Harlow and colleagues (1971) and subsequent researchers such as Kraemer and co-workers (1997) and Higley and Linnoila (1997) have provided cogent data in regard to depression and aggressive and impulsive behaviour in primates.

In ethological terms suicidal behaviour could be interpreted as displacement activity, as an innate releasing mechanism or as a fixed-action pattern. With regard to displacement activity, a persuasive theory has been postulated by Jones and Daniels (1996) about the re-direction of aggression towards oneself when it is either not socially appropriate to be angry at others, or when there are other powerful barriers to the expression of aggression. Such a hypothesis has some clinical utility, particularly when considering some institutional populations, such as jails, where there are not only constraints upon behaviour but also social isolation.

Suicidal behaviour also acts as a stimulus, which could be interpreted as an innate releasing mechanism, which elicits a response, the fixed-action pattern, in other people. Alternatively, it could be interpreted as the fixed-action pattern, whereby the behaviour itself is precipitated

women have greatest reproductive value, and their appeals are more likely to be met altruistically.

A parallel can also be drawn between suicidal behaviour, particularly in young women, and "ritual agonistic behaviour", or the settlement of dispute by exchange of signals, which are often concluded by so-called "yielding behaviour", rather than by physical violence. In this regard the concept of "resource-holding potential" is pertinent. This implies that the result of ritual encounters between members of the same species depends on the individual's ability to use and conserve attributes such as size, skill and previous success. In essence this means whether or not individuals consider themselves more powerful than competitors. In humans it has been described as "social attention-holding power", which is "the ability to attract attention and investment from other members of the group" (Stevens and Price, 1996). This has implications in terms of a person's self-esteem and capacity to form social affiliations, be they in the work place or with a partner. Stevens and Price (1996) have stated that "A subjective social attention holding power assessment which results in a perception of oneself as being both powerless and unattractive will activate that ancient biological mechanism responsible for the yielding subroutine, with all its depressive and behavioural consequence". A further dimension to this sequence of events is the concept of "entrapment" described by Williams (1997), when the individual perceives no other options than to yield. Williams suggested that a sense of entrapment is "central to suicidal behaviour", and that it results in "long-term demobilisation, a biological state involving chemical changes".

This appears to indicate that yielding behaviour is disadvantageous. However, that that may not necessarily be the case has been suggested by Sloman and Price (1987) who observed that "acceptance of loss or defeat requires a certain level of developmental maturity". They noted that most people learn both healthy assertion and appropriate yielding in family and group contexts, and that it was normal under certain circumstances to accept defeat or yield during ritual agonistic encounters. It is further pertinent that yielding behaviour is similar to female courtship behaviour, as the female who is able to yield and turn an agonistic encounter with a male into a sexual encounter provides biological advantage to her species. Not uncommonly such an outcome is observed in suicidal behaviour in young women.

The previous speculations have been based primarily on naturalistic observation of individuals, both human and animal. A broader application of ethological principles—urban ethology—involves a community-wide examination of behaviour. For example, what mechanisms could underline the marked changes in the pattern of suicide for certain groups, such as young males, in some countries over a relatively short period of time?

A concept which may be of relevance is that of the "tipping point" (Tittle and Rowe, 1973; Goldney, 1998), which implies that there is a background or base rate of a behaviour, probably as a result of many factors, but that there is a threshold or "tipping point" which, once breached, allows for a dramatic increase in that behaviour. Although this concept is derived from a sociological background, its implications are strikingly similar to a model of suicide based on studies of chaos theory, dynamic systems and self-organization, where it was noted that "in an open system, abrupt changes in the very nature of the structure may take place" (Mishara, 1996).

These concepts are applied to suicidal behaviour in an attempt to understand such behaviour in an overall scientific climate, which is becoming increasingly aware that certain processes in nature, although given different names by different disciplines, share many features in common. For example, they are consistent with the "principle of universality", which has been applied to a number of different physical and organizational systems, where it has been observed that a critical point may be reached beyond which sudden changes in many systems occur (Buchanan, 1997). This appears to be particularly germane to suicidal behaviour, as it often emerges in a dramatic and ostensibly unexpected manner as a response to multiple stressors.

RECENT NEUROBIOLOGICAL PERSPECTIVES

For many years it was believed that the human brain could not regenerate and that there was an inevitable loss of nerve cells from early adulthood onwards. Indeed, the view of the Spanish neurologist Ramon y Cajal in 1913 that "In adult centres the nerve paths are something fixed, ended, immutable. Everything may die, nothing may be regenerated" (quoted by Lowenstein and Parent, 1999) remained influential for most of the twentieth century. However, in the last 20 years increasing data have emerged which have demonstrated clearly an association between external stressors, behaviour and neurobiological changes.

For example, in his seminal article "Transduction of psychosocial stress into the neurobiology of recurrent affective disorder", Post (1992) provided a cogent description of the development of depressive conditions after stressors had produced changes in biochemical and neuro-anatomical substrates. This model implies that the experience of depression leaves behind a memory trace, which predisposes to further episodes of depression. Consequently, subsequent stressors do not need to be so severe, and a point comes when depression may be spontaneous, without external stressors. In fact, it is as if a critical point or tipping point has been breached.

Such a theory is consistent with the "gluco-corticoid cascade" hypothesis, (O'Brien, 1997), whereby prolonged hypothalamic/pituitary/adrenal (HPA) activity produces hippocampal damage, as demonstrated in vervet monkeys subjected to prolonged social stress (Uno et al, 1989). Hippocampal damage produces impairment in cognition, and that may contribute to what Williams (1996) has described as the "mnemonic interlock" phenomenon, which is a subtle inability of suicidal subjects to recall specific events. It is also consistent with the cognitive science perspective provided by Segal and colleagues (1996), who suggested that the voluntary deployment of attention in order to prevent the escalation of mild depressive states may have an underlying neuro-biological basis, which in essence counteracts the development of affective disorders as postulated by Post. Such hypotheses are attractive, as they allow a reconciliation between differing hypothetical paradigms.

ANIMAL STUDIES

There have been a number of recent animal studies which are pertinent in providing a link between early clinical observations and the biology of behaviour. Of particular relevance is the work of Insel (1997), who described "a neurobiological basis of social attachment" in a study of the mouse-like mammals, the prairie (*Microtus ochrogaster*) and montane (*Microtus montanus*) voles. Although the prairie and montane voles belong to the same species, they have markedly different social behaviours. Prairie voles are monogamous and highly affiliative with strong pair bonds and both males and females participate in parental care. Puberty for the female does not occur at any specific age, but only after exposure to a signal in the urine of an unrelated male, following which she becomes sexually receptive and forms an enduring monogamous bond. By contrast montane voles are isolated, have little social contact, are not monogamous and females frequently abandon their young.

It is important that there are marked differences in oxytocin- and vasopressin-receptor distribution in their brains, although after parturition the female montane vole's oxytocin-receptor binding changes to resemble that of the more parental prairie vole. Following a series of elegant experiments, Insel concluded that "Remarkably, the neurohypophyseal neuropeptides oxytocin and vasopressin appear to be important for the formation of social attachments, including pair bonding in monogamous mammals, the initiation of parental care in both males and females and possibly some aspects of the infant's attachment behavior".

These findings should probably not be considered remarkable, as Liu and co-workers (1997) have demonstrated in rats that early maternal behaviour appeared to programme HPA responses to stress in off-spring. They reported that rat pups, which received more rather than less maternal licking and grooming, showed reduced plasma adreno-corticotropic hormone and cortico-sterone responses to restraint stress. Furthermore, the greater the frequency of maternal licking and groom-ing during infancy, the lower the HPA response to stress in adulthood.

Kraemer and colleagues (1997) have also investigated changes in HPA activity and brain micro-structure in association with isolation and self-injurious behaviour in monkeys, as well as serotonin metabolism because of the consistent observation that serotonin activity, as meas-ured by cerebrospinal fluid 5-hydroxyindoleacetic acid (CSF 5-HIAA), was low in violent suicide attempters in humans (Nordström et al, 1994). In a review of their studies they described a reduction in dendritic branching of nerve cells in various regions of the brain, including the hippocampal neuronal microstructure, and suggested that the behavioural effects of isolation could be related to the degen-eration of brain neurotransmitters and associated denervation hyper-sensitivity. In regard to serotonin metabolism, they reported no association between self-injurious behaviour in isolate-reared monkeys and lowered serotonin activity because of pharmacological manipulation. This was unexpected, and in a series of studies they explored this phenomenon further and found that the behavioural effect of the pharmacological manipulation of CSF 5-HIAA was depen-dent on social-rearing factors. Whereas there was no effect with ser-otonin-lowering drugs on those monkeys who had been reared in isolation, there was an effect on the socially reared monkeys. This led them to postulate a "failure to connect" hypothesis related to early maternal deprivation, with a disruption of the usual relationship between the noradrenergic, dopaminergic and serotonergic systems, probably as a result of changes in cellular morphology and synaptic density.

Similar work has been conducted by Higley and Linnoila (1997), who reported that there was a high degree of stability of CSF 5-HIAA concentration over time in both humans and monkeys. Consistent with the association of lowered CSF 5-HIAA with violent suicide in humans, they reported that in rhesus monkeys there was excess mortality because of violence by those with low CSF 5-HIAA, and that those same monkeys were observed to be socially isolated and alienated from their peers. They noted that maternal input was critical in the development of the serotonin system, and concluded that "genetic tendencies for low CSF 5-HIAA concentrations can be attenuated or augmented by early rearing experiences, particularly parental deprivation".

Consistent with this work is the demonstration of an association between measures of sociability and serotonin metabolism in rhesus macaques (Mehlman et al, 1995), with CSF 5-HIAA concentration being positively correlated with the total time spent grooming others and being in close proximity with other group numbers, and with the number of close neighbours. This demonstrates that certain indicators of social competence are related to CSF 5-HIAA in primates, and these findings are consistent with a recent study in non-depressed persons given a selective serotonin re-uptake inhibitor which reduced negative effect and increased affiliative behaviour (Knutson et al, 1998). Quite clearly this behavioural change is advantageous in terms of an individual's social attention-holding power described previously.

The importance of these reports is that they are congruent with molecular and cellular theories of depression in humans, such as those proposed by Post (1992) and more recently by Duman and colleagues (1997). Indeed, the latter stated that "stress can decrease the expression of brain-derived neurotrophic factor and lead to atrophy of these same populations of stress-vulnerable hippocampal neurons". Duman and co-workers (1997) went on to hypothesize, in a manner consistent with the earlier work of Post (1992) and which is entirely compatible with developmental theory, that "one possibility is that many individuals who become depressed may have had a prior exposure to stress that causes a small amount of neuronal damage, but not enough to precipitate a behavioural change. If additional damage occurs, either as a result of normal ageing or further stressful stimuli, these effects may then be manifested in the symptoms of a mood disorder".

For obvious reasons such research is difficult to carry out in humans, but it is interesting to reflect on recent findings in other species. In his presidential address to the American Psychiatric Association, Hartmann (1992) referred to the work of the neurobiologist, Fernald and his colleagues who have recently published further work which demonstrates that changes in the social state of an African cichlid (*Haplochromis burtoni*) fish are associated with changes in neuronal size (Fox et al, 1997). They demonstrated that how a male fish interacted with other males, in regard to whether it was socially dominant or meek, had an effect on the brain cells regulating the fish's size, colour and capacity to reproduce. The dimensions of those brain cells were seen to be plastic and if an aggressive fish met a larger and/or more aggressive fish, the hypothalamic neurones of the defeated male rapidly shrank. After the hypothalamic cells had shrunk, the male testes followed suit, decreasing the fish's apparent desire and ability to breed. In the laboratory situation some male fish were environmentally pushed from dominators to meek types and cellular changes followed. Fernald and his colleagues found that key behavioural changes occurred first and drove the brain changes and it was quite evident that social changes altered the brain cells.

Such work is consistent with what Edelman (1987) has termed "Neural Darwinism", an obvious evolutionary reference to organisms responding to the environment. This has been reviewed further by Gynther and co-workers (1998) who concluded that "While the most dramatic examples of neuroplasticity occurred during a critical period of neural development, neuroplasticity can also occur in adult neocortex. Neuroplasticity appears to be activity-dependent: synaptic pathways that are intensively used may become strengthened, and conversely, there may be depression of transmission in infrequently used pathways". They observed that the most profound examples of activity-dependent plasticity were seen in the first few months following birth, and referred to experiments in newborn kittens deprived of visual input in one eye where marked changes were observed in the functional organization of their visual cortex.

These findings are similar to those reported by Brainard and Knudsen (1998) in experimental work on young barn owls wearing prisms that displaced their visual field horizontally. The owls were able to adjust to auditory stimuli so that they could correctly orientate themselves to the source of the sound, despite wearing the prisms. That adjustment was mediated by changes in the response properties of neurones in the central auditory pathway and the phenomenon could be reversed. It is of note that there was a time after which the brains of the owls could not adjust adaptively to prismatic displacement of the visual field, depending on the animals' environment. However, spectacle-reared owls could return to normal after removal of the spectacles during their lifetime, but their capacity to do so depended on the environment. Those mature owls who were able to regain normal sound localization

Nevertheless, the results of the few human studies to date, as well as those from animal research, appear to be sufficiently robust to warrant the pursuit of intensive study of maternal and peri-natal factors in order to provide an additional link in our understanding of the suicidal process.

CONCLUSION

It could be argued that the ethological paradigm has been extended beyond its limits in some of the studies referred to. However, there is a logical connection between the early ethological observations and hypotheses, the more recent delineation of biochemical and neuro-physiological data associated with developmental issues in other species and in man, and the naturalistic longitudinal cohort observations of factors associated with subsequent suicidal behaviour.

Clinicians can be reassured that as a result of this research derived from ethological principles we are closer to understanding the nexus between early adverse life events and the neurobiology associated with developmental issues. However, we cannot yet draw definite conclusions from such studies. Indeed, as persuasive as some of these hypotheses and analogies may appear, they remain at the level of hypotheses, albeit hypotheses now on a firmer theoretical base than when tentative ethological speculation was made 40 years ago. Importantly, an ethological approach has provided a bridge between sociological and psychological theories, on the one hand, and those theories based more on biological sciences, on the other. Even if it were for that reason alone, the value of an ethological approach in the conceptualization of the suicidal process is assured.

REFERENCES

Barker, D.J.P., Osmond, C., Rodin, I., Fall, C.H.D. and Winter, P.D. (1995) Low weight gain in infancy and suicide in adult life. *British Medical Journal*, **311**: 1203.

Bowlby, J. (1958) The nature of the child's tie to his mother. *International Journal of Psychoanalysis*, **39**: 350–373.

Brainard, M.S. and Knudsen, E.J. (1998) Experience affects brain development. *American Journal of Psychiatry*, **155**: 1000.

Buchanan, M. (1997) One law to rule all. *New Scientist*, **2107**: 30–35.

Duman, R.S., Heninger, G.R. and Nestler, E.J. (1997) A molecular and cellular theory of depression. *Archives of General Psychiatry*, **54**: 597–606.

Edelman, G.M. (1987) *Neural Darwinism: The Theory of Neuronal Group Selection*. New York, Basic Books.

Elbert, T., Pantev, C., Wienbruch, C., Rockstroh, B. and Taub, E. (1995) *Science*, **270**: 305–307.

Engel, G.L. (1962) Anxiety and depression–withdrawal. *International Journal of Psychoanalysis*, **43**: 89–97.

Farberow, N.L. and Shneidman, E.S. (1961) *The Cry for Help*. New York, McGraw-Hill.

Fergusson, D.M. and Woodward, L. (1999) Breast feeding and later psychosocial adjustment. *Paediatric and Peri-natal Epidemiology*, **13**: 144–157.

Fox, H.E., White, S.A., Kao, M.H.F. and Fernald, R.D. (1997) Stress and dominance in a social fish. *The Journal of Neuroscience*, **17**: 6463–6469.

Goldney, R.D. (1980) Attempted suicide: an ethological perspective. *Suicide and Life-Threatening Behavior*, **10**: 131–141.

Goldney, R.D. (1998) Variation in suicide rates: the "Tipping Point". *Crisis*, **19**: 136–138.

Goldney, R.D. and Bottrill, A. (1980) Attitudes to patients who attempt suicide. *Medical Journal of Australia*, **2**: 717–720.

Gynther, B.D., Calford, M.B. and Sah, P. (1998) Neuroplasticity and psychiatry. *Australian and New Zealand Journal of Psychiatry*, **32**: 119–128.

Harlow, H.F., Harlow, M.K. and Suomi, S.J. (1971) From thought to therapy: lessons from a primate laboratory. *American Science*, **59**: 538–549.

Hartmann, L. (1992) Presidential address: reflections on humane values and bio-psycho-social integration. *American Journal of Psychiatry*, **149**: 1135–1141.

Henderson, S. (1974) Care-eliciting behavior in man. *Journal of Nervous and Mental Disease*, **159**: 172–181.

Higley, J.D. and Linnoila, M. (1997) Low central nervous system serotonergic activity is traitlike and correlates with impulsive behavior. In D.M. Stoff and J.J. Mann (Eds), *The Neurobiology of Suicide*. New York, Annals of The New York Academy of *Sciences*, Volume 836.

Insel, T.R. (1997) A neurobiological basis of social attachment. *American Journal of Psychiatry*, **154**: 726–735.

Jacobson, B. and Bygdeman, M. (1998) Obstetric care and proneness of offspring to suicide as adults: case-control study. *British Medical Journal*, **317**: 1346–1349.

Jones, I.H. and Daniels, B.A. (1996) An ethological approach to self-injury. *British Journal of Psychiatry*, **169**: 263–267.

Jones, I.H. (1982) Self-injury: toward a biological basis. *Perspectives in Biology and Medicine*, **26**: 137–150.

Knutson, B., Wolkowitz, O.M., Cole, S.W., Chan, T., Moore, E.A., Johnson, R.C., Terpstra, J., Turner, R.A. and Reus, V.I. (1998) Selective alteration of personality and social behavior by serotonergic intervention. *American Journal of Psychiatry*, **155**: 373–379.

Kraemer, G.W., Schmidt, D.E. and Ebert, M.H. (1997) The behavioural neurobiology of self-injurious behavior in Rhesus monkeys. In D.M. Stoff and J.J. Mann (Eds), *The Neurobiology of Suicide*. New York, Annals of The New York Academy of Sciences, Volume 836.

Lester, D. (1991) Childhood predictors of later suicide: follow-up of a sample of gifted children. *Stress Medicine*, **7**: 129–131.

Lester, D. and Goldney, R.D. (1997) An ethological perspective on suicidal behavior. *New Ideas in Psychology*, **15**: 97–103.

Liu, D., Diorio, J., Tannenbaum B., Caldji, C., Francis D., Freedman, A., Sharma, S., Pearson, D., Plotsky, P.M. and Meaney M.J. (1997) Maternal care, hippocampal glucocorticoid receptors, and hypothalamic-pituitary-adrenal responses to stress. *Science*, **177**: 1659–1662.

Lowenstein, D.H. and Parent, J.M. (1999) Brain, heal thyself. *Science*, **283**: 1126–1127.

Mehlman, P.T., Higley, J.D., Fauches, I., Lilly, A.A., Taub, D.M., Vickers, J., Suomi, S. J. and Linnoila, M. (1995) Correlations of CSF-5-HIAA concentration with sociality and the timing of emigration in free-ranging primates. *American Journal of Psychiatry*, **152**: 907–913.

Mishara, B. L. (1996) A dynamic model of suicide. *Human Development*, **39**: 181–194.

Montgomery, S.M., Bartley, M.J. and Wilkinson, R.G. (1997) Family conflict and slow growth. *Archives of Diseases of Childhood*, **77**: 326–330.

Neeleman, J., Wessely, S. and Wadsworth, M. (1998) Predictors of suicide, accidental death, and premature natural death in a general-population birth cohort. *Lancet*, **351**: 93–97.

Neugebauer, R. and Reuss, M.L. (1998) Association of maternal, antenatal and perinatal complications with suicide in adolescence and young adulthood. *Acta Psychiatrica Scandinavica*, **97**: 412–418.

Nordström, P., Samuelsson, M., Åsberg, M., Träskman-Bendz, L., Aberg-Wistedt, A., Nordin, C. and Bertilsson, L. (1994) CSF 5-HIAA predicts suicide risk after attempted suicide. *Suicide and Life-Threatening Behavior*, **24**: 1–9.

O'Brien, J.T. (1997) The "gluco-corticoid cascade" hypothesis in man. *British Journal of Psychiatry*, **170**: 199–201.

Post, R.M. (1992) Transduction of psychosocial stress into the neurobiology of recurrent affective disorder. *American Journal of Psychiatry*, **149**: 999–1010.

Rampon, C., Ya-Ping, T., Goodhouse, J., Shimizu, E., Kyin, M. and Tsien, J.S. (2000) Enrichment induces structural changes and recovery from nonspatial memory deficits in CA1 NMDAR1 – knockout mice. *Nature Neuroscience*, **3**: 238–244.

Salk, L., Lipsitt, L.P., Sturner, W.Q., Reily, B.M. and Levat, R.H. (1985) Relationship of maternal and perinatal conditions to eventual adolescent suicide. *Lancet*, **1**: 624–627.

Seager, C.P. (1978) What's in a name? Attempted Suicide. *British Journal of Psychiatry*, **132**: 206–207.

Segal, Z.V., Williams, J.M., Teasdale, J.D. and Gemar, M. (1996) A cognitive science perspective on kindling and episode sensitisation in recurrent affective disorder. *Psychological Medicine*, **26**: 371–380.

Simpson, M.A. (1976) Self-mutilation. In E.S. Shneidman (Ed.), *Suicidology*. New York, Grune and Stratton.

Sloman, L. and Price J.S. (1987) Losing behavior (yielding sub-routine) and human depression: proximate and selective mechanisms. *Ethology and Sociobiology*, **8**: 99S–109S.

Stengel, E. (1962) Recent research into suicide and attempted suicide. *American Journal of Psychiatry*. **118**: 725–727.

Stengel, E. and Cook, N.G. (1958) *Attempted suicide: Its social significance and effects*, Maudsley Monograph Number 4. Oxford, Oxford University Press.

Sterr, A., Muller, M.M., Elbert, T., Rockstroh, B., Pantev, C. and Taub, E. (1998) Changed perceptions in Braille readers. *Nature*, **291**: 134–135.

Stevens, A. and Price, J. (1996) *Evolutionary psychiatry: a new beginning*. London, Routledge.

Tittle, C.R. and Rowe, A.R. (1973) Moral appeal, sanction threat and deviance: an experimental test. *Social Problems*, **20**: 488–498.

Trivers, R.L. (1971) The evolution of reciprocal altruism. *Quarterly Review of Biology*, **46**: 35–57.

Uno, H., Tarara, R., Else, J.G., Suleman, M.A. and Sapolsky, R.M. (1989) Hippocampal damage associated with prolonged and fatal stress in primates. *Journal of Neuroscience*, **9**: 1705–1711.

Westcott, W.W. (1885) The suicide of animals. In *Suicide: Its History, Literature, Jurisprudence, Causation and Prevention*. London, H.K. Lewis.

Williams, J.M.G. (1996) The specificity of autobiographical memory in depression. In D. Rubin (Ed.), *Remembering Our Past: Studies in Autobiographical Memory*. Cambridge, Cambridge University Press.

Williams, M. (1997) *Cry of Pain: Understanding Suicide and Self-harm*. London, Penguin.

Chapter 8

TOWARDS A PSYCHOBIOLOGICAL MODEL OF THE SUICIDAL PROCESS

Kees van Heeringen

INTRODUCTION

Although suicidal behaviour rarely occurs without a context of psychiatric problems, there are several reasons to separate the study of suicidal behaviour from that of psychiatric disorders. Cross-sectional and longitudinal studies have shown that the occurrence of suicidal behaviour is not limited to the boundaries of classical psychiatric diagnostic categories. Almost all psychiatric disorders are characterized by an increased risk of suicidal behaviour. Hence, the existence of one or more suicidal syndromes has been proposed independently of psychiatric disorders (Ahrens and Linden, 1996). Moreover, familial transmission of suicide occurs independently of the transmission of psychiatric disorders (Brent et al, 1996). There is thus no simple linear causal association between psychiatric problems and suicidal behaviour.

Evidence is accumulating that suicidal behaviour results from the interaction between stressor-induced state-dependent characteristics such as psychiatric problems, and trait-like factors, which may include characteristics related to personality. Based on currently available knowledge a stress–diathesis model can be used to describe this interaction (e.g. see Mann et al, 1999). In this model, the "stress" concept refers to psychiatric, psychological or biological phenomena, which occur

Understanding Suicidal Behaviour. Edited by Kees van Heeringen
© 2001 John Wiley & Sons Ltd.

following the exposure to stressful life events (see also Chapter 3). The term "diathesis" is used to describe a persistent vulnerability or pre-disposition to suicidal behaviour. A diathesis for a disorder can be defined as the genetic predisposition and the biological traits produced by genetic programming, biological stressors or both (Zuckerman, 1999).

In this chapter an attempt will be made to integrate the results of the studies that were reviewed in the various chapters of the first part of this book by developing a model to describe the interaction between stress and a diathesis for suicidal behaviour. This psychobiological model will incorporate the stress–diathesis and process approaches to the understanding of suicidal behaviour.

The chapters in the first part of this book have made clear that many aspects of these models can be defined in biological (see Chapters 3 and 4), psychological (see Chapter 5) or psychiatric (see Chapter 6) terms. However, an increasing amount of research findings indicates a con-siderable overlap between these approaches, thus justifying the de-scription of a psychobiological basis for the explanation of suicidal behaviour. The findings as described in the first part of this book can be used to develop a psychobiological stress–diathesis model to explain the occurrence of suicidal behaviour across classical psychiatric diagnostic boundaries. Moreover, evidence is accumulating that this psychobiological basis is not a static phenomenon, but rather should be regarded as a dynamic system, in which stress and diathesis influence each other and which can be influenced by various factors.

This chapter will describe how the changes occurring according to these influences might be responsible for the course of the suicidal process, thus justifying an integration of the stress–diathesis model and the suicidal process approach in a psychobiological model of the suicidal process. First, current knowledge about the stress and diathesis components of the stress–diathesis model will be summarized accord-ing to psychiatric, psychological and biological points of view, respec-tively. Second, currently available knowledge about the ways in which these components may influence each other will be reviewed. Finally, it will be argued that diathesis is to be regarded as a dynamic organiza-tion of characteristics, which can thus be influenced by a variety of factors. These factors may include influences with a detrimental effect on the vulnerability for suicidal behaviour, which thus may be respons-ible for the progression of the suicidal process. However, the assump-tion of a dynamic nature of the diathesis implies that it can also be influenced by protective factors such as treatment. Implications with

events (see also Chapter 4 and below). Second, a psychiatric component of the diathesis may consist of personality-related characteristics. Personality characteristics in association with suicidal behaviour have been described in categorical terms (e.g. see Haw et al, in press; Suominen et al, 2000). However, the categorical approach to personality is associated with important methodological limitations (e.g. in terms of overlaps between categories and heterogeneity with regard to outcome) which are not present in a dimensional approach. In Chapter 6 Apter and Hofek have provided an example of such a dimensional approach by describing personality constellations in association with suicidal behaviour. Personality dimensions, which were found in other studies in association with suicidal behaviour, have been described as aloofness (Shaffer, 1974), low reward dependence in terms of Cloninger's psychobiological model of personality (Van Heeringen et al, 2000) or high stability as measured by means of the Marke–Nyman Temperament (MNT) Scale (Engström et al, 1996a; see also Chapter 3). Persons who score low on reward dependence or high on stability are characterized by being aloof and detached. Noteworthy in this respect is the finding of Ferdinand and Verhulst (1995), who studied the stability of emotional and behavioural problems from adolescence into young adulthood and the effect of these problems on the occurrence of psychopathology during an 8-year follow-up. They found that suicidal behaviour was particularly associated with a pervasive behavioural pattern (the "withdrawn syndrome"), which was characterized by withdrawal from contact with other people, sadness and a preference for being alone. It thus appears that a personality characteristic, which can be defined in terms of reward dependence, is associated with an increased risk of suicidal behaviour. This personality characteristic, which is hypothetically at least in part heritable (Cloninger et al, 1993), may be responsible for the development of interpersonal problems which are known to commonly precipitate suicidal behaviour. Kendler and colleagues (1993) have recently shown that the occurrence of such problems is, at least partially, under genetic control, and it is conceivable that reward dependence plays a role in the occurrence of interpersonal problems by interfering with affiliative capacities. In Chapter 3 Träskman-Bendz and Westrin referred in a similar way to genetic influences on the availability of social support, which may play a role in the development of suicidal behaviour (see also Chapter 15).

As was described by Apter and Ofek in Chapter 6, a trait related to impulsivity and the regulation of aggression has also been shown to have an effect on the occurrence of suicidal behaviour. Amsel and Mann in Chapter 9 will discuss the potential benefits of including the aggression/impulsivity trait in the assessment of the risk of suicide. However, there appears to be a complex relationship between anxiety, aggression, impulsivity, depression and suicidal behaviour. The discussion of the association between trait-dependent characteristics—such as impulsivity and aggression—and suicidal behaviour may well be confounded by a lack of equivocal definitions of these characteristics. This issue will be discussed in more detail in Chapter 15.

Research in the *psychological* domain has demonstrated that patients with a history of non-fatal suicidal behaviour show a number of characteristics that, as described by Williams and Pollock in Chapter 5, apparently are trait dependent. These characteristics include perceptual characteristics (i.e. attentional biases towards being a loser) and the sense of being entrapped when confronted with particular stressors such as those described above. The term "entrapment" refers to the sense of being caught in a particular situation, which may lead to feelings of hopelessness. Williams and Pollock (2000) have convincingly argued that this sense of being entrapped is associated with (most probably) trait-dependent deficiencies in problem-solving skills, which in turn appear to depend upon deficits in autobiographical memory. A final cognitive psychological characteristic, typical of attempted suicide patients, is their lack of positive rescue factors (i.e. the possibility to generate positive future events). As described in Chapter 5, Williams and co-workers were able to demonstrate that hopelessness correlated significantly with the lack of generating future positive events, and not with an excessive anticipation of negative things in the future.

With regard to the *biological* aspects of the diathesis for suicidal behaviour, a dysfunction of the serotonergic system has received most attention. The association between the occurrence of suicidal behaviour and dysfunctioning of the serotonergic (5-HT) system is indeed one of the most replicated findings in biological psychiatry. The nature of this association is, however, still not yet totally clear. A dissection of the serotonergic system as proposed by Deakin (1996) can be helpful in explaining some of the serotonergic findings in association with suicidal behaviour by describing the divergent roles of the $5\text{-}HT_{1a}$ and $5\text{-}HT_2$ systems. The $5\text{-}HT_{1a}$ system, which projects from the brainstem's median raphe nucleus, is thought to be involved in resilience to psychosocial stressors, primarily located in the medial temporal cortex and hippocampus and mediated by the $5\text{-}HT_{1a}$ system in conjunction with noradrenaline. Dysfunction of the system is associated with depressive ideation and low self-esteem. The $5\text{-}HT_2$ system, which consists of projections from the dorsal raphe nucleus to the prefrontal cortex and amygdala, is thought to be involved primarily in executive functions, and works in conjunction with the dopaminergic system. Dysfunction of the $5\text{-}HT_2$ system is characterized by social anxiety and hopelessness. Further evidence supporting the involvement of the serotonergic system in suicidal behaviour has been provided by studies of the brains of suicide victims and by studies using platelets or challenge techniques. Based on a review of research findings, Van Praag concluded in Chapter 4 that suicidal behaviour is associated with disturbances in serotonin metabolism and in serotonin receptor functions. A recent neuro-imaging study by means of SPECT (Single Photon Emission Computerized Tomography) using a highly selective receptor radioligand confirmed the involvement of the $5\text{-}HT_2$ system in suicidal behaviour by showing a reduced binding potential of $5\text{-}HT_{2a}$ receptors in the prefrontal cortex of patients who very recently attempted suicide (Audenaert et al, 2001). The binding potential was significantly more decreased in attempters who used violent methods than in those who deliberately poisoned themselves. This finding thus adds to the evidence for involvement of the serotonergic system in suicidal behaviour, and suggests that the disturbance of the serotonergic system is more prominent in violent than in non-violent suicidal behaviour.

A second issue with regard to trait-related biological aspects of the diathesis concerns the possibility of a hyper-reactivity of the HPA axis as the cause of the increased production of cortisol following exposure to stressful life events (see Chapter 4). Our finding of a significant negative correlation between reward dependence scores on Cloninger's Temperament and Character Inventory (TCI) and free urinary-cortisol concentrations indicates that this temperamental dimension plays an important role in the processing of events that may precipitate suicidal behaviour (Van Heeringen et al, 2000). Noteworthy is the study of Engström and colleagues (1996b) who found a similar correlation between high scores on the MNT dimension stability (reflecting emotional distance from others) and urinary cortisol secretion. In other words, the lower the score on reward dependence (or the higher the score on stability) the stronger the stress response. Evidence is accumulating that this stressor-induced increase in cortisol production may play a crucial role in the development of the diathesis, and may determine the course of the suicidal process to a considerable extent. There is indeed evidence that particular stressors interfere with serotonergic neurotransmission, most probably because of the effects of increased cortisol secretion (Deakin, 1996). The course of the suicidal process and the factors that may influence this course will be described in more detail in the second part of this chapter.

Diathesis for suicidal behaviour: two components

In the stress–diathesis model, which is elaborated in this chapter on the basis of the results of the studies as described in the first part of this book, it is hypothesized that the probability of occurrence of suicidal behaviour is associated with the existence of disturbances in at least two components, or, in other words, that the diathesis consists of at least two components. The first component can be regarded as the faculty that regulates the interaction between an individual and his/her environment, and thus may contribute to the development of inter-personal problems and resilience towards such stressful events. The second component mediates the behavioural reactions to problems, such as those arising from this interaction. These two components influence each other through anatomic and neurobiological connections (Table 8.1).

The involvement of the first component in the development of suicidal behaviour can be described at two levels, because the interaction between an individual and his/her environment includes both the way in which an individual reacts to changes in the environment and the way in which an individual contributes to the characteristics of the environment. First, individuals who are at increased risk of suicidal behaviour are characterized by a sensitivity for particular stressors. As described above, stressful life events associated with the occurrence of suicidal behaviour are commonly of an interpersonal

Table 8.1 Two components of a diathesis for suicidal behaviour

Approach	Social-interaction component	Behavioural-inhibition component
Psychiatric	Suicidal ideation	Hopelessness/anxiety
Biological	5-HT$_{1a}$/noradrenaline	5-HT$_2$/dopamine

Personality:
  TCI   temperament
            character
  MNT
	Low reward dependence
	Low self-directedness
	High stability
		High harm avoidance
		Low self-directedness
		Low validity

Neuro-anatomical	Medial temporal cortex/hippocampus	Prefrontal cortex/amygdala
Cognitive psychological	Sensitivity to signals of defeat	Entrapment and absence of rescue factors
Neuropsychological	Attention	Autobiographical memory

TCI = Temperament and Character Inventory (Cloninger et al, 1993).
MNT = Marke–Nyman Temperament Scale (Engström et al, 1996).

or psychosocial nature, and the sensitivity is determined by the way these events are processed in the receptive brain (in the brain's medial temporal cortex in conjunction with the hippocampus), and more specifically by the extent to which they are perceived as a threat to the integration of the individual in the system in which he or she lives. Cloninger and colleagues (1993) have suggested that biases in the perception of events in the interpersonal realm are determined by the temperamental dimension reward dependence.

From a neurobiological point of view this first component is probably mediated by the 5-HT$_{1a}$ system in conjunction with noradrenergic projections, as proposed by Deakin (1996) and described earlier in this chapter. Cortisol has been shown to have a cytotoxic effect on hippocampal cells (McEwen, 1999; see p. 155). Sustained exposure of the 5-HT$_{1a}$ system to increased levels of cortisol thus may be responsible for or contribute to a disturbed 5-HT$_{1a}$ functioning in the first component as described above, thus leading to decreased resilience to stressors. This might explain, at least partially, the increasing behavioural responsivity over time, as indicated by the finding that life events become less important in triggering depressive episodes when the number of episodes increases.

The second component that might be involved in the diathesis for suicidal behaviour is thought to be responsible for the behavioural reaction to perceived stressful events. In the brain such behavioural reactions are mediated by the executive function of the prefrontal cortex. Deakin (1996) has pointed at the crucial role of the 5-HT$_2$ system with regard to this executive function. It thus comes as no surprise that post-mortem and neuro-imaging studies have revealed disturbances in the 5-HT$_{2a}$ system in the prefrontal cortex of individuals who showed suicidal behaviour. It is, however, not clear yet in what way these serotonergic disturbances contribute to the occurrence of suicidal behaviour. In the stress–diathesis model, which was recently proposed by Mann and colleagues (1999), a serotonin-mediated impulsivity and deficiency in the regulation of aggression plays a crucial role. Our recent neuro-imaging studies of the 5-HT$_{2a}$ system in attempted suicide patients and healthy volunteers (Van Heeringen et al, submitted) showed a significant correlation between prefrontal 5-HT$_{2a}$ receptor binding potential, levels of hopelessness and scores on the temperamental dimension harm avoidance (reflecting at least partially heritable biases in behavioural inhibition, Cloninger et al, 1993). The results thus suggest that a cluster made up of 5-HT$_{2a}$ dysfunction, hopelessness and behavioural inhibition characterizes attempted suicide patients. If serotonin-mediated behavioural inhibition indeed plays a crucial role in the development of suicidal behaviour, it is tempting to speculate that this inhibition is responsible for the "arrested flight" situation as described by Williams and Pollock in Chapter 5, and related to problem-solving deficits which cognitive psychologists have described as a core phenomenon in the development of suicidal behaviour. It can further be speculated that these problem-solving deficits are the consequence of a deficient-working memory, a short-term component of the autobiographical memory function of the prefrontal cortex. As will be described in more detail in Chapter 15, studies in which neuropsychological assessments are combined with sophisticated functional neuro-imaging techniques may provide support for these speculations.

The association between the proposed components of the diathesis and the important concept of self-disclosure, which was addressed in Chapters 1 and 6, is not yet clear. Self-disclosure reflects the ability to communicate personal feelings, or to share intimate feelings with others. Self-disclosure may have an important impact on the course of the suicidal process by determining, among others, the threshold (or the level of the dotted line in Figure 1.1) which the suicidal process is not observable to others so that no therapeutic or preventive actions can be undertaken. As was described in Chapter 6 by Apter and Ofek, limited self-disclosure is associated with loneliness and with (lethal) suicidal behaviour, anxiety and aggression. It may thus be that aspects of both components of the diathesis (i.e. the social interaction and behavioural inhibition components) may be involved in the ability for self-disclosure.

The causes of a diathesis for suicidal behaviour

With regard to the causes of a diathesis-like vulnerability or predisposition, it has been suggested that genetic factors and early traumatic life events play a role. With regard to *genetic factors*, it must be taken into account that most behavioural characteristics are heritable (McGue and Bouchard, 1998), and there is little doubt about a genetic effect on the occurrence of suicidal behaviour, including suicide attempts and completed suicide (Roy et al, 2000). With regard to genetic influences on the risk of suicide, the serotonergic system has been the subject of considerable research interest (Roy et al, 2000). For example, Du and colleagues (1999, 2000) indeed recently demonstrated an association between the allelic distribution of the serotonin transporter and the 5-HT_{2a} receptor genes and suicidal behaviour and ideation, respectively. The development of a diathesis-like vulnerability may be determined genetically also through the familial transmission of personality characteristics. Biological approaches to personality disorders are receiving increasing attention, and genetic contributions to a growing number of personality dimensions have indeed been identified. Cloninger and co-workers (1993) have suggested a genetic effect on the temperamental dimensions of their psychobiological personality model, including those which have been shown to be involved in suicidal behaviour, as will be described in more detail (see p. 153). A recent twin study of the heritability of personality dimensions showed a broad range of heritability estimates, with the highest estimate (i.e. 64 per cent) for narcissism (Livesley et al, 1993), identified by Apter and Ofek in Chapter 6 as one of the core personality factors associated with suicidal behaviour.

Less information is available with regard to the effect of *early life events* on the development of a trait-dependent vulnerability or diathesis. A vast amount of studies have investigated the effect of early life events on the occurrence of suicidal behaviour; however, without specifying in which way such events may increase the probability of suicidal behaviour. For example, Yang and Clum (1996) have recently reviewed a large number of studies of the relationship between suicidal behaviour and negative life events during childhood or adolescence. They showed a clear and consistent association between adult attempted suicide and sexual or physical abuse and emotional neglect during childhood or adolescence. Moreover, attempted suicide patients were found to more commonly report parental divorce or separation, and premature death, suicidal behaviour or chronic psychiatric disorders in one or both parent(s). It is, however, not clear yet in which way such experiences of parental problems influence the probability of suicidal behaviour in offspring. Yang and Clum (1996) suggest a cognitive link by hypothesizing that the exposure to early negative life experiences leads to cognitive disturbances such as low self-esteem, hopelessness and deficient problem-solving skills. Many questions, however, remain unanswered (e.g. about the role of genetic effects). It is indeed possible that early experiences with a demonstrated effect on the occurrence of suicidal behaviour (i.e. parental divorce or separation and psychiatric disorders or suicide in one or both parents) reflect heritable parental characteristics related to personality (such as deficient affiliative capacities, deficits in interpersonal problem-solving skills, or impulsivity) or to a vulnerability to develop psychiatric disorders.

Perhaps even more important than the question whether a diathesis results from the presence or absence of early negative experiences, and more in keeping with the concept of a continuous diathesis (see p. 150), is the growing insight into how an individual's resilience towards stress is determined by the interaction between the individual and his/her caretaker in early life. As stated by Kandel (1999), differences in an infant's interactions with its mother—differences that fall in the range of naturally occurring individual differences in maternal care—are crucial risk factors for an individual's future response to stress. In view of the role of the personality dimension reward dependence, which has a (hypothetical) genetic origin (Cloninger et al, 1993), in the development of suicidal behaviour, it is tempting to speculate that a low level of reward dependence (reflecting emotional distance) in the mother will affect the interaction with her child, and thus influence the child's resilience towards stress. As was described by Goldney in Chapter 6, on the basis of his review of ethological findings, early experiences indeed may alter the set point for a biological response to stress. Research data suggest that there are 'windows in time' (e.g. early, middle or late childhood, puberty and mid-adolescence) when a gene is dependent on a certain type of environmental influence to determine its expression (Gabbard, 2000). It may well be that traumatic experiences during unstable periods of brain development can produce a form of regression to an earlier stage of neural function and structure. There is currently no information about such a "window in time" with regard to the development of the proposed vulnerability for suicidal behaviour. Evidence has recently been found of an effect of a lack of positive parent–child interaction during middle childhood on the occurrence of adult depression (Lindelöw, 1999), but the relevance of findings like these for the development of suicidal behaviour remains to be shown.

The interaction between stress and diathesis

Stress–diathesis models may take different forms depending on as- sumptions made about the roles of the stress and the diathesis, such as whether they are necessary, sufficient or contributing but not neces- sary causes (Zuckerman, 1999). Such models can be additive or inter- active, depending on the way in which the stress and diathesis, individually or in combination, may influence the occurrence of a disorder. The interactive model postulates that the diathesis is a neces- sary but not sufficient condition for the disorder. The additive model of stress–diathesis interaction suggests that stress may have some influ- ence in producing the disorder, but that it takes much more stress in a person with a weak or absent diathesis than in someone with a strong diathesis (Zuckerman, 1999). A diathesis can be dichotomous (i.e. present or absent) or continuous. Variation in neurotransmitter levels, for example, rather than a specific neural deficit, will allow for degrees of diathesis. Stress–diathesis models may further differ accord- ing to the degree of interdependency of the stress and the diathesis.

While certain kinds of stress may be unrelated to the diathesis, other types of stress, such as those produced by defective interpersonal skills, may have a direct relationship with the diathesis.

Based on the research findings as reviewed in Part I, a hypothetical model can be proposed to explain suicidal behaviour as the consequence of an interaction between stress and a diathesis.

From a neuro-anatomical point of view the two described components are thought to be connected via the uncinate fasciculus (Deakin, 1996). It is still unclear whether disturbances in this connection are involved in the pathogenesis of suicidal behaviour. As described by Van Praag in Chapter 4, somewhat more is known about neurobiological interactions by means of studies of the effect of cortisol on the serotonergic system. Dinan (1994) has suggested that changes in central monoaminergic pathways, as found in depression, occur as a direct consequence of overactivation of the HPA axis and associated hypercortisolaemia. It has been shown that sustained hypercortisolaemia reduces the metabolism of serotonin, possibly via activation of the enzyme tryptophan pyrrolase and shunting of large amounts of tryptophan to the kinurenine pathway, thus leaving insufficient amounts of tryptophan available for synthesis of serotonin (see Chapter 4). Animal studies have shown effects of steroids on both the 5-HT_{1a} and 5-HT_{2a} systems (López et al, 1997). The results of such studies have suggested that a balance between hippocampal 5-HT_{1a} receptors, which are hypothetically involved in the first component of the diathesis, and cortical 5-HT_{2a} receptors (possibly involved in the second component of the diathesis), is essential for the ability to respond to stress (McKittrick et al, 1995). It is not yet clear whether the 5-HT_{1a} and 5-HT_{2a} receptor changes observed in hypercortisol states represent an adaptive response to stress or a breakdown of this adaptive mechanism (López et al, 1997).

THE SUICIDAL PROCESS AND ITS COURSE OVER TIME

The chapters in Part I have reviewed the increasing amount of knowledge resulting from studies of epidemiological, psychological, biological, psychiatric and related characteristics of the suicidal process. However, almost all of these studies have been retrospective or cross-sectional in design, and consequently far less evidence is available regarding the course of such characteristics over time. In order to discuss the psychological, biological and/or psychopathological underpinnings of the suicidal process one thus has to rely upon information on the course of psychiatric disorders associated with suicidal phenomena. However, insight into the evolution of the neurobiological substrate over time is increasing, and suggests that the diathesis is continuous and not dichotomous.

The course of psychopathological manifestations of the suicidal process

The evolution of psychopathological characteristics during the course of the process is not yet totally clear. Williams and Pollock described in Chapter 5 how initial phases of the process can be characterized by high levels of protest, which may become apparent as increased levels of anxiety or anger. Later in the process, when escape potential following the confrontation with adverse circumstances is perceived as reduced, despair may gradually gain the upper hand, which may be reflected by more marked symptoms of depressed mood and increased levels of hopelessness. Empirical data on the psychopathological characteristics of particular phases in the process and their course over time are scarce and fragmentary. The available data appear to support, however, Williams and Pollock's hypothetical description of the process. Bettes and Walker (1986), for instance, showed that male adolescent patients who expressed suicidal thoughts in the absence of behaviour were more likely to be rated as anxious when compared with suicide attempters. With regard to later phases of the process, studies of survivors of medically serious suicide attempts, which commonly occur in later phases of the suicidal process, may provide insight into the psychopathological characteristics of these later phases. These studies have shown that the prevalence of mental disorders is similarly high for non-fatal serious suicide attempts and for completed suicide, and underline the important role of mood disorders in medically serious suicide attempts (Beautrais et al, 1996; O'Donnell et al, 1996). The proposed gradual evolution from anxiety-related signs early in the process to depressive symptoms in later phases of the suicidal process mirrors findings from studies outside the suicidological area, showing that depressive disorders are commonly preceded by anxiety disorders, in particular those reflecting social anxiety (Fava et al, 2000).

In view of the common association between affective disorder and divergent components of suicidality, including suicidal ideation, suicide attempts and completed suicide, the relationship between the course of affective disorders and that of the suicidal process deserves further study. Affective disorder is a highly recurrent illness, and the number of lifetime episodes of major depression is significantly

of suicidal behaviour, and its potential involvement in the suicidal process merits further consideration.

As described above, the probability of occurrence of suicidal behaviour at a certain moment in an individual's life appears to be defined by the interaction between stressful life events and a two-component diathesis, which mediates the perception of these events (and thus reflects a sensitivity to environmental influences) and determines the behavioural reaction to such stressors, respectively. These systems most probably are functionally intertwined, and influence each other by means of, for example, neuro-endocrine mechanisms.

Based on currently available knowledge, the neurobiological substrate of these two systems can be described, and evidence for their involvement in the development of suicidal behaviour is increasing. The proposed stress–diathesis model underlines that individual characteristics and the environment do not stand in opposition, but act rather in a reciprocal fashion. The effect of influences such as genetic factors or neuro-endocrine mechanisms is thereby probabilistic rather than deterministic, and shaped by environmental influences. This overview has also indicated a considerable overlap in findings from research with apparently diverging backgrounds such as psychology and biology, thus justifying a psychobiological approach to the treatment and further study of suicidal behaviour. It is remarkable how findings from such diverging research approaches converge by pointing at the crucial role of memory and learning in the development of suicidal behaviour.

Memory, diathesis and the suicidal process

By assuming an interaction between stress and diathesis the stress–diathesis approach contributes to an explanation for the differences between individuals in their response to stressors. In other words, the diathesis can be considered of major importance in the process of defining the behavioural reactions to stressors by determining the significance and salience of perceived stressors. Cloninger and colleagues (1993) have provided a model, the usefulness of which in suicide research was summarized by Williams and Pollock in Chapter 5. The definition of a diathesis in terms of memory and learning is a major characteristic of Cloninger's psychobiological model (1993). This psychobiological model of personality is based on the constructs of temperament and character that are involved in perceptual processes and the development of concepts, respectively. During the process of determining the significance and salience of perceived stressors human beings convert sensory inputs (i.e. percepts) into abstract symbols (i.e.

concepts). Stimulus-response characteristics thus depend on the conceptual significance and salience of perceived stimuli (Cloninger et al, 1993). The involved perceptual and conceptual memory systems correspond to procedural and declarative memory systems.

This conceptualization of a diathesis in terms of personality traits and memory systems may contribute substantially to an integration of many of the abovementioned findings with regard to the vulnerability to suicidal behaviour, thus allowing for development of a psychobiological model of suicidal behaviour. Temperament dimensions play a major role in this model, as was indicated earlier in this chapter, by describing the role of, for example, reward dependence and harm avoidance in the two components of the diathesis.

An important aspect of the procedural memory system concerns its involvement in perceptual learning and the learning of habits and skills. As such, temperament can be defined in terms of individual differences in associative learning in response to novelty, danger or punishment, and reward, reflecting the temperamental dimensions novelty seeking, harm avoidance and reward dependence, respectively (Cloninger et al, 1993). Temperament determines direct perceptual experience and thus unconscious automatic responses to stimuli. While genetic influences on the development of temperamental characteristics are increasingly identified, additional influences most probably occur during infancy. Animal studies have clearly shown that stress early in life, by separation of the infant from its mother, produces a reaction in the infant that is stored primarily by the procedural memory system. This is the only well-differentiated memory system that the infant has early in its life, but this action of the procedural memory system leads to a cycle of changes that ultimately damages the hippocampus and thereby results in a persistent change in declarative memories (Kandel, 1999).

The declarative memory system might be involved in the development of suicidal behaviour at several levels because of its role in autobiographical memory and in the development of self-concepts via insight learning. The first component of the diathesis in the model as described above implicates a role of the medial temporal lobe and the hippocampus. These structures are involved in one component of the declarative memory system (i.e. episodic or autobiographical memory). In addition to the medial temporal cortex and the hippocampus, the prefrontal cortex is also involved in the storage of declarative memory. This part of the brain has, in general, three functions: (1) working memory (a short-term component of episodic or autobiographical memory), (2) preparatory set (the priming of sensory and especially motor structures for performance of an act that is contingent on a prior event, and thus on the content of working memory) and (3) inhibitory control (inhibition of distracting memories or stimuli) (Fuster, 1997). The combination of the first two functions leads to reconciliation of the past with the future, or of behaviour with goals. As such, the prefrontal cortex plays a role in cognitive, emotional and motivational aspects of human behaviour, and changes in its executive functioning lead to changes in the reactivity to external stimuli, and thus in interactions with other people. Adequate functioning will provide individuals with the capacity to, for example, formulate goals with regard to long-term consequences, generate multiple response alternatives and initiate goal-directed actions (Malloy et al, 1998). The important role of impulsivity, problem-solving deficits and reactivity to the environment has been described at several points in the first part of this book, which may underline the crucial involvement of the prefrontal cortex in the development of suicidal behaviour and indicate the effect of its functions on the course of the suicidal process.

Animal studies have shown that lesions in the *orbital region* of the prefrontal cortex lead to an inability to deal with aggression, following which the animal loses its stand in its community (Fuster, 1997). As described in Chapters 4 and 5, respectively, both the regulation of aggression and a decrease in social ranking may play a role in the development of suicidal behaviour, thus suggesting that (dys-)function in this area is involved in suicidal behaviour. Lesions in the *dorsolateral area* of the prefrontal cortex may influence cognitive functions to such an extent that this may result in an inability to sort out sensory stimuli, to generate multiple response alternatives and to inhibit the response tendency to flee (Fuster, 1997). The similarities in the description of these functions of the prefrontal cortex and that of the dysfunctions found in association with suicidal behaviour, including problem-solving deficits and the "arrested flight" concept, are striking, thus indicating the urgent need for further study of the role of the prefrontal cortex in the development of suicidal behaviour. Diagnostic advances in the area of neural science offer intriguing possibilities for such research, and relevant research methods and strategies will be described in detail in Chapter 15.

Such studies may provide insight into the association between the evolution of the suicidal process and changes in the neurophysiological systems and their functions, as described above. For example, the question arises to what extent repeated exposure to specific stressors gradually undermines the escape potential. This escape potential may be a crucial factor in the choice of suicidal behaviour as the response to an unbearable situation of living, because reduced escape potential is determined by the perception of being closed in ("entrapment"). The stronger this perceived entrapment is, the higher the level of hopelessness and the risk of suicidal behaviour. The gradual undermining of the escape potential might well be the consequence of the cytotoxic effects of the corticoid stress hormone on involved memory systems (McEwen, 1999). As was described by Goldney in Chapter 7, such effects have indeed been demonstrated in cells of the hippocampus. The hippocampus is thought to play a role in resilience to psychosocial stressors as a part of the first component of the psychobiological model, as described on pp. 144 and 145. These cytotoxic effects may indeed gradually diminish the capacity to generate multiple responses to stressors or to put stressful life events in context, thus explaining the evolution from "protest" to "despair" or from anger/ anxiety to hopelessness during the suicidal process. Goldney's "tipping point" hypothesis (see Chapter 7) remains to be tested in the context of the suicidal process. It may thus be that during the process of such a gradual decline, a threshold or tipping point may be breached following which a dramatic change in the process may take place. Such a change may become manifest as a sudden outburst of self-harming behaviour, whether or not with a fatal outcome.

If functioning well, declarative memory systems may thus serve to modify the unconscious automatic responses to stimuli as determined by temperamental characteristics, and thus decrease reactivity to the environment by providing a context in which stressful life events may occur (the hippocampus is thought to play a major role in providing this context). By using information that is stored in the autobiographical memory system, conceptual insights may thus modify habitual responses and decrease the reactivity to the environment, which are determined by temperamental characteristics. Cloninger and colleagues (1993) have used the term "character" to describe the conceptual organization of perception. Character develops through a maturation process, which involves insight learning or the development of new adaptive responses as a result of conceptual reorganization of experience. Character thus may allow individuals to control, regulate and adapt behaviour to fit the situation in accordance with individually chosen goals, or, in other words, to make choices among alternative responses. By modifying automatic, unconscious or habitual responses, character thus needs to mature in order to increase self-directedness and reduce reactivity to environmental influences. Referring to common precipitants of suicidal behaviour in Chapter 7, Goldney cited Sloman and Price (1987) who stated that acceptance of loss or defeat requires a certain level of developmental maturity. Insight learning thus may provide a fruitful component of the treatment and prevention of suicidal behaviour. Thus, while temperament dimensions may be modified by pharmacological interventions, as will be discussed in Chapter 13, psychological treatments may be relevant for the development of character. Examples of psychotherapeutic approaches will be provided in Chapter 14. However, it is now clear that glutamate and gamma-aminobutyric acid (GABA) neurotransmitters are involved in the development of declarative memory (Nutt, 2000), which is a crucial aspect of psychotherapeutic strategies aiming at gaining mastery over temperament-driven behaviour (Gabbard, 2000). Drugs that influence these neurotransmitter systems may thus have an impact on the ability to learn from psychotherapy. This issue will be discussed in more detail in Chapter 15.

CONCLUSIONS

This chapter has reviewed the evidence in support of a hypothetical psychobiological model of suicidal behaviour, which is based on a stress–diathesis model, but encompasses a process-based approach. In short, suicidal behaviour is believed to be the consequence of the interaction between stressors, which are commonly of a social or interpersonal nature, and a diathesis. This diathesis is suggested to consist of two components. These components determine, first, social interaction, the occurrence of social stressors and the resilience to such stressors, and, second, the capacity of problem solving and the behavioural reaction in case of inadequate problem solving. Recent advances in the area of neural science are providing a rapidly increasing insight into the neuro-anatomical and neurobiological underpinnings of these components. While the model described in this chapter is mainly based on observations in humans, it is intriguing to note the similarity between these findings and those from animal studies, which indicate that a balance between these components is essential for the ability to respond adequately to (social) stress.

The dissection of a diathesis for suicidal behaviour in two components or subsystems may help to explain a number of observations which have been commonly made with regard to suicidal behaviour. Most importantly, it may provide insight into the reasons why not all depressed individuals who experience suicidal ideation (in association with a dysfunction of the first component) engage in suicidal behaviour, because of adequate functioning of the second component. It may also explain why not all individuals who are exposed to negative life experiences develop emotional disorders (as a result of the resilience function of the first component) or show suicidal behaviour (as a result of the adequate function of the second component).

Emphasis was put on the role of memory and learning in these components of the diathesis, and on how they are shaped by genetic influences and (whether or not early) life experiences. The diathesis is considered to be continuous (i.e. not dichotomous), and experiences may influence the diathesis to such an extent that resilience to stressful life events may gradually diminish, thus explaining the suicidal process as it is commonly preceding a completed suicide.

Although much more research is needed to support this hypothetical dissection of the diathesis for suicidal behaviour into two components, it may also provide insight into suicidal behaviour that is necessary for development of new approaches to treatment and prevention. Research strategies and implications for treatment and prevention will be discussed in detail in Chapter 15.

REFERENCES

Ahrens, B. and Linden, M. (1996) Is there a suicidality syndrome independent of specific major psychiatric disorders? Results of a split half multiple regression analysis. *Acta Psychiatrica Scandinavica*, **94**: 79–86.

Åsberg, M. (1997) Neurotransmitters and suicidal behavior: the evidence from cerebrospinal fluid studies. In D.M. Stoff, and J.J. Mann (Eds), *The Neurobiology of Suicide: from the Bench to the Clinic*. New York, New York Academy of Sciences.

Åsberg, M., Träskman, L. and Thorén, P. (1976) 5-HIAA in the cerebrospinal fluid: a biochemical suicide predictor? *Archives of General Psychiatry*, **33**: 1193–1197.

Audenaert, K., Van Laere, K., Dumont, F., Slegers, G., Mertens, J., Van Heeringen, C. and Dierckx, R.A. (2001) Decreased frontal serotonin 5-HT$_{2a}$ receptor binding potential in deliberate self harm patients. *European Journal of Nuclear Medicine*, **28**: 175–182.

Beautrais, A.L., Joyce, P.R., Mulder, R.T., Fergusson, D.M., Deavoll, B.J. and Nightingale, S.K. (1996) Prevalence and co-morbidity of mental disorders in persons making serious suicide attempts: a case-control study. *American Journal of Psychiatry*, **153**: 1009–104.

Bettes, B.A. and Walker, E. (1986) Symptoms associated with suicidal behavior in children and adolescents. *Journal of Abnormal Child Psychiatry*, **14**: 591–604.

Brent, D., Bridge, J., Johnson, B. and Connolly, J. (1996) Suicidal behavior runs in families. A controlled family study of adolescent suicide victims. *Archives of General Psychiatry*, **53**: 1145–1149.

Cloninger, C.R., Svrakic, D.M. and Przybeck, T.R. (1993) A psychobiological model of temperament and character. *Archives of General Psychiatry*, **30**: 975–990.

Deakin, J.F.W. (1996) 5-HT, antidepressant drugs and the psychosocial origins of depression. *Journal of Psychopharmacology*, **10**: 31–38.

Dinan, T.G. (1994) Glucocorticoids and the genesis of depressive illness: a psychobiological model. *British Journal of Psychiatry*, **164**: 365–371.

Du, L., Bakish, D., Lapierre, Y.D., Ravindram, A.V. and Hrdina, P.D. (2000) Association of polymorphism of serotonin 2A receptor gene with suicidal ideation in

Part II

THE SUICIDAL PROCESS APPROACH: IMPLICATIONS FOR THE UNDERSTANDING AND TREATMENT OF SUICIDAL BEHAVIOUR

Chapter 9

SUICIDE RISK ASSESSMENT AND THE SUICIDAL PROCESS APPROACH

Lawrence Amsel and J. John Mann

INTRODUCTION

Despite the advances in suicide research the prediction of suicide remains a difficult problem. The process approach to suicidal behaviour that we describe draws on insights from the "stress–diathesis model" that we have proposed and from advances in the field of risk-factor research. In this chapter we will review the prediction problem from a traditional statistical perspective, and examine how these new approaches may contribute to suicide-risk assessment. Where possible, we will illustrate these points using neurobiological risk factors associated with increased suicidal behaviours.

THE PREDICTION PROBLEM

Although there are a number of well-established risk factors for suicidal behaviours, the prediction of suicide in individual cases remains difficult. A recent review article for the general clinician in the *New England Journal of Medicine* (Hirschfeld et al, 1997) on identifying suicidal patients illustrates this problem. Whereas the article mentions a number of risk factors, it does not give a single quantitative estimate for these risk factors, a practice that would be eschewed in a similar

Understanding Suicidal Behaviour. Edited by Kees van Heeringen
© 2001 John Wiley & Sons Ltd.

article dealing with any general medical condition. No quantitative estimates are given because there are no reliable data in the literature.

Nearly 15 years ago, the late Jacob Cohen (1986) described some of the statistical and clinical reasons for the difficulties in suicide prediction. The predictive value of any given risk factor is dependent on the base rate of the outcome of interest. Cohen pointed out that even among individuals who are prone to suicide (i.e. those who suffer from say depression, schizophrenia and borderline personality disorder), the base rate for completed suicide is about 2 per cent per year. In such a population, even a hypothetical super-predictor with a sensitivity and specificity of 90 per cent would have a positive predictive value of only 16 per cent. That means that 84 per cent of those categorized as positive are wrongly categorized. Since missing a potential suicide is a tragedy, high sensitivity is clearly desirable. However, it comes at the cost of low specificity, which means many false positives and an enormous potential dilution in effort and resources.

Pokorny (1993) made a similar point based on a longitudinal study of patients with an even lower base rate of suicide. In a sample of 4800 consecutively admitted in-patients followed up for 5 years, he found a suicide rate of 0.3 per cent per year. That this base rate of suicide was low is not surprising given that he studied a consecutive series of admissions. Using a comprehensive battery of clinical and demographic variables and a stepwise regression modelling technique, he developed an "optimal" weighted-sum prediction scale. While this achieved a specificity of 95 per cent, the sensitivity was only 29 per cent. Pokorny concluded that, as a predictive instrument, such scales have no clinical usefulness. He also examined the effect that a hypothetical instrument with 95 per cent sensitivity and 95 per cent specificity would have on his sample. He concluded that even such an instrument would be clinically useless, unless there was a much higher base rate of suicide in the population to which it was applied. He suggests that a useful test would need a population in which the base rate of suicide was greater than 30 per cent. That rate is higher than in any known high-risk population.

While there is no arguing with these numbers, the measure of an instrument's usefulness depends on the purpose to which it is put, a point we will return to below (Feinstein, 1985).

Another reason for prediction difficulties according to Cohen (1986) was inadequate case finding. This is not merely a problem of subjects being lost to follow-up, but of the fact that, for any given subject at any given time, their ultimate status in unknown. This runs up against the basic rule of test development, the requirement for a gold standard for comparison (Feinstein, 1985). It also introduces the time dimension as a key variable in any predictive or explanatory model. Unlike many general medical conditions in which the natural history and course of progression is well understood, the time factor in suicidality seems almost random. This also raises the question of which aspects of suicidal behaviour we want to predict. Since our prediction capacity will differ for completed suicides versus attempted suicide versus degree of medical damage (Mann, 1998), we may do better when we attempt to predict intermediate events.

Suicide studies in particular tend to screen large cohorts for many potential predictor variables and may generate chance findings. Moreover, even where replication across studies verifies the statistical significance of a risk factor, many clinically unimportant variables may survive in our models as a result of large sample sizes. It would be better, Cohen contends, if the research were more hypotheses-driven, thus increasing confidence in the results and reducing the need for replication of unexpected findings.

Another challenge is the complex causal structure of risk factors in suicide research. The multiple variables used as putative risk factors have highly complex interactions with each other, as well as with the outcome of interest. Unmeasured common-causal variables, redundancy of predictors and psychometric unreliability all contribute to this challenge. In particular it is important to find risk factors that are orthogonal (i.e. causally independent). Nor can statistical care alone solve the problem, as we need to understand these causal interrelationships prior to setting up statistical models.

Cohen (1986) suggests that we should use linear models that are hierarchically organized to reflect causal structure. In addition, to clarify causal relationships, he recommends the use of structural models such as those used in path analysis and econometrics. Finally, he advocates that biological factors should be added to the psychometric and demographic ones traditionally employed.

The problems, as raised by Cohen and Pokorny, are closely interrelated. In dealing with rare events it is often futile to try and improve a single diagnostic test or measure (Fleiss, 1986). In order to raise the predictive accuracy, we need multiple tests that are orthogonal (i.e. causally independent). If we have two tests that are independent, we can apply the first, and subsequently apply the second only to those who tested positive. This in effect raises the base rate for the second test, the elusive goal to which Pokorny refers. For example if both tests had sensitivity and specificity of 90 per cent in a population with a 2 per cent suicide rate, after applying the first test the base rate in the positive subgroup would be 16 per cent. Taken together the two tests would yield a sensitivity of 80 per cent. The sensitivity decreases because the criteria for being positive are more stringent. However, the specificity rises to 99 per cent and the positive predictive value is 62 per cent as compared with a positive predictive value of 16 per cent for a single test.

At the other extreme, if the tests were in complete agreement then their sequential application is redundant and adds no information. Most of the scales we deal with in suicide research lie somewhere between these extremes. While this point may seem obvious it is worth emphasizing because in the realm of explanatory research we are often precisely interested in proving that two measures of risk overlap.

In fact, the goals of explanation, prediction and those of prevention may require different models. Explanation, by Occam's razor, calls for the fewest possible variables (i.e. for aggregating variables where possible). From the perspective of prediction the more independent the causes, and the higher the dimensionality, the better chance we have of predicting. Redundant variables, however, including intermediate causal variables, add nothing to our prediction accuracy, and in practice the more variables there are, the more difficult it is to correctly estimate the model parameters. In prevention, however, the intervening variables that make up the detailed causal pathway are valuable because they offer more potential nodes for intervention. O'Carroll (1993) pointed out that, in the prediction or prevention setting, strategies that focus on the "real" explanatory cause of suicide might have less practical value than multi-causal models.

THE STRESS–DIATHESIS MODEL AND THE SUICIDAL PROCESS MODEL

The stress–diathesis model of suicide has been described in detail as an etiological and explanatory model for suicidal behaviour (Mann et al, 1999). It posits an underlying diathesis (i.e. a lifelong stable trait of aggression/impulsivity tied to hypo-serotonergic functioning), that interacts causally over a lifetime with stressors such as episodes of major depression, adverse life events or psychosis to lead to suicidal behaviours. As described in Chapter 1, the suicidal process model can be regarded as:

> a concept that is used to describe the development and progression of suicidality as a process within the individual and in interaction with his surroundings. The process may involve thoughts about taking one's life,

which evolve through often-recurrent suicide attempts with increasing lethality and suicide intent and end with completed suicide. The concept assumes the existence of an underlying and persistent vulnerability that is constituted of biological and psychological trait characteristics, and which may become clear under the influence of specific stressors.

Thus, these two models have a great deal of conceptual overlap, with the process model focusing on describing the clinical consequences and developing the prevention strategy of the more explanatory stress–diathesis model. One difference is the implication in the process model of a progression from ideation through attempts to suicide completion. The stress–diathesis model we have proposed does not see the pathway to suicide as necessarily including suicide attempts. Rather we recognize that about three-quarters of suicides complete on the first attempt. Thus, it is more precise to consider the interaction of the stressor and diathesis as resulting in suicidal ideation, and, in turn, a suicide attempt or completion may follow. However, serious suicide attempts (i.e. those resulting in severe medical consequences) have correlates or predictors similar to those of completed suicide. Thus, the stress–diathesis model and the process model share important features and also differ in important ways. In the rest of this chapter we will focus on their common features.

The stress–diathesis and process models also draw from advances in risk-factor research where the process approach to causal risk factors has also been an active area of research. By virtue of including both state and trait variables interacting over time, the stress–diathesis and process models guide assessment of the risk of suicide.

First, the models divide the probability function into two more or less orthogonal parts, one of which is time-dependent, the other being dependent on personal characteristics. Thus, the risk structure might on first approximation look like: $L_{suicide}(t) = L_{stress}(t) \times P_{diathesis}$. In the language of risk analysis this would read: the risk intensity function of suicide is equal to the risk intensity function of experiencing a severe stressor multiplied by the fractional prevalence of the aggressive/impulsive personality type. A risk intensity function $L(t)$ is the conditional probability of an event occurring in the short interval after time t, given the status of the subject prior to time t. This gives an immediate indication of why not all depressives, or all subjects with aggressive/impulsive characteristics, are suicidal, and begins to model the low base rate in the overall population. For example, it models the fact that for subjects with equal scores on the Hamilton Depression Scale, aggressive/impulsive characteristics distinguish attempters from non-attempters (Mann et al, 1999). The independence of the risk factors in the stress–diathesis and process models are extremely important as we saw above in Cohen's critique. This allows us to increase our predictive accuracy by developing scales for stress and diathesis independently, and applying them sequentially.

In contrast, many theories of suicide ultimately load all psychological risk factors into a single dimension, which is conceptualized as an intolerable level of pain that motivates suicide. Shneidman (1998) stated this explicitly, but many other theories do this implicitly (see Lester, 1994). The stress–diathesis and process models recognize that most persons experiencing a severe stressor do not commit suicide, or even attempt suicide, because of powerful inhibitory factors. The stress–diathesis and process models sort psychological risk factors according to independent dimensions: protection or predisposition (diathesis), and motive supplied by the stressor.

Both the diathesis and stressors are viewed as having psychological and biological components. Thus, the model does not segregate psychological and biological into independent factors. However, it has been possible to extract biological markers related to low serotonergic function for the aggression/impulsivity diathesis that are largely independent of the stressor diagnosis (Mann et al, 1999).

The diathesis factor is proving amenable to measurement both at the psychometric and at the neurobiological level. The vicissitudes of the stress factor, however, are clearly more difficult to predict (e.g. we are just beginning to be able to predict relapse in depression, Van Londen et al, 1998). Interestingly, Alnaes and Torgersen (1997) reported that the rates of depressive relapse may depend on personality style and thus may also be trait-like. Thus, relapse prediction for depression and other psychiatric disorders will need to be incorporated into our predictive and preventive models.

RISK-FACTOR RESEARCH

While risk-factor research is not a new idea, being probably as old as the concept of causation (Kazdin, 1997), within health care it has taken on a new quantitative formalism and is emerging together with prevention science as an independent discipline (see the report *Plan for Prevention Research* published by the National Institute of Mental Health, Bethesda, Maryland, USA, No. NIH 96-4093; also see reviews by O'Carroll, 1993; Kazdin et al, 1997; Kraemer et al, 1997).

The distinguishing characteristics of risk-factor research are that its goals are focused on prevention in populations, its methodology is probabilistic and not deterministic, it seeks to operationalize its concepts and it is concerned with modelling the intervening paths between a risk factor and its associated outcome. It serves as the quantitative framework for the suicidal-process approach. We will cover these points in turn.

RISK-FACTOR RESEARCH—A FOCUS ON POPULATION AND PREVENTION

As outlined by Mrazek and co-workers (1997) risk-factor research recognizes three types of prevention, which have replaced the primary, secondary and tertiary nomenclature. The first involves low-cost, universally targeted, prevention strategies. All public-service announcements fall into this category (e.g. depression-awareness programmes). The second type involves selective preventive interventions with subgroups identified as being at high risk. The third type involves interventions with persons already affected or in imminent risk thereof.

Risk factors are most useful for the targeted approach, in which a risk factor is used to divide the population into two groups, one being at higher risk. Since it is impossible to parse the groups perfectly, the goal is not to identify individuals who will have the adverse outcome, but rather to divide a given population into two subgroups. One of the subgroups will be enriched for the outcome of interest compared with the initial group and the other will be impoverished for this outcome. The key is to identify a subgroup of the population sufficiently enriched for the adverse outcome such that a preventive intervention can have a measurable impact.

We think of a risk factor as a discriminator or test whose properties are described by its sensitivity and specificity for the predicted outcome. We can estimate the effectiveness of such a test by using the following form of Bayes' theorem: (pre-test odds) × (likelihood ratio) = (post-test odds). The pre-test odds are the baseline odds of the outcome in our population, the likelihood ratio is the ratio of the true positive rate to the false positive rate and the post-test odds are the enriched odds of the outcome in our high-risk subgroup. When the probabilities are below 0.05, odds and probabilities are very close, and we can substitute the probabilities for the odds without changing the outcome. The formula is: (pre-test probability) × (likelihood ratio) = (post-test probability). Thus, the likelihood ratio is simply a multiplier that defines by how much the post-test group is enriched for the particular outcome (Sackett et al, 1991).

An example will make this clearer. Assume we have a population of 1000 persons with a suicide rate of 2 per cent per year, and we have a risk factor with a sensitivity and specificity of 67 per cent, and thus a likelihood ratio of two. Then the test will divide our sample into two groups, where the group that tests positive has 336 persons with a probability of suicide of 4 per cent. The group that tests negative contains 664 persons and has a probability of suicide of 1 per cent. Thus, the group that tests positive has a fourfold increase over the group that tested negative.

Under this approach, rather than having no clinical use, existing risk factors in suicide are actually very helpful. The usefulness of this approach can be seen in the following scenario. Assume we have 1000 psychiatric admissions available per year. We use these admissions to prevent suicide and simultaneously to treat psychopathology. At this point in time it is not possible to disaggregate these functions. A reasonable estimate of an acute-care psychiatric stay in the USA is about $10 000, and thus our total budget is $10 million. The rule is we admit patients on the basis of usual clinical criteria until the money runs out. While this scenario may have seemed artificial a few years ago, it has recently become quite realistic. Let us assume the rate of suicide for these patients is about 2 per cent per year if they were not hospitalized. Thus, if our intervention is 100 per cent successful at preventing suicide, we have saved 20 lives. We have also treated 980 serious, but ultimately non-suicidal, patients. The total cost is allocated for these functions simultaneously as we do not know a priori for whom we are having the life-saving effect, and for whom we are "merely" treating a major mental illness. This makes it difficult in practice to estimate what our real budget for suicide prevention is, and to compare it with, say, the cost for a life-saving cardiac intervention, where the same limitations in information exist.

For this example, however, let us assume that the treatment can be divided into two components. The first is the treatment of the primary psychiatric disorder, and the second is the treatment designed to reduce the diathesis for a suicidal act. The second component is the one we strive to offer only to the truly high-risk patients. That would include elements such as monitoring the patient for suicidal ideation, psychotherapy and perhaps prescribing serotonin-enhancing medications to reduce impulsive behaviours, and for attempt preparations, removing the means for suicide.

With this focus we can do a better job at suicide prevention with existing tools. Assume, as above, that we have a risk factor that was independent of our initial clinical criteria and that has a sensitivity of 67 per cent and a specificity of 67 per cent. We could then screen 2969 patients with this test and select a high-risk subgroup of 1000 patients with a suicide rate of 4 per cent. Using this risk factor as an additional screen, we could endeavour to save 40 lives at the same cost constraint. That would, however, leave 1969 low-risk patients still needing treatment for their psychopathology. In the interest of saving lives we will have directed our limited resources to the higher risk group. This approach has a further price.

Of individuals categorized by the screening test as positive, 96 per cent are not going to make a suicide attempt, and of those categorized as negative 1 per cent are in fact suicidal. Thus, in admitting our thousand patients we needed to screen 2969 and we turned away 1969, of whom 19 go on to commit suicide. But from the population perspective we prevented 40 suicides rather than 20, a 100 per cent gain in saved lives over the standard triage method. Thus we disagree with the conclusions of Cohen and Pokorny that screening tests are clinically useless. As Feinstein (1985) has pointed out, we cannot judge a diagnostic test in the abstract, but only in relation to how it will be used. Note that our reluctance to act on these numbers stems from our clinical focus on the patients in front of us. We are reluctant to accept the failures of screening, thus we tend not to screen and to leave out of our calculations those who are not screened at all and go on to suicide. We must remember that there are over 30 000 suicides each year in the USA. We must believe that ultimately improved screening will result in better testing of new treatments and ultimately in fewer suicides.

The levels of 5-hydroxyindoleacetic acid (5-HIAA), a metabolite of serotonin, in the cerebrospinal fluid (CSF) has promising properties as a discriminator for completed suicide. In a 1-year follow-up design, with completed suicide as the outcome, Nordström and colleagues (1994) found that low CSF 5-HIAA had a sensitivity of 73 per cent and specificity of 53 per cent, with a likelihood ratio of 1.6. Similarly, Träskman and co-workers (1981) found a likelihood ratio of 2.13 on an earlier subset of the same patient group, while Edman and colleagues (1986) found a likelihood ratio of 1.4 in a larger subsample of the same group. Roy and colleagues (1986) found a likelihood ratio of 1.4 in an independent study. Thus, CSF 5-HIAA has approximately the discriminating power we estimated above for our hypothetical triage test.

To complete the example we can include the cost of screening lumbar punctures. Assuming the cost of a lumbar puncture to collect CSF to be $1000, including the averaged cost of any morbidity. We could screen 2289 patients and hospitalize 771 of them at the same $10 million cost constraints as given above. Among the hospitalized patients there would be 31 whose lives we save by hospitalization. We would turn away 1518 of whom 15 go on to suicide. Although the loss of these 15 lives is tragic, this procedure of identifying higher risk subjects through CSF 5-HIAA would save an additional 11 lives over the usual procedures because we can treat more high-risk patients at the same cost. What is important is that a test such as CSF 5-HIAA is not redundant with information already available to the triage team from the clinical interview. Certainly we are aware of no regularly used screening tool that has this predictive value; however, as we will discuss below, using appropriate clinical scales might also provide additional non-redundant screening criteria.

Under this approach the goal is to target an intervention to an identified high-risk group and reduce its rate of suicide. As pointed out by O'Carroll (1993), we are not just interested in the most theoretically important risk factor or the ones with the highest correlations. Rather we are also interested in risk factors that can be changed within an identifiable subgroup in such a way as to prevent suicides. Sometimes the obscure risk factor can be the most useful. Mann and colleagues (1999) found that smoking was a risk factor for attempter status, with a sensitivity of 69 per cent and a specificity of 56 per cent and a likelihood ratio of 1.6. If this could be generalized to the population as a whole, then smokers would have an approximately 50 per cent increased risk of making an attempt. Thus, any population-based prevention strategy should target this subgroup. As it turns out this example is not without external validation as Kazdin and co-workers (1997) report that smoking may also be a marker for delinquency and aggression, while several studies report that smoking is associated with completed suicide. Of course, the intervention would target psychopathology and not smoking cessation.

RISK-FACTOR RESEARCH: OPERATIONALIZING RISK

Risk-factor research has recognized the need to classify risk factors by their evidentiary status and by their function in a causal chain. Kraemer and colleagues (1997) have identified six levels of risk factors in the causal hierarchy. This typology depends on the current state of evidence and can change with additional evidence. To begin with, we must have a measurable characteristic of a population and a well-defined outcome. If the characteristic can be used to divide the population into two groups in which the probabilities of the outcome are significantly different, then the characteristic is termed a correlate of the outcome. If it can be further established that the characteristic precedes the outcome, it is called a risk factor. In retrospective studies, we can do no better than establish correlates, as the temporal sequence between the outcome and its correlate may not be known. As an example, both aggression/impulsivity and a history of childhood abuse have been shown to be associated with and precede suicide-attempter status, and are thus risk factors for attempter status. However, it is much more difficult to establish whether childhood abuse precedes the aggression/impulsivity trait or is a consequence of it, or if both result from a third, common cause such as genetic or familial effects (Mann et al, 1999).

Risk factors can be further subdivided depending on whether or not they can change or be changed experimentally. Only those that can change, and whose change affects the probability of the outcome, can be called true causal risk factors. These distinctions are important as illustrated by the smoking example above. It makes sense to target a group for intervention on the basis of smoking habit, but there is no evidence to support the idea of reducing suicide by smoking cessation.

Another example is that hypo-serotonergic function is correlated with aggression/impulsivity and with suicidal behaviour. We also know that hypo-serotonergic function and aggression/impulsivity are trait factors that precede suicidality, and thus are risk factors for suicidality. However, despite its appealing logic, we do not have direct evidence that reducing aggression/impulsivity will reduce suicidal behaviour as well. It is possible that hypo-serotonergic function is independently a cause of both suicidal behaviours and aggression/impulsivity as separate characteristics (e.g. Malone and colleagues, 1998 have shown an association between subtypes of aggression and treatment response in adolescents). While Linehan (1997) has shown that reducing self-injury in borderline personality disorder does reduce suicidality, the treatment was too multi-factorial to definitively answer our question. In addition to clinical trials aimed directly at changing serotonin function, clinical trials that specifically target aggression/impulsivity either with medication or with psychotherapy are needed.

RISK-FACTOR RESEARCH: DEFINITIONS OF STATE AND TRAIT

A further attempt to operationalize risk factors involves the concepts of state and trait variables. Kraemer and colleagues (1997) point out that we are not able to study trait and state aspects of our subjects except through instrumental measures. They suggest therefore that we define state and trait aspect of our measures rather than think of them as characteristics of our subjects. Trait variables are defined as those that have negligible variance within a subject over a given time frame but large variance across the sample. State variables are those that show large variances within the same subject over time but whose average over time may be similar between subjects. Thus Kraemer's formal definitions focus on whether the variance of a variable is best accounted for by the time dimension or by the subject dimension. Under these definitions certain characteristics can be thought of as having both state and trait aspects insofar as they might be measured by both a state and a trait variable.

In the stress–diathesis and process models, for example, the stressor is generally thought of as a state variable. If we think of a subject whose stressor is recurrent major depression, however, it seems that there are two measures involved: the lifetime diagnosis, which is a trait variable, and the time dependant episodes, which are state variables. In other words, depression or any other chronic psychiatric condition is a lifetime risk factor for having episodic stressors. We might then modify our equation above to read: $L_{\text{suicide}}(t) = L_{\text{episode}}(t) \times P_{\text{diagnosis}} \times P_{\text{aggressive diathesis}}$. Thus suicidal behaviour, being time dependent, is a state variable made up of a risk intensity function and two trait (i.e. time-invariant) variables.

Looked at this way it is little wonder that we have difficulty predicting individual suicides. The problem is formally similar to that of predicting earthquakes as described by Ellis (1985). In the approach of Ellis we abandon the idea of exact prediction. Instead we monitor high-risk cities for their level of risk over time and call an alert when the risk goes over a certain threshold. Similarly, if we wanted to establish a suicide surveillance procedure we would need to proceed in two steps. The first is to segregate the population on the basis of the trait variables, just as we would identify cities in which to locate an earthquake surveillance system. This is represented above by $P_{\text{diagnosis}} \times P_{\text{aggressive diathesis}}$. Second, we define the risk intensity function, which is the same as probability of an outcome at time t conditional on having information about the system up to time t. Thus $L_{\text{episode}}(t)$ determines the time-dependent or state-dependent component of risk. When the risk intensity goes over a certain threshold we call an alert.

In our case the risk intensity function is, for example, the probability of a depressive relapse in the next month based on a monthly collection of clinical status. The problem reduces to estimating this moving risk. The difficulty is that we cannot estimate this very reliably or accurately. Nevertheless the formalism developed by Ellis for earthquakes could help us recognize what kind of information we may need in order to generate the appropriate time-dependent risk estimates. In any case, it seems too ambitious to predict a lifetime risk for suicide in an individual based on measures at a single point, when we are not even sure how to estimate the local risk based on continuously updated information.

In discussing the distinction between state and trait measures in suicide research it is important to recognize that biological markers may be either. Thus CSF 5-HIAA is believed to be a trait marker (Mann, 1998). On the other hand, Pandey (1997) found that the serotonin receptor 5-HT_{2A}, which is contained on the surface of platelets, was increased in density in suicidal subjects independent of their psychiatric diagnosis. Moreover the increase in 5-HT_{2A} density was significantly higher in subjects with a recent attempt versus those with past suicide attempts. This raises the intriguing possibility that platelet 5-HT_{2A} receptor number is a state-dependent marker of suicidality.

Similarly, clinical rating scales can be both state and trait. In fact, Beck and colleagues (1999) recently raised the possibility that a single scale can be both, depending on how it is administered. They reported that the Scale for Suicidal Ideation (SSI), if modified to focus on the subject's worst episode (SSI-W), becomes a significantly better predictor of eventual suicide with an odds ratio of 13.8 versus 5.4. Thus while the SSI is a highly variable state measure the SSI-W has the stability of a trait measure. Consistent with this notion we have reported that hopelessness is more severe in depressed patients with a history of a suicide attempt compared with non-attempters, and that this difference persists into the remitted state, even though both groups report a big improvement in hopelessness on remission (Rifai et al, 1994).

RISK-FACTOR RESEARCH: PROCESS, PATHS AND CAUSAL CHAINS

A central contribution of risk-factor research has been the notion of process analysis or path analysis, which is an examination of how risk factors interact over time to lead to a particular outcome. According to O'Carroll (1993), our traditional focus has been on the most proximate and most primary risk factors (i.e. the beginning and the end of the causal chain) instead of focusing on stages or elements in the life process that culminate in suicide.

The interactions between risk factors along such a chain of events is often highly complex, and not a simple linear progression. Any causal factor may have multiple antecedent risk factors and in turn may have multiple consequences, many of which may be causally unrelated to the outcome of interest. Nevertheless each of these factors will be either a correlate or a risk factor for the outcome (e.g. the number of years of education was a risk factor for attempter status in the study by Mann and colleagues, 1999). Yet this may simply be a tangential consequence of aggression/impulsivity, birth difficulties, child abuse, head injury, parenting and be causally unrelated to attempter status.

For our purposes there are a few key contributions that path and causal analysis can make. First is the ability to explain the complex interactions of already identified risk factors. We have seen that suicidal ideation as measured by the SSI is a predictor of eventual suicide and SSI-W (Beck et al, 1999) is a stronger predictor. We also know that the aggression/impulsivity trait is a predictor of attempter status. But we are only beginning to understand the relationship between these variables and between cognitive states and behaviour (e.g. Mann and colleagues (1999) have shown that suicidal ideation and aggression/impulsivity are largely independent components of suicidal acts). Another example is the suggestion that CSF 5-HIAA levels may behave differently relative to suicidal risk in bipolar disorder than in unipolar depression. Thus, we need to better understand the effect that mood-disorder subtype may have on the connection between serotonin hypofunction and suicidal outcome. This observation may extend to aggression/impulsivity, which does not differentiate suicide attempters within a group of patients suffering from bipolar disorder, but does so in those suffering from unipolar depression (Oquendo et al, 1997).

Second, this approach calls for component analysis. This can be thought of as the disaggregation of the multiple elements that may exist in what we think of as a unitary risk factor. To take an obvious but illustrative example, we had long known that gender is a risk factor for osteoporosis. But what is it about femaleness that is the "active ingredient" in its being a risk factor? We now know that one such component is postmenopausal estrogen level, yet this may not completely explain the variations known to exist. In this example, because gender is an unchanging trait, it can never be shown to be a causal risk factor. Only mutable aspects of gender, like hormone levels, can be shown to be causally related to the outcome. For suicide research the disaggregation of gender is particularly important because some component of femaleness is a risk for higher rates of depression, while another component is protective of completed suicide. Thus, females have about one-third the suicide rate of men and do not have the substantial increase in suicide rates seen in men in the eighth decade of life.

Third, drawing on the developmental approach, risk-factor research has focused on microanalysis of the causal chain of cognitive–behavioural events that lead to a suicide. Thus, each intermediate step can be studied as an outcome of preceding steps, and as a risk for succeeding steps. At each stage (mediator variable) of such a process we can examine what factors facilitate or thwart movement into the next stage (moderator variables). We currently think of prior suicidal attempts as an important risk factor for eventual suicide. But does each attempt add to the risk or is attempter status merely a marker which, once exposed does not change? Clark and co-workers (1989) reported the latter, but Leon and colleagues (1990) found that each successive attempt added to the risk. On the other hand, it has been shown that high-lethality attempts are psychometrically and neurobiologically different from low-lethality attempts (Mann et al, 1997). We might speculate that only the high-lethality attempts are fixed markers for eventual completed suicide, while lower lethality attempts may be additive, but this would need verification. Risk-factor research addresses these intermediary risks, correlations and causes in detail.

While this may begin to sound far from psychiatric practice, Linehan and co-workers (1993) have actually introduced this sort of microanalysis into their therapeutic strategy for "chronically parasuicidal borderline" women. By insisting that patients do a detailed behavioural analysis of each self-destructive act, dialectic behaviour therapy is examining the intermediate, cognitive–affective–behavioural stages in such behaviours. In effect this exposes the moderator variables over which the patients have control, if only they could identify them.

SOME METHODOLOGICAL ISSUES IN THE USE OF BIOLOGICAL MARKERS AS PREDICTORS IN SUICIDALITY

Cohen (1986) suggested that the introduction of biological variables would reduce the prediction problem. Yet, as Cohen pointed out in the case of psychometric variables, even if we were to develop a biological "test" with a 90 per cent specificity and 90 per cent sensitivity we would still be plagued by the base-rate problem. In this sense individual biological predictors should not be expected to improve the prediction problem. It is the anticipation that biological variables will be a source of independent variables that makes them more useful in prediction. Yet the biological markers we develop are often defined in terms of measurable behaviours. In other words, from the point of view of explanation, the usefulness of biological variables is enhanced if they are redundant with clinical variables rather than independent. For prediction, the opposite is true.

As an example, Mann and co-workers (1997) found in a sample of 22 depressed in-patients who had made prior suicide attempts that low CSF 5-HIAA could discriminate the low-lethality attempters from the high-lethality attempters. In this sample low CSF 5-HIAA had a sensitivity level of 93 per cent and a specificity of 63 per cent for discriminating prior degree of lethality. Mann also demonstrated that the measurable trait of impulsivity correlates with both suicidal behaviour and CSF 5-HIAA (Mann, 1998), thus demonstrating a plausible behavioural mechanism. This is an essential part of constructing a neurobiological model in psychiatry. Thus, the very success of a neurobiological marker may eventually make it a redundant predictor.

Currently, however, the reason we do not use CSF 5-HIAA is not because we could assess level of aggressivity. Efficient methods for the measurement of aggression/impulsivity have not as yet been developed. Moreover, we do not know how such instruments would perform relative to CSF 5-HIAA in the prediction of future suicide attempts. It is also worthy of note that while a positive suicidal history is an important predictor, a negative history has little predictive value, because three-quarters of all suicides do not make a previous suicide attempt. Thus, other predictors must be identified. Time-independent or trait predictors offer an advantage in this regard.

Overall, the current status of biological markers of suicide risk is reminiscent of the early history of laboratory tests in internal medicine. At first, clinical observation remained a better discriminator. Eventually, however, the lab tests became not only more accurate but able to detect disease much earlier in its course, before the clinical markers, with their concomitant morbidity, were manifest (Sox et al, 1988).

CONCLUSIONS

There are reasons to be optimistic that current lines of research will improve our risk assessment of suicidality in a way that will save lives. First, our clinical instruments are improving. Recent reports by Beck on the importance of assessing not only current suicidal ideation but also its worst occurrence in the past and by Mann on aggression/impulsivity show promise as effective discriminators of subgroups that are at high risk for suicidal behaviour. Second, while still in their infancy, biological predictors are showing promising specificity, sensitivity and discriminatory power. The limitation to their clinical use is due in part to the redundancy of information, and in part to our reluctance to use relatively invasive procedures in behavioural settings. Third, to achieve these benefits we may need to think more in the paradigms of populations and probabilities rather than focusing on individual prediction. Finally, it is not the state of knowledge that is lacking at this moment, but its translation into practice. Clinical guidelines for the assessment of the risk of suicide commonly do not even mention the assessment of aggressivity or recommend a systematic investigation of suicidal ideation of the sort that we know to be an effective predictor. What is required is more intensive translational research to make our growing understanding of suicidal behaviours applicable in everyday practice.

ACKNOWLEDGMENTS

This work was supported by Public Health Service Grants (NIMH) MH46745, MH56390, MH48514 and MH40210 to Dr Mann, and by Stanley Foundation Center for Applied Neuroscience of Bipolar Disorders at Columbia University.

REFERENCES

Alnaes, R. and Torgersen, S. (1997) Personality and personality disorders predict development and relapses of major depression. *Acta Psychiatrica Scandinavica*, **95**: 336–342.
Beck, A.T., Brown, G.K., Steer, R.A., Dahlsgaard, K.K. and Grisham, J.R. (1999) Suicide ideation at its worst point: a predictor of eventual suicide in psychiatric outpatients. *Suicide and Life-Threatening Behavior*, **29**: 1–9.
Clark, D.C., Gibbons, R.D., Fawcett, J. and Scheftner, W.A. (1989) What is the mechanism by which suicide attempts predispose to later suicide attempts? A mathematical model. *Journal of Abnormal Psychology*, **98**: 42–49.
Cohen, J. (1986) Statistical approaches to suicidal risk factor analysis. *Annals of the New York Academy of Sciences*, **487**: 34–41.
Edman, G., Åsberg, M., Levander, S. and Schalling, D. (1986) Skin conductance habituation and cerebrospinal fluid 5-hydroxyindoleacetic acid in suicidal patients. *Archives of General Psychiatry*, **43**: 586–592.
Ellis, S.P. (1985) An optimal statistical decision rule for calling earthquake alerts. *Earthquake Prediction Research* **3**: 1–10.

Feinstein, A. (1985) *Clinical Epidemiology: The Architecture of Clinical Research.* Philidelphia, W.B. Saunders.

Fleiss, J. (1986) *Statistical Methods for Rates and Proportions.* New York, Wiley.

Hirschfeld, R.M. and Russell, J.M. (1997) Assessment and treatment of suicidal patients. *New England Journal of Medicine,* **337**: 910–915.

Kazdin, A.E., Kraemer, H.C., Kessler, R.C., Kupfer, D.J. and Offord, D.R. (1997) Contributions of risk-factor research to developmental psychopathology. *Clinical Psychology Review,* **17**: 375–406.

Kraemer, H.C., Kazdin, A.E., Offord, D.R., Kessler, R.C., Jensen, P.S. and Kupfer, D.J. (1997) Coming to terms with the terms of risk. *Archives of General Psychiatry,* **54**: 337–343.

Leon, A.C., Friedman, R.A., Sweeney, J.A., Brown, R.P. and Mann, J.J. (1990) Statistical issues in the identification of risk factors for suicidal behavior: the application of survival analysis. *Psychiatry Research,* **31**: 99–108.

Lester, D. (1994) A comparison of 15 theories of suicide. *Suicide and Life-Threatening Behavior,* **24**: 80–88.

Linehan, M.M. (1997) Behavioral treatments of suicidal behaviors. Definitional obfuscation and treatment outcomes. *Annals of the New York Academy of Sciences,* **29**: 302–328.

Linehan, M.M., Heard, H.L. and Armstrong, H.E. (1993) Naturalistic follow-up of a behavioral treatment for chronically parasuicidal borderline patients. *Archives of General Psychiatry,* **50**: 971–974.

Malone, R.P., Bennett, D.S., Luebbert, J.F., Rowan, A.B., Biesecker, K.A., Blaney, B.L. and Delaney, M.A. (1998) Aggression classification and treatment response. *Psychopharmacological Bulletin,* **34**: 41–45.

Mann, J.J., Waternaux, C., Haas, G.L. and Malone, K.M. (1999) Toward a clinical model of suicidal behavior in psychiatric patients. *American Journal of Psychiatry,* **156**: 181–189.

Mann, J.J. (1998) The neurobiology of suicide. *Nature Medicine,* **4**: 25–30.

Mann, J.J. and Malone, K.M. (1997) Cerebrospinal fluid amines and higher-lethality suicide attempts in depressed inpatients. *Biological Psychiatry,* **41**: 162–171.

Mrazek, P.J. and Hall, M. (1997) A policy perspective on prevention. *American Journal of Community Psychology,* **25**: 221–226.

Nordström, P., Samuelsson, M., Asberg, M., Träskman-Bendz, L., Åberg-Wistedt, A., Nordin, C. and Bertilsson, L. (1994) CSF 5-HIAA predicts suicide risk after attempted suicide. *Suicide and Life-Threatening Behavior,* **24**: 1–9.

Oquendo, M.A., Waternaux, C., Malone, K.M. and Mann, J.J. (1997) Characteristics of bipolar suicide attempters and non-attempters. Paper presented at the *1997 ACNP Annual Meeting, Hilton Waikoloa Village Kamuela, Hawaii.*

O'Carroll, P. (1993) Suicide causation: pies, paths, and pointless polemics. *Suicide and Life-Threatening Behavior,* **23**: 27–36.

Pandey, G.N. (1997) Altered serotonin function in suicide. Evidence from platelet and neuroendocrine studies. *Annals of the New York Academy of Sciences,* **836**: 182–200.

Pokorny, A.D. (1993) Suicide prediction revisited. *Suicide and Life-Threatening Behavior,* **23**: 1–10.

Rifai, A.H., George, C.J., Stack, J.A., Mann, J.J. and Reynolds, C.F. III (1994) Hopelessness in suicide attempters after acute treatment of major depression in late life. *American Journal of Psychiatry,* **151**: 1687–1690.

Roy, A., Agren, H., Pickar, D., Linnoila, M., Doran, A.R., Cutler, N.R. and Paul, S.M. (1986) Reduced CSF concentrations of homovanillic acid and homovanillic acid to 5-hydroxyindoleacetic acid ratios in depressed patients: relationship to suicidal behavior and dexamethasone nonsuppression. *American Journal of Psychiatry*, **143**: 1539–1545.

Sackett, D.L., Haynes, R.B. and Tugwell, P. (1991) *Clinical Epidemiology: A Basic Science for Clinical Medicine*. New York, Williams & Wilkins.

Shneidman, E.S. (1998) Perspectives on suicidology. Further reflections on suicide and psychache. *Suicide and Life-Threatening Behavior*, **28**: 245–250.

Sox, H.C., Blatt, M.A., Higgins, M.C. and Marton, K.I. (1988) *Medical Decision Making*. Boston, Butterworth-Heinemann.

Träskman, L., Åsberg, M., Bertilsson, L. and Sjostrand, L. (1981) Monoamine metabolites in CSF and suicidal behavior. *Archives of General Psychiatry*, **38**: 631–636.

Van Londen, L., Molenaar, R.P., Goekoop, J.G., Zwinderman, A.H. and Rooijmans, H.G. (1998) 5-year prospective follow-up of outcome in major depression. *Psychological Medicine*, **28**: 731–735.

Chapter 10

THE SUICIDAL PROCESS
AND SOCIETY

Unni Bille-Brahe

INTRODUCTION

When people ask *"why* did this person want to kill himself or herself?"*,
the immediate answer usually begins with the word *because:* because of
a broken heart, because he or she was suffering from depression,
because he or she went bankrupt, because of *tedium vitae.* However,
not everybody suffering from a broken heart, a depression or *tedium
vitae* will kill himself or herself, so clearly more questions and answers
are needed.

Albert Camus (1942) has frequently been quoted for stating that the
question of suicide is the most fundamental of all philosophical questions. Although the person grasping the rope or a glass of pills hardly
regards the consideration to kill himself or herself as a philosophical
question, the views on life and death in force in society most certainly
influence not only the attitudes towards self-killing in general, but also
the decision he or she is going to make.

Menno Boldt (1988) summed this up nicely by stating that "Meaning
goes beyond the universal psychological criteria for certifying and
classifying self-destructive death: It refers to how suicide is conceptualized in terms of cultural normative values. Some examples of particular
socio-cultural conceptualizations of suicide are that it is an unforgivable
sin, a psychotic act, a human right, a ritual obligation, an unthinkable
act, and so on. The meaning of suicide is derived from cultural experiences and encompasses the historical, affective qualities that the act

Understanding Suicidal Behaviour. Edited by Kees van Heeringen
© 2001 John Wiley & Sons Ltd.

symbolizes for a cultural group". In other words, the meaning of suicide emerges from and is part of the complex pattern of beliefs, attitudes, norms, traditions, etc. that we refer to when we talk about culture – and which is varying over time, between societies and even within societies. Of special relevance in our context are the views in force on life and death and how they influence the attitudes towards suicidal behaviour.

As pointed out elsewhere (Bille-Brahe, 2000), the meaning of suicide has changed considerably over time and between societies from being a proper way to end one's life in antiquity, to a mortal sin during the Middle Ages, later a psychotic act, and today a rational act or even a human right. Accordingly, the attitudes towards suicidal behaviour have varied from tolerance and acceptance to the deepest condemnation, to scorn and contempt, and again to increasing tolerance and acceptance. Noteworthy is, however, the fact that when the Catholic Church decreed suicide a mortal sin, it had a decisive effect on the conception of the meaning of suicide and on the attitudes towards killing oneself that has been dominating for centuries. Only gradually was the suicidal act to be seen in relation to the individual and/or societal circumstances: suicidal behaviour came to be regarded as a more or less understandable reaction to traumatic events and pain, and the individual who committed suicide to be looked upon not as a *sinner*, but rather as a *victim* of certain conditions.

The other point of relevance is the predominant view on man. Throughout history, man has lived and survived through co-existing and co-working with fellow human beings. According to Émile Durkheim (1895, 1897), among others, man is first and foremost a social being, and accordingly the social "I" is the most important and also the most valuable part of man. During later years, and especially during this century, individual-oriented attitudes have gained ground, placing the individual "I" as the most important part: the ideal was to be the free and autonomous *individual*. Gradually, however, the original conception of freedom, as a *freedom from* discrimination or suppression in order to be *free to* achieve and accomplish, was reduced to be *free from* (period!). Man became the centre of his own universe and his motto the Archimedean outburst: "Don't disturb my circles!" In short, in the emerging so-called "ego-society" there has been a growing tendency in the individual to withdraw from involvement and responsibilities. In the extreme this has made psychiatrists start talking about narcissism and borderline symptoms.

This development has been strongly enhanced by the general secularization that has taken place in most modern societies and which, by reducing or almost eliminating the importance of the church as the body of social control, has had a detrimental effect on the old-fashioned moral and spiritual fibre of the psychological climate of societies. Linked to this is the change in viewing death as an inevitable and natural event. Most people born in our part of the world during the first part of this century would, before they were 15 years of age, have experienced death in their near family, and the death would most probably have taken place at home. Today, most of us do not experience death among our dear ones until we ourselves are growing old, and these deaths most often take place behind curtains in a hospital. Our knowledge of—and thereby conception of—death is first and foremost based on what we know from the media, especially what we see on television, be it in news reports from battlefields and catastrophes or as entertainment in crime or splatter films. The lack of reality and personal relevance of these presentations are, to an increasing degree, influencing our attitudes towards both life *and* death, making the meaning of life questionable to many and the topic of death taboo.

Norms, values and attitudes are not static; in fact, they are perpetually changing. Usually these changes have taken place slowly and also rather smoothly; there has been a kind of built-in inertia securing overlapping and time for internalization of new norms. When, however, changes take place with speed and violence, old values and norms are rejected before new ones are established and internalized; the well-known and familiar "rules of the road" are thrown away before any replacements are in shape, generally accepted and internalized.

This is what Émile Durkheim termed "anomie", one of the four conditions that may increase the frequency of suicide in a society, the others being altruism, fatalism and egoism (Durkheim 1897, see also e.g. Bille-Brahe, 1987). Literally, the word "anomie" means normlessness, which, of course, makes it rather meaningless in this connection, as it is precisely the existence of common norms that constitutes groups or societies and binds them together. Instead, Durkheim used the term to describe the situation where changes are taking place so rapidly that the group/society is no longer able to create, maintain and enforce the norms and values that procure the necessary solid and reliable frames for life of, and in, the society. However, man needs these "rules of the road" for support and to be able to feel safe and belonging somewhere. When changes take place with an accelerating speed there are no reliable frames of support and man feels insecure; without support from the well-known cultural pattern and the guidelines of his society, life becomes an unpredictable and ego-oriented enterprise.

Against this background, one of the key concepts in approaching an understanding of the reasons why people want to kill themselves is closely related to the question of change, especially changes that take place with accelerating speed and violence so that the mechanism of inertia, which usually applies to the setting of norms, is more or less inactive. The result is that not only are existing norms rejected before new norms are generally accepted and internalized, but also that in post-modern societies such as ours, with their advanced information technology, the supply of norms and values is boundless. *One of the main characteristics of most societies today is precisely that changes are taking place with accelerating speed and that most of the changes that take place in our societies are of a very radical nature.* The term "societies in transition" (coined by the Ukrainian psychologist Alexander Mokhovikov) does not only apply to the New Independent States in Central-Eastern Europe; countries all over the world, the Western countries not being an exception, are experiencing upheavals in social order, changes in socio-economic conditions and in cultural patterns, and shifts in the systems of beliefs, norms and values.

It seems reasonable to assume that these changes may be experienced differently in various layers of the social structure and thereby affect various groups differently, which in turn may cause both undercurrent and open tensions, and conflicts between groups (e.g. age groups). In this context, it is relevant that societal changes have been concurrent with the changing age composition of the population in most countries, indicating that changes may also have different meanings and impacts on various age groups.

To conclude this rather long introduction, *this chapter will discuss how changes in norms and values and in social conditions may influence the risk of suicide.* The importance of *change* was underlined in some (unpublished) studies carried out at the Danish Centre for Suicidological Research in the 1980s on correlations between suicide rates and basic societal parameters such as rate of unemployment, rate of divorce, per-capita income, rate of female economical activities, etc. These studies indicated only weak, if any, correlation between the *level* of parameters and suicide rates, but highly significant correlations between the abruptness and/or violence of the *changes* in these parameters and the frequency of suicide.

Questions will be posed regarding the ways in which these cultural and societal changes and changes in age composition interact to redefine the roles, images and self-consciousness of the various age groups and, in continuation of this, whether and how *this in turn may influence the risk of suicide or rather the propensity for suicidal behaviour in the various age groups*. Thus, while taking its point of departure in the societal development on a macro level, the focus will be on what we may call the *mezzo* level, that is on the interplay between the macro level and individuals or (age) groups of individuals (i.e. the micro level). Changes in Danish society and Danish data on suicide and attempted suicide will be used to illustrate the argument.

TRENDS IN SOCIETAL DEVELOPMENT

The changes in Danish society during recent decades correspond with some of the major developments that have taken place in many other countries as well: the change in age composition caused by the baby boom in the mid-1940s, the explosive growth in affluence and welfare during the booming 1960s, the similarly explosive growth in the educational system from the late 1950s and the development of new information technology.

The age distribution

As in most Western countries, the age composition of the Danish population has changed markedly during this century. Figure 10.1 illustrates these changes from the neat pyramid-shaped distribution for both sexes at the beginning of the 1920s to the more oval-shaped distribution in the mid-1990s caused by increases in the numbers of men below the age of 50 years and of women above the age of 65 years.

For example, in Denmark 75 years ago, elderly people above the age of 65 years constituted approximately 10 per cent of the total population, today they constitute about 20 per cent, and when the baby-boomers from the mid-1940s reach the age of retirement, they will total more than one-third of the Danish population. The changes in age composition are not only due to the fact that more people live longer, but are also caused by a decline in fertility. In Denmark two large-scale and prolonged decreases have taken place with regard to this latter phenomenon. First, there was a decrease from 4.5 live-born babies per woman in the beginning of the 1890s to 2.1 at the beginning of the 1930s, whereafter the level increased and stabilized at about 2.6. Next, attitudes towards family planning and norms regarding contraception and abortion changed; the generations of women born after the war decided their own "fertility level" and after the mid-1960s the level

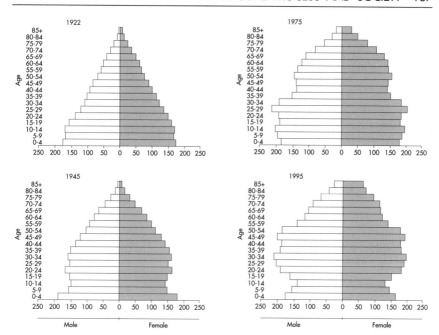

Figure 10.1   Changes in age distribution of the Danish population in the period 1922–1995.

dropped to less than 1.5 live-born babies per woman. During the 1990s an increase to about 1.8 has taken place.

At a practical level this means that the number of "breadwinners" (i.e. the economically active) relative to those to be supported has decreased markedly from nine breadwinners per one retired person before the Second World War to less than 4 : 1 today. According to prognosis, this number will further decrease to 3 : 1 within the next 10–15 years, and it can be expected that this development may have severe stressing effects on both parties. It may also imply that the growing number of "non-breadwinners" will have increasing political power and more say about the setting of norms and values in our society.

According to, among others, the American demographer Easterlin (1968, 1978, 1980), these changes are of substantial relevance, as the relative size of a birth cohort may in the end influence the individual cohort's rate of suicide. Huge cohorts need more space than small cohorts, and consequently members of huge cohorts are exposed to the risk of being "squeezed in", and thus to severe psychological stress, eventually resulting in crime, abuse and suicidal behaviour. (For a more

Figure 10.2   Per-capita income in Denmark 1916–1996.

detailed description of the theories on the relative size of the cohort (RSC) and its effect on the frequency of suicidal behaviour, see Bille-Brahe, 2000.)

Affluence and welfare

The relationship between suicide rates and various socio-economic factors, including the level of unemployment, has been the subject of many studies for more than a century. Figure 10.2 gives an overview of the development of per-capita income in Denmark during a period of 80 years (the definition of per-capita income was based on the term "available amount" in the national budget, calculated in millions of Danish Kroner, adjusted for the years 1940–1945 and deflated to 1980 DKK).

The steep increase in affluence during the "booming 1960s" was beneficial to literally all groups in Danish society. Nevertheless, analyses of co-variations with rates of suicide showed a clear *positive* correlation ($p < 0.001$), i.e. the more affluence, the higher the frequency of suicide. It is, however, important to note the fact that the differences in income from one year to another also became more and more pronounced. Economic instability thus became another characteristic feature of Danish society.

During the 1960s Denmark developed into a welfare society. The new social policy meant a break from the traditional poor-relief system with its strong stamp of degrading charity and a change to viewing public support as something all citizens are entitled to when in need. Albeit, affluence and welfare also gradually changed Denmark, as with many other Western countries, into a materialistic consumer society.

Education and information technology

The third main characteristic concerns the increasing level of education. Table 10.1 illustrates the effect of the strengthening of the educational system starting in the late 1950s. While at the beginning of the 1960s very few Danes had more than the compulsory basic schooling (which at that time meant 7 years), by the mid-1990s about one-third of the younger generations had a further 3–5 years of schooling. A similar development can be seen among older age groups, in which the proportion of people taking further education increased from 2 to 18 per cent. During the 20th century, technology in general progressed not only rapidly, but also with accelerating speed (Toffler, 1981; Naisbitt, 1982). This has particularly been the case in the last few decades with the advent of information technology. Telecommunication, PCs, access to e-mail and the Internet now play a part in the everyday life of most Danes.

During these processes the structure of Danish society changed. On the one hand, society became more homogeneous. Both rural/urban and social-class differences became less pronounced as a result of increasing mobility—socially, occupationally as well as geographically. At the same time, the country opened up towards the rest of the world, not only regarding trade and commerce, but also tourism in general increased and going "interrail" (rail travel throughout continental

Table 10.1 Changes in level of education

	1962		1996	
	BS* (%)	USS** (%)	BS* (%)	USS** (%)
20–29	94	6	64	35
30–39	95	5	71	30
40–49	96	4	73	26
50–59	97	3	82	18
60–69	98	2	87	13

 * Only basic (compulsory) school (9 years).
** Upper secondary school (3–5 years).

Europe) became popular among the young. On the other hand, various subgroups formed with their own particular lifestyles, based on special norms and values, such as hippies, Hell's Angels, feminists and various grass-root and/or political movements, some of them rather fanatical.

Norms and values changed and multiplied dramatically: most kinds of conduct and behaviour became accepted and very few directly "forbidden". In short, people were largely left with few of the necessary common "rules of the road", a situation described by Durkheim as anomic. The lack of social control, brought about by the rejection of traditions and authority following the youth revolution in 1968, and also increasing secularization led to the anomic state. At the same time, a rather extreme individualism evolved from individual-oriented attitudes, which were characteristic of the 20th century, stemming from the general demand for liberation. It should perhaps be added here that even though anomic and egoistic states do not necessarily coincide, they are rarely totally independent of each other. The social control necessary to prevent anomie is exercised via, among others, the family group, groups of friends and colleagues or in social surroundings. The more the individual feels that he or she belongs to the group, the more easily the norms and values of the group are internalized. Consequently, if ego-oriented attitudes (i.e. the cultivation of the individual "I") predominate, the individual's interest in and sense of obligation towards the norms and values of the community will weaken. It is exactly for that reason that the ability of the group or community to maintain its norms and values (i.e. to exercise the necessary amount of social control) will weaken correspondingly.

GENERAL TRENDS IN THE FREQUENCY OF SUICIDAL BEHAVIOUR

Figures 10.3 and 10.4 show age-specific rates of suicide during the period 1922–1996 and of attempted suicide in the years 1989–1997. Age-specific rates of suicide were calculated on the basis of data from the Register of Suicide, the Danish Centre for Suicidological Research in Odense (data on 5-year age bands of individuals aged 65 and older were available only from 1943). Data on attempted suicide were available from the Register of Suicide Attempts, collected by the monitoring group of the WHO/Euro Multicentre Study on Parasuicide carried out in the county of Funen (Fyn).

Figure 10.3 confirms the well-known pattern showing that the occurrence of suicide increases with age as far as males are concerned, while among females rates peak in the middle age groups. However, the

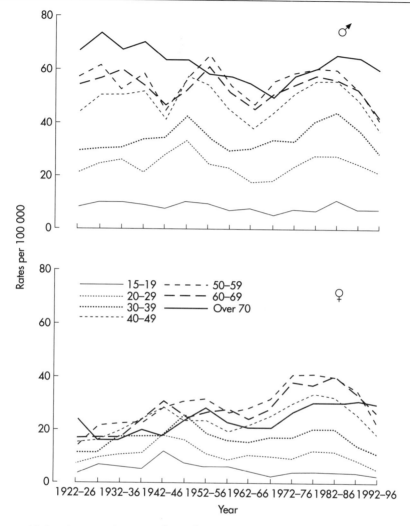

Figure 10.3 Age-specific rates of suicide in the years 1922–1996 by gender (5-year average).

figure also shows that throughout the years—*except for the last period* (i.e. 1992–1996)—there has been an increased risk for suicide among adult men, and particularly among those in their early middle age. It is also interesting to note that, since the beginning of the 1980s, frequencies of suicide have been increasing among old elderly men (70 years and over). With regard to females, there was a steep relative increase in the occurrence of suicide among adult women and women in their early middle age in the 1970s and 1980s. Particularly noteworthy is,

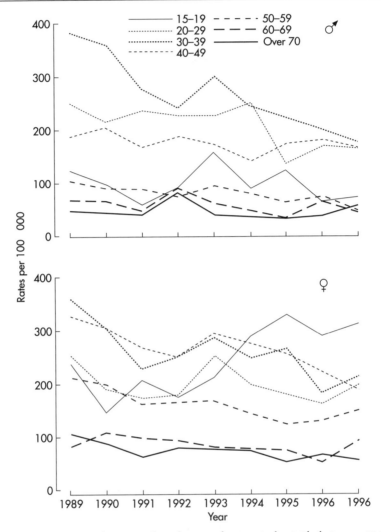

Figure 10.4 Age-specific person-based rates of attempted suicide between 1989 and 1997, by gender.

however, the marked increase in frequency among relatively older females during the subsequent period.

Likewise, Figure 10.4 illustrates the well-known fact that, contrary to completed suicide, suicide *attempts* are carried out by younger people. The frequency of attempted suicide has, in general, decreased, as is the case for completed suicide, *but with one exception*: the frequency of suicide attempts among young girls aged 15–19 has doubled during a 5-year period in the 1990s.

We can now formulate our questions more specifically: Did anything happen in Danish society during the last decades that can make us better understand *why there has been an increasing trend in frequency of suicide among old elderly men and young elderly women and why people reaching their forties during the 1980s apparently were increasingly prone to react to problems and pain with suicidal behaviour? The same question applies to young girls during the 1990s.*

SUICIDE AMONG THE ELDERLY

It is a well-known fact that the risk of suicide increases with age. As the number of elderly people in most populations is increasing, there has been growing concern regarding future trends in suicide among elderly people. It has, however, also been maintained that the *proportion* of suicides among the elderly did not increase, at least not as much as expected. In Denmark, for example, during the first part of the 20th century, elderly people above the age of 65, constituting about 10 per cent of the total population, committed about 25 per cent of all suicides. Today, elderly people constitute about 25 per cent of the total population, but they still are responsible for about one-quarter of all suicides. The explanation for this apparent paradox may be that the process of getting old has changed too. In many studies of suicidal behaviour among the elderly, *the elderly* are defined as persons aged 65 years and over. Thus, all persons above the age of 65 years are regarded as one homogeneous group, at times commonly characterized as being poor, lonely, in poor health or miserable. In real life, however, elderly people not only differ from each other as much as other people, but there are also huge differences between the various age groups of the elderly. A so-called young elderly person aged 65 has very little in common with an old elderly celebrating his/her 80th or 90th birthday. In addition to this, we should note that being 70 years old today is quite different from being 70 years old 25 or 50 years ago. Results from a comprehensive study of three cohorts of future Danish elderly, carried out in the mid-1980s (Bille-Brahe, 1989; Schroll, 1989), indicated that marked changes are taking place in their lifestyles, life standards, attitudes and various health aspects were concerned. Longitudinal studies of the health of 70-year-olds have shown an increasing improvement of health, so that 70-year-olds today are in much better physical and mental health than those at the same age 20 years ago. They also live longer. (For a more detailed discussion of the changing situation of the elderly see Bille-Brahe, 2001).

Figure 10.5 underlines the fact that, at least as far as the risk of suicide is concerned, people of 65 years and older cannot be seen as a homogeneous group. The differences between various age groups are especially pronounced among elderly men. The increase in the rate of suicide among *old* elderly men (80+) around 1980 was steeper than that for the young elderly, and the frequency remained at this high level while rates among the young elderly decreased.

During the 1970s, suicide rates increased in all age groups among females, especially among those aged 30 years and older. The increase was followed by a general decrease starting in the mid-1980s. However, while female rates of suicide used to reach their peak among the middle-aged (as shown in Figure 10.2), rates of suicide have now been increasing for *old* elderly women (80+); in 1996 these rates reached 19.6 per 100 000, compared with 15.0 per 100 000 among the middle-aged.

Most elderly are today aware of the problems arising from the change in age distribution, and they are also aware of the fact that because they will probably live longer, they will at some point also be more fragile and in need of care. As they are used to a high standard of living, they will make some demands for more and better services. They are, however, also aware that, because of the small sizes of the exhorts embarking on their working lives, there will be a decreasing number of people to carry the burden of support, i.e. to procure the resources needed to meet these demands. The problem is also growing because increasing numbers of elderly people are opting for early retirement at the age of 60.

The effect of this development may have an influence on the rate of suicide, i.e. the theories on the relative size of a birth cohort may have some relevance: it can be shown that, in spite of increasing good health and vigour, the increasing size of the elderly population co-varies with the risk of suicide among the elderly. Two-way variance analysis indicates, however, that only a small part of the variance in rates of suicide can be explained by the relative size of cohorts.

This brings us to two other aspects which are of importance when trying to understand the risk of suicide among elderly people. The first concerns the feeling of alienation that still prevails among many of the old elderly. They do not feel themselves able to follow what is going on in modern society or to understand the many things that are happening (e.g. in the computer world). They feel useless, outdated and, as their peers disappear, more and more lonely, because no one "talks their language" any longer. Here again the young elderly are in a different position: in Denmark, training courses in the use of computers

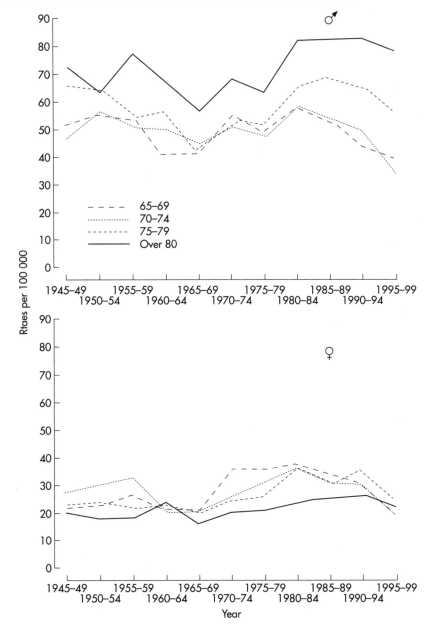

Figure 10.5   Age- and gender-specific rates of suicide for various groups of the elderly.

and the Internet are offered free or at a very low cost for retired people.

The second aspect deals with the question raised by both David Clark (1992) and Ad Kerkhof (1994) in their studies on suicide among the elderly: Could it be that suicide among the elderly is less motivated by, for example, alienation, loneliness or general misery than by a fear of becoming dependent on others? According to the studies carried out by Clark and Kerkhof, respectively, the elderly who commit suicide are no more miserable than most other elderly individuals, but it seems that they belong to a special type of personality who places great value on independence. It can be argued that the development of modern society and its individual-oriented views on humans have promoted this personality type, who is especially prone to stress the need for being an independent individual. The topic of being elderly is frequently discussed in the media, and especially on television where focus is on increasing frequency of dementia and depression among the elderly and on the detrimental effect of these conditions on individuals in general, and the elderly in particular. The new elderly are used to being self-reliant even when getting older, and consequently an increasing number seems to abhor the idea of being left like a wilting vegetable at the mercy of some care person or other. For example, the discussion in the Netherlands, prior to the introduction of access to assisted suicide, bears witness to this development and to the development of attitudes, resembling those prevailing among the Stoics and the Epicureans, praising *mors voluntaris* as the (only) decent way to end one's life.

THE BABY-BOOMERS

This term refers to the huge cohorts born around the mid-1940s, a phenomenon well known in many countries in the West. In Denmark, there was a general increase in the frequency of suicidal behaviour during the 1960s and 1970s, and this increase was in particular relatively marked among the baby-boomers. This can be illustrated by showing the so-called "cumulative incidence proportion" (CIP, Table 10.2) of the cohorts (i.e. the total number of suicides committed by this cohort through their lifespan or up to a certain age). The CIP is defined as

$$\text{CIP} = 10^5 \left(1 \div \pi \frac{N_{ij} - n_{ij}}{N_{ij}} \right)$$

where N = the population and n = the number of suicides, both calculated as sliding means.

Table 10.2 Cumulative incidence proportions by age for cohorts born between 1931 and 1960 (sliding means)

				Year				
Males (age)	1946–50	1951–55	1956–60	1961–65	1966–70	1971–75	1976–80	1981–86
50–54								489
45–49							**427**	418
40–44						350	**357**	320
35–39					260	253	**283**	226
30–34				164	195	198	168	158
25–29			97	111	126	116	114	84
20–24		47	49	58	63	66	50	49
15–19	17	9	15	14	21	16	17	17
Females (age)								
50–54								251
45–49							**215**	181
40–44						**174**	152	139
35–39					122	123	**174**	81
30–34				75	84	75	62	46
25–29			43	51	51	46	32	21
20–24		24	21	22	25	22	14	9
15–19	8	5	7	7	6	6	4	5

CIP values increase, of course, by age, but the table shows that the rate of increase is especially steep for baby-boomers when they reach their forties. Figure 10.6 reflects this increase in the frequency of suicide during the 1960s and 1970s by showing CIP values for males and females when they were 35–39, 40–44 and 45–49 years old in 1960, 1980 and in 1996, respectively.

The variation in frequency of suicide *relative* to other cohorts is perhaps demonstrated more clearly in Figure 10.7, which shows the increasingly high frequencies among both men and women born in the 1940s when they reached their forties (i.e. during the 1970s and 1980s). It should be noted that the high CIP values for women in 1945 (see Figure 10.3) are usually explained by referring to the relatively high number of unhappy or unfortunate relationships between Danish women and members of the German occupational forces.

Unfortunately, we are in no position to calculate CIP values or other long-term measures on suicide attempts, but, as shown in Figure 10.8, we know from earlier studies that the frequency of attempted suicide increased markedly among adult men and women during the last part of the 1970s (Bille-Brahe and Juel Nielsen, 1986).

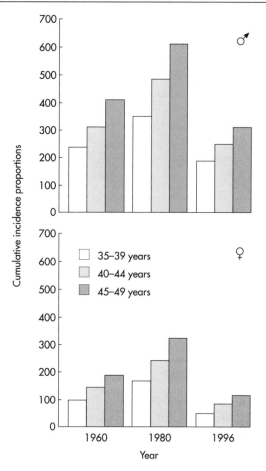

Figure 10.6   Cumulative incidence proportions at certain ages during the period 1960 to 1996.

Normally we do not consider the fact that the concept of *adolescence* is something new and that only recently in human history has there been a need for a term covering the period between childhood and adult life. This need became especially evident as the baby-boomers grew up. As mentioned above, researchers have been discussing the implication for society of the relative size of a cohort using various frames of reference. For example, Hendin (1987) explained the highly significant correlation between suicide rate and relative cohort size in the USA by pointing to problems arising when huge numbers of young people simultaneously are seeking education, looking for a job, a place to live, etc. In Denmark, however, the new huge cohorts born in the mid-1940s were welcomed with open arms, as they were dearly needed

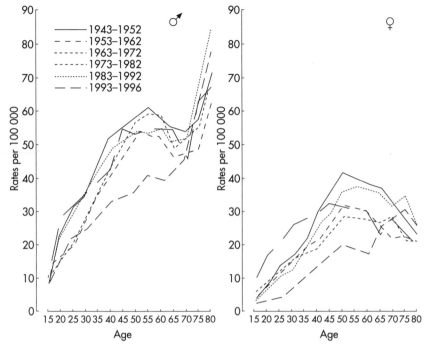

Figure 10.7   Rates of suicide during the period 1943–1966, by gender and age.

at the time of growth and expanding economical and technological activities during the 1960s. There was plenty of room for these cohorts, and they were given more power than any generation of young people before them had experienced. Accordingly, fashions and lifestyles, norms and values were to an increasing degree on their terms; "the young" became the trendsetters, not only for their own generation, but also for the younger *and* older generations as well.

The implicit consequences of this development in Denmark were both far reaching and long lasting. Danish society changed with a velocity never before experienced, and by the late 1960s this accumulation of change gave vent to the so-called youth revolt or "revolution of 1968", which in Denmark, as in many other Western countries, came to stand for revolt against predominant authoritarian bureaucracies and old-fashioned, rigid and, in the eyes of the young, meaningless traditions. They were against war and for love, for free sex and women's liberation, etc. Politically, the young generation moved left, not least at universities and other institutes of higher education, where teaching and research to a very high degree were carried out within a Marxist

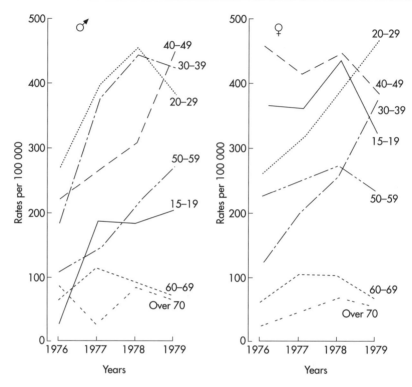

Figure 10.8   Age-specific person-based rates of attempted suicide between 1976 and 1979, by gender.

frame of reference. At the same time, however, materialism in combination with increasing affluence enhanced the development of a consumer society where, for example, the Church and several traditional Christian institutions became less and less important.

One of the effects of this development was that traditional family life was gradually disrupted. Divorce and cohabitation of unmarried partners became common. On the basis of regular interviews with the Danish population aged 16 or over, the Danish Central Bureau of Statistics estimated that the number of common-law marriages increased in a single decade by 250 per cent. Also, family life itself became unstable; more and more families came to consist of a series of changing partners and changing numbers of *my* children, *your* children and *our* children, or became single-parent families (recent reports from the Danish Ministry of Social Affairs indicate that approximately 15 per cent of all children below the age of 18 live in a single-parent family). During the 1960s and especially during the 1970s married Danish women entered the labour market at such a speed that by the end of the 1970s in most families both parents were working full-time, while children were taken care of by various institutions such as day-care centres, nurseries, kindergartens and after-school facilities. Theories on upbringing and education were greatly affected by the prevailing anti-authoritarian ideas advocating the principle of "free upbringing".

However, when the baby-boomers reached their late thirties and early forties, the norms and values in force in Danish society were changing again, and so was life for the baby-boomers. Out were the carefree Bob Dylan inspired folk singers with their long hair and high ideals of peace and flower power—in had come individual-oriented consumers with their 'keep-up-with-the-Joneses' syndrome. The yuppies had entered the stage, and owning a house, a thoroughbred dog and a family station wagon (preferably Volvo) with room for at least two children became the standard.

I find it reasonable to argue that these changes had a double-sided negative effect on the baby-boomers: an ideological and emotional down trip or deroute following the more or less conscious denouncement of former ideals, and increasing stress caused by striving to keep up with the new way of life, which too often was met by various ways of trying to cope (e.g. pills or alcohol). Thus, the baby-boomers became more and more vulnerable, and they were thus more exposed to an increased risk of suicide. Unfortunately, this development coincided with ongoing changes in attitudes towards suicidal behaviour. From being a taboo topic and something definitely not acceptable, suicide came gradually to be seen as an understandable reaction to problems and pain, or even as a human right. There was, in short, no longer either in the religious or in the more secular everyday norm system any deterrent to using suicide as a "way out".

YOUNG GIRLS

As described above, the average rates of both suicide and attempted suicide have decreased during the last 10–15 years in Denmark, as in most other countries in Western Europe (Schmidtke et al, 1996; Bille-Brahe, 1998). In Denmark, however, a notable exception has been the frequency of suicide *attempts* among young girls. As shown in Figure 10.9, the rate of suicide attempts among young girls aged 15–19 more than doubled over a 5-year period in the 1990s.

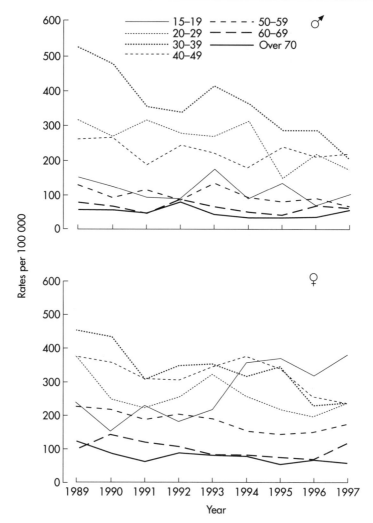

Figure 10.9 Age- and gender-specific event-based rates of attempted suicide in the county of Funen (Fyn) between 1989 and 1997.

The frequency of suicide attempts among 15–19-year-old girls reached its peak in 1995. This was followed by a decrease in 1996, but even then the rate of events had more than doubled over the period. The question thus has to be posed why this increase in frequency of suicide among young girls occurred, and why they react, to whatever it is, so differently from all other groups, including boys of the same age group?

Table 10.3 Person-based rates of attempted suicide and suicide among 15–19-year-old girls and 15–19-year-old boys, 1990–1996

	15–19-year-old girls				15–19-year-old boys			
	Suicide attempt		Suicide		Suicide attempt		Suicide	
	N	Rate	N	Rate	N	Rate	N	Rate
1990	23	140	—	—	15	88	2	12
1991	32	200	—	—	9	54	—	—
1992	25	162	—	—	14	86	—	—
1993	30	198	1	7	25	159	2	13
1994	39	268	1	7	12	78	—	—
1995	39	276	—	—	15	103	1	7
1996	35	257	—	—	8	57	—	—

Table 10.3 shows that rates of suicide attempts have been higher for 15–19-year-old girls than for 15–19-year-old boys throughout the whole period. Since 1994 the difference has even been increasing, and in 1996 the rate for girls was 4.5 times higher than the rate for boys of the same age. Table 10.3 also shows, on the other hand, that the frequency of *completed* suicide is higher among boys than among girls. The ratio of attempted suicide to completed suicide among these young people is much higher than the 8–10 : 1, generally assumed in the literature, especially among girls where the ratio on average is higher than 110 : 1. For boys the ratio is "only" 20 : 1. Gender-specific differences in suicidal behaviour have received much attention in the literature, where the "hows" and "whys" have been discussed within various frames of reference. So, this discussion will not be pursued here, and only a brief description based on Danish data will be included.

One interesting difference between the two groups emerging from Danish data concerned the reasons given by girls and boys, respectively, for their suicide attempt. The girls would typically and very freely explain that they had attempted suicide because they had problems with their boyfriend or partner. The boys, on the other hand, would be more reluctant to speak about the reason why; they would more often talk about having too many problems, and also—relative to the girls—they would more often state that they simply "wanted to get away", that life was not worth living, etc. This information does not, however, bring us closer to any answers; according to the girls, the reason why they tried to kill themselves was trouble with their partner, but it is hardly conceivable, when compared with 5–10 years ago, that twice as many girls suffer from a broken heart or that a broken heart is twice as painful nowadays.

Perhaps we should try and rephrase our question: Could there be something during their childhood and upbringing that has affected *the propensity* of especially young girls to react to problems in this peculiar and rather dramatic way?

Being 15–19 years old in the period 1990-1996 means that these young girls were born between 1971 and 1981; that is, they were children of the baby-boomers, the generation who had come into age in "the booming sixties", when Denmark developed into an affluent consumer society with an increasingly high level of welfare. During the childhood and upbringing of these young girls, their parents were themselves in the middle of abrupt changes in traditional norms and values, which left them without any common "traffic regulations" (i.e. in a state of anomie and also of egoism). As the parents of these young girls were both promoters of and subject to the anomic state of society, it stands to reason that they were neither able to provide a stable framework for their children nor to transmit to them a set of "rules for the road" or commonly shared norms and values.

A possible explanation of why an increasing number of young girls attempt suicide may therefore be found in the anomic and egoistic states in our society during their upbringing and in the inability of the parental generation to provide their children with common norms and rules and a sense of belonging within a solid and reliable framework. In line with the anti-authoritarian attitudes of their parents, children were given very free reins and extensive freedom to choose for themselves, the legacy of the parental generation only amounting to a distorted echo of Sartre's "choosing oneself", namely staging oneself. What happens when a generation is no longer taught common norms and values is that they tend to create them themselves. However, without a solid ballast in the form of security, care and love, guidance and support this freedom is a very heavy burden for young shoulders, and it does not always prepare the young to meeting hardships and tackle problems.

Another particular feature of the 1970s was the markedly increasing frequency in suicidal behaviour. Registration surveys indicate that during the latter half of the 1970s the rates of attempted suicide increased in Denmark by at least 10 per cent per year, the increase being particularly pronounced among adults. The frequency of suicide also increased dramatically, the rates in 1980 being the highest ever registered in Denmark. The increase took place in all age groups, but again the increase was relatively high among adults, as described above. About 1980 every fourth death in the parental generation was due to suicide, and suicide was the most frequent cause of death after cancer among 35–49-year-olds.

According to most theories on learning, children learn by watching the behaviour of others, particularly the behaviour of significant others (usually the parents), and this holds to some extent for suicidal behaviour as well (Bille-Brahe, 1991). Suicidal behaviour may then be something one learns as a special language or way of communication, and as a way to solve problems. Thus, having experienced suicidal behaviour in the family is a very potent risk factor. A study carried out on about 3500 Danish students showed that the risk of considering taking one's own life more than doubled if the student had experienced suicide in the family, and the risk of attempting suicide was three times higher (Jessen et al, 1996).

However, even if such considerations may indicate why some young people today are at an increased risk of suicidal behaviour, they do not, of course, explain why there are these striking differences between girls and boys. The information we have on the personal and social characteristics of young suicide attempters and any differences between the boys and girls is, however, scarce. After being adjusted for age, differences can be summarized as follows: among boys suicide attempters were more often repeaters, more often living alone or in institutions, they had moved more often, were more often economically active, but also more often unemployed. Among girls suicide attempters were more commonly living with their parents, had a better schooling and were more often in the process of training. This information, however, does not help us in answering our question. On the contrary, relating this information to what is known about risk factors, we would have expected the boys to have the highest frequency of attempted suicide.

Looking at a normal population of youngsters, however, as in the above-mentioned study on students, some interesting differences between boys and girls emerge. Significantly more girls than boys had seriously considered attempting suicide and significantly more had made one or more suicide attempts. At the same time, more girls than boys thought that one should always try and prevent suicide, while the boys argued that suicide was a human right. Thus, boys and girls clearly showed different attitudes towards suicidal behaviour, and they attached different meanings to the phenomenon. Also, more girls than boys said they experienced or had experienced emotional problems, but apparently, contrary to boys, girls would seek and receive help with their problems from family or friends.

Combined with the differences in attitudes towards suicidal behaviour this may be interpreted as follows. Girls seem to associate suicidal behaviour first and foremost with attempted suicide (one should always try and prevent suicide), and a suicide attempt is more likely to be seen as a cry for help or attention (girls seek help with their problems). Contrary, boys seem to associate suicidal behaviour with a human right to commit suicide, thus putting an end to problems and pain. This notion is supported by the data presented above: the ratio of attempted suicide to completed suicide was $20:1$ among 15–19-year-old boys, but as high as $120:1$ for girls.

Girls also more freely admitted that, when exposed to teasing or bullying in school or among friends, they would be upset and sometimes reduced to tears, while boys would either laugh or pay back in some more or less aggressive way. Psychologists seem to agree that when something goes wrong, girls are in general inclined to blame themselves, while boys tend to put the blame on others, and that this could be the reason why girls react inwardly by crying, feeling helpless and lost, while boys react outwardly, usually in a more or less aggressive way.

Developing a personal identity is an important part of growing up. The process takes place in interplay with others, and successful development depends on responses from others, again in particular from the so-called significant others, and of the unambiguous character of the signals transmitted by them. Apparently, decades of campaigning for sex equality have not been able to change the fact that boys and girls are different, among other things in their ways of acting out, and these differences seem to be particularly pronounced among the young. The women's liberation movement in Denmark during the 1970s was at times both rather militant and fanatic. The declared goal was complete equality with men. Consequently, women did not so much create a new role of their own based upon their own norms and values, rather they adopted premises prevailing in the male world. There was a lot of talk about a new feminine identity, but in fact the new female image was more or less deliberately devoid of any traits, including fashion, attitudes and behaviour in public as well as in private life that could be defined as especially feminine. This, however, left daughters especially in a kind of vacuum in which creation of their own identity *as a girl* was problematic. The blurring of sex in everyday life led to bewilderment and uncertainty: both parents in jobs, both changing diapers, using the vacuum cleaner, cooking the food, etc. However, messages received from the male world were more unambiguous than those from women. Fathers may be doing some housework, but they are still more interested in football.

The important issue here is the fact that the male world provides a more solid framework for the creation of a male identity, and also creates more opportunities for acting out than does the female world. In recent years, more and more boys in Denmark participate actively in various sports, and sport is playing an increasingly important part in the masculine world. Sport provides great opportunities for acting out, either as an active participant or as an onlooker screaming his head off in some stadium, and both ways stimulate the feeling of being part of a group. Alternative ways of acting out are the use or abuse of alcohol and drugs, and these too are most prevalent among boys.

Finally, boys also act out more often through crime, especially gang crime, usually connected with violence. This last difference in particular points to a tentative answer to our question. According to statistics, the average frequency of crime has been decreasing (just like the average frequency of attempted suicide), *but not among young boys*: the rate of crimes of violence committed by 15–19-year-old boys doubled during the period under study. Figure 10.10 shows how the frequency of attempted suicide among young girls and the frequency of crimes of violence among young boys follow the same thought-provoking pattern.

A tentative conclusion could therefore be that conditions during their upbringing in the fast-changing society in the 1970s have made both girls and boys vulnerable, and their parents (or caretakers) have not provided them with the ability to cope with problems in a rational and

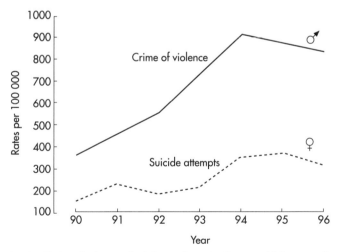

Figure 10.10 Rate of crimes of violence for 15–19-year-old boys and rate of attempted suicide for 15–19-year-old girls.

realistic way. They react then upon the same experiences, but in different ways. This difference is, of course, of importance when dealing with young people, but far less so when trying to understand those factors that promote these kinds of reaction.

CONCLUSIONS

An overview of the frequency of suicidal behaviour in Denmark has shown that during recent decades some notable movements have taken place in the rates among three groups in particular: the old elderly, the baby-boomers and very young girls.

The aim of this chapter has been to try and understand such a phenomenon by relating the variation to some of the changes that coincidentally have taken place in Danish society.

In Denmark, as in most other countries, cultural, social, economical, technological and demographical changes have taken place during the past century, and especially after the Second World War with an accelerating speed and violence, resulting, as argued by Durkheim, in among others anomie and egoism. Edwin Shneidman, another leading suicidologist, has also used the concept of egoism when he described three types of suicide: the egoistic suicide, which is seen as a result of an intra-psychic process during which what is going on in the individual overshadows everything else, the dyadic (or social) suicide that relates to unmet needs in relation to significant others, and the sociological suicide, occurring when a person has lost his sense of coherence and of being part of a continuum.

Although the three age groups described in this chapter have been exposed to the same periodical events (i.e. the same development), their age and cohort membership will have coloured the way they perceive the events. It therefore seems reasonable to assume that most of the changes that have taken place within the last decades have affected the various groups in different ways. On the other hand, however, a common denominator for all groups seems to be that the effect has been one of increased vulnerability. Thus it may be said that all three groups in some way may be seen as *victims* of the development. The present old elderly have had very little influence on what has taken place during recent decades, and they experience difficulty in coming to terms with what is going on in modern society, which may make them feel impotent and superfluous. The baby-boomers, who in reality were the initiators of most of the changes, were, as they grew older, in a way victims of what they themselves had initiated. Finally, adolescents find themselves in the wake of all the changes and also, we should add, at the mercy of ongoing changes, the situation resembling the story of the *Sorcerer's Apprentice*.

However, some of the changes in norms and values have apparently had a somewhat similar effect on all three groups. I am referring to views and attitudes on life and death in general, and towards killing oneself in particular. There are still different opinions as to the acceptability of suicide, but in general Danes have adopted a very tolerant view on suicide, and in all three age groups there seems to be an increasing number advocating suicide as a basic human right. Furthermore, it seems that younger people to an increasing extent find it acceptable to use non-fatal suicidal behaviour as a form of communication or a way of problem solving.

REFERENCES

Bille-Brahe, U. and Juel Nielsen, N. (1986) Trends in attempted suicide in Denmark 1976–1980. *Suicide and Life-Threatening Behavior*, **16**: 46–55.

Bille-Brahe, U. (1987) Suicide and Social Integration. A pilot study on the integration levels in Norway and Denmark. *Acta Psychatrica Scandinavica*, **76** (suppl. 336): 45–62.

Bille-Brahe, U. (1989) *Nye tider – nye ældre. Holdninger og forventninger (New Times – New Elderly. Attitudes and Expectations)*. EGV Foundation, Copenhagen.

Bille-Brahe, U. (1991) Langtidsvirkninger af stigninger i forekomsten af suicidal adfærd. Suicidal adfærd blandt børn og unge (Long-term effects of increases in the occurrence of suicidal behaviour. Suicidal behaviour among children and adolescents). *Nord. Psychiat. Tidssk*, **45**: 185–188.

Bille-Brahe, U. (1998) *Suicidal Behaviour in Europe. The Situation in the 1990's*. World Health Organization, Regional Office for Europe, Copenhagen.

Bille-Brahe, U. (2000) Sociology and suicidal behaviour. In K. Hawton and K. Van Heeringen (Eds), *The International Handbook of Suicide and Attempted Suicide*. Chichester, Wiley.

Bille-Brahe, U. (2001) Suicide among the Danish elderly. In D. De Leo and A. Schmidtke (Eds), *Suicide in Older Adults: A Transcultural Comparison*. London, M. Dunitz, in press.

Boldt, M. (1988) The meaning of suicide: implications for research. *Crisis*, **9**: 93–108.

Camus, A. (1942, 1991) *The Myth of Sisyphos*. London, Penguin.

Clark, D.C. (1992) Narcissistic crisis of aging and suicidal despair. Presidential address to the *25th Conference of the American Association of Suicidology*. Chicago, Rush-Presbyterian-St Luke's Medical Center.

Durkheim, É. (1895) *Les règles de la méthode sociologique*. Danish translation, Fremad, Copenhagen, 1972.

Durkheim, E. (1897) *Suicide. A Study in Sociology*. The Free Press, New York.

Easterlin, R.A. (1968) *Population, Labor Force and Long Swings in Economic Growth*. New York, National Bureau of Economic Growth.

Easterlin, R.A. (1978) What will 1984 be like? Socioeconomic implications of the recent twist in age structure. *Demography*, **15**: 397–432.

Easterlin, R.A. (1980) *Birth and Fortune: The Impact of Numbers on Personal Welfare*. New York, Basic Books.

Hendin, H. (1987) Youth suicide: a psychosocial perspective. *Suicide and Life-Threatening Behavior*, **17**: 151–165.

Jessen, G., Andersen, K. and Bille-Brahe, U. (1996). Suicidal ideation and suicide attempts among 15-24-year-olds in the Danish educational system (Danish with English summary). *Ugeskr Læger* **158**: 5026–5029.

Kerkhof, A.J.F.M., Ormskerk, S.C.R. and Oomes, M. (1994) Assessing rationality in elderly suicidal patients: common sense versus dynamic assessment. In U. Bille-Brahe and H Schiødt (Eds), *Intervention and Prevention*. Odense, Odense University Press.

Naisbitt, A. (1982) *Megatrends: Ten New Directions Transforming our Lives*. New York, Warner Books.

Schmidtke, A., Bille-Brahe, U., DeLeo, D., Kerkhof, A., Bjerke, T., Crepet, P., Haring, C., Hawton, K., Lönnqvist, J., Michel, K., Pommereau, X., Querejeta, I., Phillipe, I., Salander-Renberg, E., Temesvary, B., Weinacker, B. and Sampaio Faria, J.G. (1996) Attempted suicide in Europe: rates, trends and sociodemographic characteristics of suicide attempters during the period 1989–1992. Results of the WHO/Euro Multicentre Study on Parasuicide. *Acta Psychiatrica Scandinavica*, **93**: 327–338.

Schroll, M. (1989) *Nye tider – nye ældre. Helbred (New Times – New Elderly. Health)*. Copenhagen, EGV Foundation.

Toffler, A. (1981) *The Third Wave*. London, Pan Books Ltd.

Chapter 11

THE TREATMENT OF SUICIDAL BEHAVIOUR IN THE CONTEXT OF THE SUICIDAL PROCESS

Keith Hawton

INTRODUCTION

Effective treatment of suicidal individuals is a key element in suicide prevention. This chapter will focus specifically on the treatment of patients who have deliberately self-harmed. This includes patients who have taken overdoses and those who have self-injured in some way. The term "deliberate self-harm" (DSH) avoids implying any specific single motivation, as is the case, for example, with the term "attempted suicide". Despite extensive knowledge of the characteristics of DSH patients, treating them often proves difficult and there is very little hard evidence regarding efficacy and effectiveness to guide the clinician when making treatment decisions.

Deliberate self-harm appears to be an increasing problem in many countries. In the UK, for example, rates of DSH have risen in the past 10–15 years such that the number of general hospital presentations per year has increased from approximately 100 000 to at least 150 000 (Hawton et al, 1997; Kapur et al, 1998). There is wide variation between countries in Europe regarding rates of DSH presentations to general hospitals, as is clearly illustrated by findings from the WHO/Euro Multicentre Study of Suicidal Behaviour (Schmidtke et al, 1996). There is also marked variation in the rates in different age

Understanding Suicidal Behaviour. Edited by Kees van Heeringen
© 2001 John Wiley & Sons Ltd.

groups, with some countries such as the UK and France having particularly high rates in the very young (especially females) and other countries having relatively high rates in somewhat older age groups (Schmidtke et al, 1996). We also know that much DSH occurs in the community but does not lead to presentation to clinicians (De Wilde, 2000). Very importantly there is a strong link between DSH and completed suicide (Sakinofsky, 2000), which underlines the need for particular care in the treatment of this patient population.

In this chapter the problems that face DSH patients and the specific state and trait characteristics of these patients, which are very relevant to planning treatment, will be considered. In addition, those factors that lead to difficulties in treatment will be highlighted. Various types of approaches to treatment, particularly in relation to the components of the suicidal process, will then be considered, together with the current evidence regarding their efficacy. Reasons for the paucity of definitive findings in this area will be put forward. A pragmatic approach to planning treatment for DSH patients dependent upon their specific characteristics will then be proposed, including making available treatments from different modalities and combined therapies. Finally, the research implications of evidence in this area will be considered.

PROBLEMS AND CHARACTERISTICS OF DSH PATIENTS WHICH ARE RELEVANT TO TREATMENT

The problems and characteristics of individuals, which may lead to DSH represent a combination of state and trait factors (see Table 11.1).

Life events and difficulties

DSH often follows life events (Paykel, 1975), which may occur against the background of more long-term difficulties (Bancroft et al, 1977). The events and difficulties cover a wide range and many patients face multiple problems. In Table 11.2 some of the more common problems found in DSH patients presenting to the general hospital in Oxford are listed and shown according to gender. As can be seen, relationship problems and occupational problems are particularly common. DSH in young people commonly occurs following disruption in a relationship with a partner or conflict with parents (Hawton et al, 1982b). This is often against a background of more long-standing family difficulties (Adam et al, 1982; Fergusson and Lynskey, 1995). Some young people

Table 11.1   Problems and characteristics of DSH patients which are relevant to their treatment needs

- Life events and difficulties
- Psychiatric disorders
   —especially depression, alcohol abuse and anxiety disorders
   —personality disorders
- Problem-solving deficits
- Impulsivity and aggression
- Hopelessness and low self-esteem
- Repetition of DSH and risk of suicide
- Motivational problems and difficulties in compliance with treatments

Table 11.2   Problems identified by clinicians in DSH patients presenting to the general hospital in Oxford in 1998

Problem	Both sexes ($n = 1049$) (%)	Males ($n = 401$) (%)	Females ($n = 648$) (%)	Difference between genders (p)
Partner	43.0	42.4	43.4	n.s.
Other family member	34.6	23.7	41.4	<0.000 01
Alcohol	28.9	38.9	22.7	<0.000 01
Employment/studies	24.5	30.9	20.5	<0.0002
Financial	19.5	25.2	16.0	<0.0005
Social isolation	17.9	20.7	16.2	=0.065
Housing	16.9	22.2	13.6	<0.0005
Bereavement	12.0	12.0	12.0	n.s.
Friends	11.7	8.5	13.7	<0.02
Physical health	9.2	10.0	8.6	n.s.
Drugs	8.9	14.5	5.4	<0.000 01

Source: Annual Report of the Oxford Monitoring System for Attempted Suicide, 1998 (unpublished) (reproduced by permission of Centre for Suicide Research, Oxford University Department of Psychiatry).
(n.s. = not significant).

are particularly troubled by social isolation. In the elderly, different types of problems seem to be more important, including physical illness and threatened loss of independence (Harwood and Jacoby, 2000).

Psychiatric disorders

Recent research in representative samples of DSH patients has shown that psychiatric disorders are extremely common, and probably more so than previously thought. Whether this represents a change in the patient population (some clinicians believe this is the case), or more sophisticated screening procedures, or both, is unclear. The most common psychiatric disorders are depression, alcohol-abuse disorders and anxiety disorders (Suominen et al, 1996; Haw et al, 2001). Personality disorders are also relatively common, being found in 40–50 percent of patients (Haw et al, 2001). In many patients there is co-morbidity of either psychiatric disorders and/or psychiatric and personality disorders (see Chapter 6). Substance abuse is very often one of the co-morbid conditions. While many patients have relatively acute affective disorders, some patients have been suffering from varying degrees of depressive symptoms for many months. Patients with such complex and persistent problems pose particularly difficult therapeutic challenges. Treatments may have to be more prolonged than in patients with more straightforward problems.

Previous research in the UK suggested that psychiatric disorders detected at the time of DSH were often transient, resolving in many cases soon after DSH (Newson-Smith and Hirsch, 1979). However, more recent research has suggested that the disorders often persist (Haw et al, 2001), including in adolescents (Burgess et al, 1998). The psychiatric disorders are often secondary to, or complicate, other problems and difficulties. This is one reason why treatment of these patients can often be problematic and may require multi-modal approaches.

Problem-solving deficits

DSH patients often have difficulties in problem solving, particularly in dealing with difficulties in interpersonal relationships (see Chapter 5; Williams and Pollock, 2000). These difficulties seem to be more marked in these patients than in other patients with psychiatric disorders who have not carried out an act of self-harm. DSH patients also often tend to adopt a passive approach to problem solving (i.e. letting problems solve themselves or relying on others for solutions, Linehan et al, 1987).

Recently it has been suggested that part of the reason for the difficulties in problem solving lies in patients having resource to relatively few specific examples of problem-solving strategies. This notion has arisen from work, described more fully in Chapter 5, in which it has been shown that autobiographical memories in these patients in response to cue words are often of a very general kind compared with control individuals, who are more likely to provide more specific autobiographical memories. Thus, in response to being presented with a stimulus word such as "happy" and being asked to indicate memories evoked by the stimulus word, DSH patients often produce generalized memories, such as "when I am with my family", rather than specific memories, such as "when I was at a party with my boyfriend last week". It is thought that this phenomenon largely represents a trait condition, which may be due to using non-specific memories to modify emotions linked to memories of adverse and unpleasant experiences during childhood and adolescence. It may, however, be exacerbated by low mood (it is common in depressed patients). The degree of overgeneralization of autobiographical memories in DSH patients appears to correlate with deficiencies in problem-solving skills (Evans et al, 1992; Sidley et al, 1997).

The facts that so many DSH patients face problems in their lives and their problem-solving skills often seem to be deficient have resulted in considerable attention regarding therapeutic procedures being devoted to problem-solving therapy. Helping the patient develop a more specific approach to defining goals and choosing strategies to achieve these may be important in countering the tendency to be overgeneral in recalling past examples of difficult situations.

Impulsivity and aggression

Van Praag (Chapter 4) has described the strong link between suicidal behaviour and aggression. Much DSH is impulsive and patients often display other evidence of impulsivity. DSH is frequently a fairly immediate response to acute or more chronic frustration in the face of seemingly (to the patient) unsolvable problems. While cognitive processes that lead to this behaviour are not entirely understood, Williams and Pollock (2000; see Chapter 5) have related this to a sense of entrapment and the need to escape from it. Therapeutic measures have been devised to try and help reduce the impulsive responses to difficult situations that characterizes many DSH patients. There is also increasing evidence that aggression (Chapter 4), and possibly impulsivity, are linked to disorder of brain serotonergic systems and that hypofunction of the systems increases vulnerability to suicidal behaviour. There is debate about whether this is primarily a state phenomenon associated with stress and low mood, or more of a trait phenomenon, possibly linked to a genetically determined vulnerability. Evidence increasingly points towards this representing a trait disorder, although manifestation of the trait may be mainly limited to certain circumstances when state phenomena (e.g. low mood) are present. Understandably, therefore, recent interest has focused on treating some DSH patients with drugs (particularly antidepressants), which alter serotonergic function.

Hopelessness and low self-esteem

Hopelessness, or pessimism about the future, is well recognized as being important in suicidal behaviour (Williams and Pollock, 2000). The key feature of hopelessness in this population appears to be a paucity of anticipated positive events rather than expectation of an excess of negative ones (MacLeod et al, 1992). Hopelessness has been shown to be a key factor in the suicidal process linking depression to suicidal acts (Beck et al, 1975; Dyer and Kreitman, 1984), is associated with increased risk of repetition of suicidal behaviour (Petrie et al, 1988) and is also a risk factor for eventual suicide (Beck et al, 1985).

Many patients who engage in DSH have a very negative view of themselves, which is usually long standing. Low self-esteem and a tendency to experience hopelessness when faced by adverse circumstances are closely linked. Both may be related to adverse early experiences, such as sexual and physical abuse. Low self-esteem is associated with risk of suicidal behaviour in adolescents (Kienhorst et al, 1990; Fergusson and Lynskey, 1995). Overholser and colleagues (1995) showed that in adolescents, low self-esteem added statistically to the risk of suicidal ideation beyond that explained by depression and hopelessness. Self-esteem problems and hopelessness are relevant to the extent to which patients engage in treatments (see p. 217). Treatment of low self-esteem and the tendency to experience hopelessness are clearly important in reducing the risk of suicidal behaviour. This may require cognitive therapeutic approaches.

Repetition of suicidal behaviour

DSH is often repeated, with some 15–25 per cent carrying out another act within a year (Sakinofsky, 2000). Repetition is particularly common during the first few weeks after a previous act. In some cases a repeated act will be fatal and the extent of history of previous suicidal behaviour is an important predictor of future suicide. Co-morbidity of psychiatric disorders and, especially, of psychiatric and personality disorders is another risk factor for repetition (Hawton et al, submitted for publication). Some patients engage in a large number of DSH acts. They are particularly difficult to manage, partly because the underlying motivation can be unclear and yet disentangling this is often essential for effective psychological treatment to be feasible. A subgroup of this population includes people who frequently self-mutilate. The motivation for such behaviour is often different to that involved in self-poisoning and it is usually related to tension relief and an attempt at reintegration with reality in an individual who has a profound sense of detachment and inner emptiness (Favazza, 1987). Direct treatment of this pattern of behaviour is likely to require specific procedures that can help modify these underlying factors or provide alternative means of reducing tension.

Prevention of repetition of suicidal behaviour, including suicide, must be a major aim in treating DSH patients.

Motivational problems and difficulties in compliance with treatment

DSH patients often appear poorly motivated to accept treatments that are offered, or fail to attend treatment sessions, possibly having initially got started in therapy. There are a number of reasons why this might be, including the fact that the motives underlying DSH are often not related to getting help (Bancroft et al, 1976, 1979; Hawton et al, 1982a), and that chronic low self-esteem and a sense of hopelessness may make an individual very pessimistic about whether treatment can help them with their problems. Social class and other important differences between the patient and the therapist may also be a barrier to engagement. The issues of motivation, engagement and compliance are very important and should be taken into account when thinking about the range of therapeutic skills and personnel needed for an effective clinical service and also the necessity for continuity of care (see p. 220).

TREATMENT APPROACHES FOR DSH PATIENTS

In this section the various treatment possibilities for DSH patients are considered, with indications of how they relate to factors in the suicidal process. The current evidence concerning efficacy is also reviewed. Information about efficacy has been provided by a review within the Cochrane Collaboration, in which all published trials of DSH patients worldwide have been reviewed (Hawton et al, 1998, 1999). Broadly speaking the treatments can be divided into those of a psychosocial nature and those involving a pharmacological approach.

Psychosocial Treatments

These encompass a wide range of approaches but can be grouped as in the following subsections.

Problem solving

Because of the reasons given above it is understandable that there has been considerable attention to treating DSH patients with problem-solving therapy. Problem solving has been described in detail elsewhere (Hawton and Kirk, 1989). In brief, it involves a careful assessment of the nature of a patient's problems, deciding which problems can and should be tackled, agreeing goals and then working out steps than can help to achieve these goals. In a stepwise approach the patient is encouraged to carry out tasks that will enable them to move towards their goals. Cognitive work is usually necessary to help deal with issues of motivation and other difficulties which may impair problem solving. The overall approach is highly collaborative and should aim to empower the patient not just to tackle their current problems but to develop more effective problem-solving approaches for the future. Attention to specific tasks may help modify the patient's tendency to think in generalized terms of previous experiences, which do not provide the patient with a repertoire of specific means of addressing problems. Problem-solving therapy is usually brief, with up to 10 sessions of treatment. The frequency of sessions should be tailored to the patient's needs, often with a short gap between sessions in the early phase and then tapering off to less frequent sessions as the patient's problems start to improve.

In the systematic review noted above, five trials were identified which included evaluation of the impact of problem-solving therapy on repetition of DSH. There has been a further trial which did not assess repetition. In each of the first five trials there was a trend towards less frequent repetition of DSH during the follow-up period in patients offered problem-solving therapy compared with those who were offered "treatment as usual". However, even when the results from all five trials were put together in a meta-analysis (Hawton et al, 1998, 1999) the difference between the treatment groups was not statistically significant (15.5 per cent repetition in patients who were offered problem-solving therapy compared with 19.2 per cent repetition in patients who had treatment as usual, odds ratio $= 0.70$, 95 per cent confidence interval 0.45–1.11). It has been argued that the main problem with trials in this field is that they have been too small (Arensman et al, in press). Power analysis indicates that much larger numbers of patients are needed to investigate whether problem-solving therapy results in a clinically significant reduction in DSH that can be detected at a statistically significant level.

A range of other outcome measures has been investigated in trials of problem-solving therapy. A meta-analysis of some of these outcomes has been conducted for the six trials mentioned (p. 218). Analysis of three variables—depression, hopelessness and problem resolution (not all the measures were included in every study)—suggests that all three outcomes improve more in patients who enter problem-solving therapy than in those offered the control treatment and that the differences are statistically significant (Townsend et al, in press). These findings are particularly encouraging. Taken together with the trends found for repetition of DSH, there appears to be growing support for the use of problem-solving therapy in some DSH patients, although clearly it is not appropriate for all. However, there is also a need for a major trial to fully evaluate this approach. There needs to be a particular focus on whether problem-solving therapy can help not just in addressing current problems but also in countering long-standing deficiencies in problem-solving skills. If this trait phenomenon can be modified then this approach offers an important clinical procedure for making a real and long-term difference to the prognosis of many DSH patients.

Increased intensity of care and outreach

Several trials have been conducted in which the main elements have included community outreach, either for all patients or just for those who had not turned up for treatment sessions, together with a relatively intense treatment programme. The design represents a response to the problems of poor motivation and compliance that were described above. Poor compliance is not a characteristic of all DSH patients so there is an important question of the extent to which outreach should be offered from the outset. In the systematic review of these treatments there was no convincing evidence of overall effectiveness in terms of reducing repetition of DSH compared with less intensive routine care. However, the trials in this group were particularly heterogeneous in nature. In one study in which non-attenders of out-patients appointments were followed up at home by a nurse who tried to encourage them to attend their appointments, promising results were found in terms of the proportion of patients in the experimental group who eventually attended appointments compared with that in the control group, where there was no community follow-up. The difference in attendance was statistically significant and there was a near-significant reduction in the rate of repetition of DSH during the year after entry to the study (Van Heeringen et al, 1995). The results of this study suggest that outreach may be a useful component of treatment, perhaps reserved for patients who are poorly compliant with aftercare or where difficulty attending a clinic is a particular issue. This approach may be especially useful in treating patients in remote rural areas.

Intensive psychological treatments

For patients with major personality problems, particularly regarding impulse control and emotional reactivity, brief therapies are unlikely to have long-term benefits. Therefore an intensive psychological approach has been developed by Linehan (1993), which is termed "dialectical behaviour therapy". The original programme includes a year of individual and group therapy, each on a weekly basis, with emergency access to the therapist between treatment sessions. The treatment addresses a range of problems, but especially problems of motivation, emotional reactivity and impulsivity, and behavioural skills, especially in relation to interpersonal difficulties. This approach was formally evaluated in a comparison with routine care in female patients with borderline personality disorders who had a history of repeated self-harm (Linehan et al, 1991). It appeared to result in a relative reduction in repetition of self-harm as well as several other positive outcomes during the year of therapy. The reduction in self-harming behaviour continued 6 months after therapy ended, although this effect disappeared in the subsequent 6 months (Linehan et al 1993). Further evaluation of this approach is ongoing.

This clinical trial has had a significant impact on attitudes towards the treatment of individuals with personality difficulties, especially those who frequently repeat acts of self-harm. It suggests that the specific vulnerabilities associated with the suicidal process in such people, which have tended to evoke therapeutic nihilism, may be amenable to modification. Further demonstrations of this are required and there needs to be development of similar procedures for male patients.

Other psychosocial approaches

Continuity of therapist may be an important factor in engaging DSH patients in treatment, through countering pessimism and vulnerability to sense of abandonment. Continuity of care was assessed in a study in Germany in which patients in one group were followed up by the same therapist who assessed them in hospital after their DSH episodes and those in another group were offered treatment with a different therapist (Torhorst et al, 1987). Attendance at treatment sessions was significantly greater in those with continuity of care. However, there was a paradoxically higher repetition rate in this group but this seems to have resulted from a failure of the randomization procedure to produce balanced groups in terms of risk factors for repetition.

Specific techniques have been assessed in individuals who self-mutilate. At present there is little evidence for the efficacy of these approaches, mainly because they have not been evaluated in randomized control trials (although the study by Linehan and co-workers (1991) did include such patients). The procedures have generally focused on providing alternative behaviours to self-injury and on reducing tension. One approach that has been suggested for individuals who repeatedly cut themselves in response to feelings of tension and/or a sense of inner emptiness is to have them wear an elastic band round their wrist which they flick sharply against their skin when these feelings are mounting. Another is to repeatedly squeeze a rubber ball (Rosen and Thomas, 1984). A cognitive behavioural model of treatment has been proposed (Hawton, 1990). It includes a combination of: specific strategies to help control cutting, relaxation techniques, help to assist ventilation of emotions, physical exercise, and help with underlying problems of low self-esteem, mood disturbances and communication difficulties. It has not, however, been evaluated, although it has some similarities to the approach used by Linehan and colleagues (see p. 220).

Group treatments have also been proposed and this was part of the approach used in the trial of dialectical behaviour therapy (Linehan et al, 1991). It could be argued that this might be very useful for individuals with difficulties in interpersonal relationships and associated emotional reactivity in that these issues can be addressed *directly* in a group context. In spite of the widely acknowledged problem of DSH in adolescents there has been relatively little evaluation of psychological treatments in this population. In a trial in the UK, family problem-solving therapy was compared with treatment as usual. There was no difference in the rates of DSH repetition in the two groups. However, patients who were *not* suffering from a depressive disorder at entry to the study showed greater reduction in suicidal ideation if they received the family problem-solving therapy (Byford et al, 1999).

Emergency cards

There has been particular interest in the UK in the possibility that providing DSH patients with cards which indicate how they can get emergency help at times of crisis will help prevent future crisis leading to further DSH. A rationale for this approach may be that some patients will only entertain the idea of involvement of helping agencies when they are in a state of crisis. Two initial but relatively small studies of this approach, one involving adults (Morgan et al, 1993) and the other young adolescents (Cotgrove et al, 1995), produced encouraging results. However, a more recent larger study in adults did not indicate any overall benefit for DSH patients given emergency cards compared with those who were not (Evans et al, 1999). A *post-hoc* analysis suggested that the card may have been helpful for individuals who had engaged in just one DSH episode, but that it may actually have been detrimental in those who were repeaters of DSH. This seemingly paradoxical result, while possibly being a chance finding, might be explicable in terms of induction of an angry response in individuals with personality disorders (and hence increased risk of repetition of suicidal behaviour) when frustrated by the fact that clinical services cannot immediately solve acute problems. Provision of emergency cards requires that there is a 24-hour service that can deal with emergency calls. Currently it would seem wise to carefully select patients who are offered this facility. For some it may provide a sense of security which could help them cope with difficulties, even if they do not actually make contact with the emergency service.

Pharmacological approaches

Treatment of DSH patients with pharmacological agents has received little evaluation. This is perhaps surprising in the light of the findings presented earlier in this chapter and elsewhere in this book. It probably partly reflects the problems of compliance with drug therapy shown by many patients in this population and partly the ethical issues of including suicidal individuals in drug trials in which one group receives placebo medication.

Psychopharmacological approaches to the suicidal process will be discussed in detail in Chapter 13. There are three aspects of the suicidal process for which pharmacotherapy might be thought to be of benefit, namely depression, aggression, and vulnerability to severe responses to stress. This section will review studies of the effects of pharmacotherapy in DSH patients.

Antidepressants

Two trials which evaluated the older antidepressants, nomifensine and mianserin, in DSH patients failed to show any benefits of the anti-depressants compared with placebo in terms of repetition of DSH (Montgomery and Montgomery, 1982; Hirsch et al, 1983).

While the obvious target of antidepressant therapy is depressive dis-order, there has been interest in whether antidepressants, especially SSRIs (Selective Serotonin Re-uptake Inhibitors), might have an impact on suicidality independent of impact on depression. The logic behind this would be that serotonergic hypofunction is thought to contribute to suicidality and aggression (see Chapter 4). While there have been reports of patients who have experienced intense suicidal ideation or sudden self-harm after starting or increasing the dose of SSRIs (Power and Cowen, 1992), meta-analysis of pooled data from treatment studies suggests less frequent emergence or worsening of suicidal ideation with SSRIs than with placebo or tricyclic antidepres-sants (Beasley et al, 1991; Montgomery et al, 1995).

A treatment study was conducted in the Netherlands in order to investigate the possible effect of an SSRI antidepressant on suicidality. In this trial, paroxetine was compared with placebo in patients who were all repeaters of DSH but who were not suffering from current depressive disorders (Verkes et al, 1998). Overall there was no differ-ence in repetition rates between the two groups. However, a *post-hoc* analysis indicated that patients with a history of between one and four episodes of DSH who received paroxetine repeated less often than similar patients who were given placebo. On the other hand, patients with a history of five or more episodes did not seem to benefit. These findings are clearly of interest, although must be treated with caution because of the nature of the analysis and because they are somewhat contrary to expectation. Interestingly, in a recent short-term trial, the serotonergic antidepressant fluoxetine seemed to decrease self-reported aggression when compared with placebo (Coccaro et al, 1997).

There is clearly more work to be done in this area. One extremely important question concerns the duration of treatment. If, for example, serotonergic dysfunction is a trait characteristic that increases vulner-ability to suicidal behaviour it can be argued that treatment with serotonergic antidepressants should be long term. Another question concerns the feasibility of encouraging patients who might benefit from medication to start and continue taking it. Psychological strate-gies similar to those used in motivational interviewing might be helpful.

Neuroleptics

In an early trial in this field the depot neuroleptic flupenthixol was given monthly in a dose of 20 mg for 6 months to patients who had a history of repeated DSH (Montgomery et al, 1979). These patients were compared with similar patients who received placebo. There was a marked difference between the two groups in terms of repetition of self-harm during the study period, with those who received the flupenthixol repeating far less. In a recent trial in a similar population of patients, the same dose of flupenthixol was compared with 10 mg monthly (Battaglia et al, 1999). There were no differences in outcome between the two groups of patients, although both showed a marked reduction in repetition compared with prior to entry to the study. Unfortunately, this trial did not include a placebo-treated group and therefore the results are difficult to interpret. The mechanism by which neuroleptics might benefit this population of patients is unclear. In terms of the suicidal process they could perhaps dampen the extent of the arousal and stress response to life events, much as seems to be the case in patients with schizophrenia exposed to emotionally laden interactions.

Many patients who self-harm will not be willing to take neuroleptic treatment. However, in patients who are, this approach may be worth trying, particularly where repetition of self-harm is especially problematic. The use of oral neuroleptics for this purpose also requires evaluation.

CLINICAL MANAGEMENT STRATEGIES

It is obvious that before treatment can be planned DSH patients must always receive a thorough and detailed assessment (Hawton and Catalan, 1987; Hawton, 2000). While evidence of efficacy and effectiveness of treatment approaches is currently rather sparse there is a range of potential treatments from psychosocial and pharmacological modalities. They should be planned having in mind the nature of the suicidal process for each individual patient. Thus, in general, briefer therapies will usually be most appropriate where a patient's problems are relatively short term and more intensive therapy where the problems are related to personality disturbances or other long-term characteristics such as chronic low self-esteem. While deficits in problem-solving skills may represent trait abnormalities, possibly exacerbated by state features (e.g. low mood), it is possible that a relatively brief therapy (e.g. problem solving) can produce persistent changes in problem-solving skills (McLeavy et al, 1994).

There is certainly a place for multi-modal therapy (e.g. a combination of antidepressant treatment and a psychosocial intervention such as problem solving). In this example the antidepressant might be used to tackle a state disorder (i.e. depression) and problem solving to assist with both current social and interpersonal difficulties and with longer term dysfunctional skills in addressing problems.

There is some evidence that continuity of care is important in encouraging attendance at treatment sessions and that outreach (e.g. through home visits) may also engage some patients in treatment when they are ambivalent about it. The general practitioner may be in an advantageous position to ensure continuity of care. This is particularly relevant to patients with long-term difficulties, and especially those who are multiple repeaters of DSH.

RESEARCH IMPLICATIONS

It will be clear that there is a major need for pragmatic trials to evaluate well-described therapies designed to address the known characteristics of this patient population which appear to make them vulnerable to suicidal behaviour. Such trials must have sufficient power in terms of inclusion of appropriate numbers of patients in the studies to provide definitive results (Arensman et al, in press). This may necessitate multi-centre treatment studies.

In view of the heterogeneity of this patient population there is a need for trials of specific therapies for subgroups of patients, such as those with substance abuse, co-morbidity, older patients and the very young. The treatments employed in such studies should reflect the particular nature of the suicidal process in the target patient population. The complex characteristics of many DSH patients suggest that multi-modal therapy, such as a combination of antidepressant and psycho-social interventions, warrants investigation. The role of neuroleptics in multiple repeaters of self-harm merits further attention. There is also a major need for evaluation of psychological and behavioural therapies for patients who repeatedly self-mutilate.

Assessment of outcome should include attention to several variables, again with a focus on those particularly relevant to the suicidal process. These include suicidal ideation, repetition of suicidal behaviour, depression, hopelessness and problem solving and resolution, plus patients' attitudes towards treatment.

CONCLUSIONS

DSH patients comprise a very challenging population for the clinician. It is essential that more effective treatments are developed and evaluated as part of the increasing attention to suicide prevention. Clinicians and researchers must remember that deliberate self-harm is not itself an illness or disorder, but a symptomatic behaviour that may occur in response to a wide range of problems and which is likely to reflect trait vulnerabilities amplified by stress, mood disturbance and alcohol abuse. Because of this, a range of treatment options are needed, the rationale for which should be modification of specific components of the suicidal process. We are becoming increasingly aware of the specific challenges for effective treatment of certain subgroups of patients, of which those with co-morbidity, especially when this includes substance abuse, perhaps represent the greatest challenge. The research needs in this area are considerable and urgent, particularly if suicide prevention through more effective treatment of this high-risk population is to be achieved.

REFERENCES

Adam, K.S., Bouckoms, A. and Streiner, D (1982) Parental loss and family stability in attempted suicide. *Archives of General Psychiatry*, **39**: 1081–1085.

Arensman, E., Townsend, E., Hawton, K., Bremner, S., Feldman, E., Goldney, R., Gunnell, D., Hazell, P., Van Heeringen, K., House, A., Owens, D., Sakinofsky, I. and Träskman-Bendz, L. Psychosocial and pharmacological treatment of patients following deliberate self-harm: the methodological issues involved in evaluating effectiveness. *Suicide and Life-Threatening Behavior* (in press).

Bancroft, J.H.J., Skrimshire, A.M. and Simkin, S. (1976) The reasons people give for taking overdoses. *British Journal of Psychiatry*, **128**: 538–548.

Bancroft, J., Skrimshire, A., Casson, J., Harvard-Watts, O. and Reynolds, F. (1977) People who deliberately poison or injure themselves: their problems and their contacts with helping agencies. *Psychological Medicine*, 7: 289–303.

Bancroft, J., Hawton, K., Simkin, S., Kingston, B., Cumming, C. and Whitwell, D. (1979) The reasons people give for taking overdoses: a further inquiry. *British Journal of Medical Psychology*, **52**: 353–365.

Battaglia, J., Wolff, T.K., Wagner-Johnson, D.S., Rush, A.J., Carmody, T.J. and Basco, M.R. (1999) Structured diagnostic assessment and depot fluphenazine treatment of multiple suicide attempters in the emergency department. *International Clinical Psychopharmacology*, **14**: 361–372.

Beasley, C.M., Dornseif, B.E., Bosomworth, J.C., Sayer, M.E., Rampey, A.H., Heiligenstein, J.H., Thompson, V.L., Murphy, D.J. and Masica, D.N. (1991) Fluoxetine and suicide: a meta-analysis of controlled trials of treatment for depression. *British Medical Journal*, **303**: 685–692.

Beck, A., Kovacs, M. and Weissman, A. (1975) Hopelessness and suicidal behavior. *Journal of the American Medical Association*, **234**: 1146–1149.

Beck, A.T., Steer, R.A., Kovacs, M. and Garrison, B.S. (1985) Hopelessness and eventual suicide: a 10-year prospective study of patients hospitalised with suicidal ideation. *American Journal of Psychiatry*, **142**: 559–563.

Burgess, S., Hawton, K. and Loveday, G. (1998) Adolescents who take overdoses: outcome in terms of changes in psychopathology and the adolescents' attitudes to their care and to their overdoses. *Journal of Adolescence*, **21**: 209–218.

Byford, S., Harrington, R., Torgerson, D., Kerfoot, M., Dyer, E., Harrington, V., Woodham, A., Gill, J. and McNiven, F. (1999) Cost-effectiveness analysis of a home-based social work intervention for children and adolescents who have deliberately poisoned themselves. Results of a randomised controlled trial. *British Journal of Psychiatry*, **174**: 56–62.

Coccaro, E.F. and Kavoussi, R.J. (1997) Fluoxetine and impulsive aggressive behavior in personality-disordered subjects. *Archives of General Psychiatry*, **54**: 1081–1088.

Cotgrove, A.J., Zirinsky, L., Black, D. and Weston, D. (1995) Secondary prevention of attempted suicide in adolescence. *Journal of Adolescence*, **18**: 569–577.

De Wilde, E.J. (2000) Adolescent suicidal behaviour: a general population perspective. In K. Hawton and K. van Heeringen (Eds), *The International Handbook of Suicide and Attempted Suicide*. Chichester, Wiley.

Dyer, J.A.T. and Kreitman, N. (1984) Hopelessness, depression and suicidal intent in parasuicide. *British Journal of Psychiatry*, **144**, 127–133.

Evans, J., Williams, J.M.G., O'Loughlin, S. and Howells, K. (1992) Autobiographical memory and problem-solving strategies of parasuicide patients. *Psychological Medicine*, **22**: 399–405.

Evans, M.O., Morgan, H.G., Hayward, A. and Gunnell, D.J. (1999) Crisis telephone consultation for deliberate self-harm patients: effects on repetition. *British Journal of Psychiatry*, **175**: 23–27.

Favazza, A.R. (1987) *Bodies Under Siege: Self-mutilation in Culture and Psychiatry*. Baltimore, The Johns Hopkins University Press.

Fergusson, D.M. and Lynskey, M.T. (1995) Childhood circumstances, adolescent adjustment, and suicide attempts in a New Zealand birth cohort. *Journal of the American Academy of Child and Adolescent Psychiatry*, **34**: 612–622.

Harwood, D. and Jacoby, R. (2000) Suicidal behaviour among the elderly. In K. Hawton and K. van Heeringen (Eds), *The International Handbook of Suicide and Attempted Suicide*. Chichester, Wiley.

Haw, C., Hawton, K., Houston, K. and Townsend, E. (2001) Psychiatric and personality disorders in deliberate self-harm patients. *British Journal of Psychiatry*, **178**: 48–54.

Hawton, K., Cole, D.C., O'Grady, J. and Osborn, M. (1982a) Motivational aspects of deliberate self-poisoning in adolescents. *British Journal of Psychiatry*, **141**: 286–291.

Hawton, K., O'Grady, J., Osborn, M. and Cole, D. (1982b) Adolescents who take overdoses: their characteristics, problems and contacts with helping agencies. *British Journal of Psychiatry*, **140**: 118–123.

Hawton, K. and Catalan, J. (1987) *Attempted Suicide: A Practical Guide to its Nature and Management* (Second Edition). Oxford, Oxford University Press.

Hawton, K. and Kirk, J. (1989) Problem-solving. In K. Hawton, P. Salkovskis, J. Kirk and D.M. Clark (Eds), *Cognitive Behaviour Therapy for Psychiatric Problems: A Practical Guide*. Oxford, Oxford University Press.

Hawton, K. (1990) Self-cutting: Can it be prevented? In K. Hawton and P. Cowen (Eds), *Dilemmas and Difficulties in the Management of Psychiatric Patients*. Oxford, Oxford University Press.

Hawton, K., Fagg, J., Simkin, S., Bale, E. and Bond, A. (1997) Trends in deliberate self-harm in Oxford, 1985–1995. Implications for clinical services and the prevention of suicide. *British Journal of Psychiatry*, **171**: 556–560.

Hawton, K., Arensman, E., Townsend, E., Bremner, S., Feldman, E., Goldney, R., Gunnell, D., Hazell, P., Van Heeringen, C., House, A., Owens, D., Sakinofsky, I. and Träskman-Bendz, L. (1998) Deliberate self-harm: a systematic review of the efficacy of psychosocial and pharmacological treatments in preventing repetition. *British Medical Journal*, **317**: 441–447.

Hawton, K., Townsend, , E., Arensman, E., Gunnell, D., Hazell, P., van Heeringen, C. and House, A. (1999) Deliberate self-harm: the efficacy of psychosocial and pharmacological interventions. In *The Cochrane Controlled Trials Register*. Oxford, Update Software.

Hawton, K. (2000) General hospital management of suicide attempters. In K. Hawton and K. van Heeringen (Eds), *The International Handbook of Suicide and Attempted Suicide*. Chichester, Wiley.

Hawton, K., Houston, K., Haw, C. and Townsend, E. Comorbidity of psychiatric and personality disorders in deliberate self-harm patients (submitted for publication).

Hirsch, S.R., Walsh, C. and Draper, R. (1983) The concept and efficacy of the treatment of parasuicide. *British Journal of Clinical Pharmacology*, **15**: 189–194S.

Kapur, N., House, A., Creed, F., Feldman, E., Friedman, T. and Guthrie, E. (1998) Management of deliberate self poisoning in adults in four teaching hospitals: descriptive study. *British Medical Journal*, **316**: 831–832.

Kienhorst, C.W.M., De Wilde, E.J., Broese van Groenou, M.I., Diekstra, R.F.W. and Wolters, W.H.G. (1990) Self-reported suicidal behavior in Dutch secondary education students. *Suicide and Life-Threatening Behavior*, **20**: 101–112.

Linehan, M.M., Armstrong, H.E., Suarez, A., Allmon, D. and Heard, H.L. (1991) Cognitive-behavioral treatment of chronically parasuicidal borderline patients. *Archives of General Psychiatry*, **48**: 1060–1064.

Linehan, M.M., Camper, P., Chiles, J.A., Strohsal, K. and Shearin, E.N. (1987) Interpersonal problem solving and parasuicide. *Cognitive Therapy and Research*, **11**: 1–12.

Linehan, M.M., Heard, H.L. and Armstrong, H.E. (1993) Naturalistic follow-up of a behavioral treatment for chronically parasuicidal borderline patients. *Archives of General Psychiatry*, **50**: 971–974.

MacLeod, A.K., Williams, J.M.G. and Linehan, M.M. (1992) New developments in the understanding and treatment of suicidal behaviour. *Behavioural Psychotherapy*, **20**: 193–218.

McLeavey, B.C., Daly, R.J., Ludgate, J.W. and Murray, C.M. (1994) Interpersonal problem-solving skills training in the treatment of self-poisoning patients. *Suicide and Life-Threatening Behavior*, **24**: 382–394.

Montgomery, S.A., Montgomery, D.B., Jayanthi-Rani, S., Roy, D.H., Shaw, P.J. and McAuley, R. (1979) Maintenance therapy in repeat suicidal behaviour: A placebo controlled trial. *Proceedings of the 10th International Congress for Suicide Prevention & Crisis Intervention*. Ottawa, Canada, June 1979.

Montgomery, S.A. and Montgomery, D. (1982) Pharmacological prevention of suicidal behaviour. *Journal of Affective Disorders*, **4**: 291–298.

Montgomery, S.A., Dunner, D.L. and Dunbar, G.C. (1995) Reduction of suicidal thoughts with paroxetine in comparison with reference antidepressants and placebo. *European Neuropsychopharmocology*, **5**: 5–13.

Morgan, H.G., Jones, E.M. and Owen, J.H. (1993) Secondary prevention of non-fatal deliberate self-harm. The green card study. *British Journal of Psychiatry*, **163**: 111–112.

Newson-Smith, J. and Hirsch, S. (1979) Psychiatric symptoms in self-poisoning patients. *Psychological Medicine*, **9**: 493–500.

Overholser, J.C., Adams, D.M., Lehnert, K.L. and Brinkman, D.C. (1995) Self-esteem deficits and suicidal tendencies among adolescents. *Journal of the American Academy of Child and Adolescent Psychiatry*, **34**: 919–928.

Paykel, E.S., Prusoff, B.A. and Myers, J.K. (1975) Suicide attempts and recent life events: a controlled comparison. *Archives of General Psychiatry*, **32**: 327–333.

Petrie, K., Chamberlain, K. and Clarke, D. (1988) Psychological predictors of future suicidal behaviour in hospitalized suicide attempters. *British Journal of Clinical Psychology*, **27**: 247–257.

Power, A.C. and Cowen, P.J. (1992) Fluoxetine and suicidal behaviour: some clinical and theoretical aspects of a controversy. *British Journal of Psychiatry*, **161**: 735–741.

Rosen, L.W. and Thomas, M.A. (1984) Treatment techniques for chronic wrist cutters. *Journal of Behavior Therapy and Experimental Psychiatry*, **141**: 520–525.

Sakinofsky, I. (2000) Repetition of suicidal behaviour. In K. Hawton and K. van Heeringen (Eds), *The International Handbook of Suicide and Attempted Suicide*. Chichester, Wiley.

Schmidtke, A., Bille Brahe, U., DeLeo, D., Kerkhof, A., Bjerke, T., Crepet, P., Haring, C., Hawton, K., Lönnqvist, J., Michel, K., Pommereau, X., Querejeta, I., Phillipe, I., Salander Renberg, E., Temesvary, B., Wasserman, D., Fricke, S., Weinacker, B. and Sampaio Faria, J.G. (1996) Attempted suicide in Europe: rates, trends and sociodemographic characteristics of suicide attempters during the period 1989–1992. Results of the WHO/Euro Multicentre Study on Parasuicide. *Acta Psychiatrica Scandinavica*, **93**: 327–338.

Sidley, G.L. and Whitaker, K. (1997) The relationship between problem-solving and autobiographical memory in parasuicide patients. *Behavioural and Cognitive Psychotherapy*, **25**: 195–202.

Suominen, K., Henriksson, M., Suokas, J., Isometsä, E., Ostamo, A. and Lönnqvist, J. (1996) Mental disorders and comorbidity in attempted suicide. *Acta Psychiatrica Scandinavica*, **94**: 234–240.

Torhorst, A., Möller, H. J., Burk, F., Kurz, A., Wachtler, C. and Lauter, H. (1987) The psychiatric management of parasuicidal patients: a controlled clinical study comparing different strategies of outpatient treatment. *Crisis*, **8**: 53–61.

Townsend, E., Hawton, K., Altman, D.G., Arensman, E., Gunnell, D., Hazell, P., House, A. and van Heeringen, K. The efficacy of problem-solving treatments after deliberate self-harm: meta-analysis of randomised controlled trials with respect to depression, hopelessness and improvement in problems. *Psychological Medicine* (in press).

Van Heeringen, C., Jannes, S., Buylaert, W., Henderick, H., De Bacquer, D. and Van Remoortel, J. (1995) The management of non-compliance with referral to out-patient after-care among attempted suicide patients: a controlled intervention study. *Psychological Medicine*, **25**: 963–970.

Verkes, R.J., Van der Mast, R.C., Hengeveld, M.W., Tuyl, J.P., Zwinderman, A.H. and Van Kempen, G.M. (1998) Reduction by paroxetine of suicidal behavior in patients with repeated suicide attempts but not major depression. *American Journal of Psychiatry*, **155**: 543–547.

Williams, J.M.G. and Pollock, L.R. (2000) The psychology of suicidal behaviour. In K. Hawton and K. van Heeringen (Eds), *The International Handbook of Suicide and Attempted Suicide*. Chichester, Wiley.

Chapter 12

SUICIDE AS GOAL-DIRECTED ACTION

Konrad Michel and Ladislav Valach

INTRODUCTION

The generally disappointing results of systematic evaluations of the treatment of suicidal behaviour, including the prevention of repeated suicide attempts as described in the previous chapter, indicate the need for a new approach towards the suicidal patient. An obvious prerequisite for establishing a trustful working relationship must be that patient and therapist have a mutual understanding of the reasons for suicidal thoughts or deliberate self-harm. Traditionally, suicidal behaviour has been understood within the framework of the biomedical-illness model. This model implies that the health professional has to find the cause of the patient's pathology and then treat the disorder. However, both suicide and attempted suicide are actions that are planned and carried out by individuals, involving conscious processes, and they are thus not mere signs of illness and pathology. An approach based on action theory may well provide an alternative framework to understand suicidal behaviour and to establish a meaningful communication between health professionals and suicidal patients. Fundamental to this approach is the assumption that a better therapeutic relationship with suicidal patients will help health professionals to become more effective in preventing suicide.

Actions are associated with cognitive and emotional processes, which involve planning, steering, monitoring and decision making. Actions are part of mid- and long-term systems consisting of projects and

Understanding Suicidal Behaviour. Edited by Kees van Heeringen
© 2001 John Wiley & Sons Ltd.

life–career aspects, or life goals. These processes are influenced by external and internal factors, such as cultural setting, early individual experiences or psychiatric disorder. Action theory not only provides a model for the study of processes resulting in an action, but also represents the way we communicate and explain our actions in everyday life, or how we make sense of actions of others.

This chapter will address an action-theoretical view of suicidal behaviour by describing, among others, preliminary results of a qualitative study of interviews with suicide attempters. Three aspects can be distinguished. First, suicide attempters in general have an impressive narrative competence. However, to allow patients to develop their narratives, the interviewer must respect the patient as the expert of his or her own actions. This requires a definition of the roles of patient and professional helper that differs from that used in the biomedical model. Second, patients understand their suicide action as a part of broader systems, which may include life–career aspects and projects, and which are goal oriented and meaningful to the patient. Suicide thus appears as a (usually temporary) goal, a possible solution, when the accomplishment of long-term goals and projects is seriously threatened. Third, the immediate goal of suicidal action is to escape from an unbearable state of mind and of psychic pain, which may amount to a state of traumatic stress, associated with dissociation, automatism and analgesia, as a result of negative and often humiliating experiences. The suicide action therefore must be understood as an attempt to preserve an individual's self-respect, or identity.

In action-theoretical terms, talking to a suicidal patient is a joint action. In a discourse about the background of a suicidal action, the interviewer becomes the co-author of the patient's narrative. An action-theoretical approach should enable patients and therapists to explore new behavioural strategies in times of emotional crises.

SUICIDE AND ATTEMPTED SUICIDE DO NOT EASILY FIT INTO THE TRADITIONAL MEDICAL MODEL

Suicide attempters constitute a special group of patients, as they are not, like other patients, admitted to a hospital because of an illness or an accident. Their admission is the consequence of an act, or an action, which clearly involves conscious planning and decision making. The question we have to ask is: Do medically trained professionals have concepts to make sense of such actions?

Usually, when a psychiatrist is called to see a patient who has attempted suicide, he tries to assess the risk of repeated suicidal behaviour by searching for clinical risk factors, particularly for signs of a psychiatric disorder, such as depression, substance abuse, severe personality disorder or schizophrenia. While there is agreement that approximately 90 per cent of suicides are associated with psychiatric disorder, reports about the frequency of psychiatric disorder in attempted suicide differ (Ennis, 1989; Suominen et al, 1996). Yet even in the case of a severe depression, it is not the disorder itself which initiates the suicidal act, but the "owner" of the depression, the individual him or herself. How then should the patient who has attempted suicide be approached?

> I got very angry when they kept asking me if I would do it again. They were not interested in my feelings. Life is not such a matter-of-fact thing and, if I was honest, I could not say if I would do it again or not. What was clear to me was that I could not trust any of these doctors enough to really talk openly about myself.

This is what a 36-year-old patient who had taken an overdose of antidepressants said following her discharge from a psychiatric ward. Various investigations have indeed demonstrated serious problems in the therapeutic relationship between suicide attempters and health professionals. For instance, suicidal patients have repeatedly been reported describing health professionals as unhelpful or even lacking awareness (Hawton and Blackstock, 1976; Wolk-Wasserman, 1987; Choquet and Menke, 1989; McGaughey et al, 1995). Others indicated that nurses and social workers had been more helpful than doctors (Treolar et al, 1993).

Although more than 50 per cent of the persons who take their own lives have seen a physician within a month before their death, suicide is addressed as a topic in only a minority of cases. Isometsä and colleagues (1995) found that, in general, in only 22 per cent of these last visits the issue of suicide had been discussed, varying from 39 per cent in psychiatric out-patients to 11 per cent in general-practice patients and 6 per cent of those who consulted other specialties. An increase in the frequency of visits to general practitioners prior to suicide and attempted suicide has been demonstrated (Appleby et al, 1996; Michel et al, 1997), suggesting that the reasons for visiting the primary-care physician are indeed related to the development of a suicidal crisis. In the Finnish study by Isometsä and colleagues (1995), 18 per cent of individuals who had contacted a physician had done so on the day of their suicide, yet even then the issue of suicide was discussed in only 21 per cent of these cases.

Thus, undeniably there is a problem of communication between suicidal patients and health professionals. This communication problem is likely to affect the aftercare of suicide attempters, and it comes as little surprise that to date we do not know how repetition of suicidal behaviour can be prevented (Möller, 1990; Hawton et al, 1998). A comparison of different aftercare strategies for suicide attempters showed that when patients were given an appointment with the doctor who had seen them first in hospital, continuity of attendance in aftercare was somewhat better. However, even then less than half of the patients showed up at their first out-patient appointment (Kurz et al, 1988).

The traditional biomedical-illness model has been the main intellectual basis for the approach of the suicidal patient. It is a linear and causal model (i.e. it assumes that there is some form of pathology, the cause of which must be identified and treated. Consistent with a causal-illness model, doctors search for the fault in the system, and they, and not the patients, are the experts in this search. Accordingly, the medically trained interviewer who sees the person admitted to a hospital ward because of a suicide attempt tries to understand the suicidal act by trying to find the underlying cause. This may be a psychiatric diagnosis, or, if the interviewer is psychologically minded, he or she may perhaps search for a psychological or psychosocial cause of the event ("What made the patient do it?").

However, the patients' explanations and the health professionals' explanations may differ considerably, as was demonstrated by Bancroft and colleagues (1979) who found a most striking disagreement between the explanations by patients and those by psychiatrists. The two reasons chosen most frequently by the observers (i.e. "communicating hostility" and "aiming to influence other people") were both rarely chosen by the patients. On the other hand, "get relief from a terrible state of mind" and "escape for a while from an impossible situation", both chosen commonly by the patients, were seldomly chosen by the observers. Psychiatrists thought that "to frighten or to make someone feel sorry", "to show desperation", and "to influence someone" were other frequent reasons. This means that psychiatrists primarily chose manipulative items, while patients tended to choose intrapersonal motives. Bancroft and colleagues discussed the possibility that the patients' choice of motives might express a wish to gain social acceptability for the suicide attempt. Evidence has now accumulated that this is unlikely to be a "retrograde falsification", but indeed a stereotypical description of a subjectively unbearable state of mind characterized by psychological pain. Assuming manipulative reasons is not only a dangerous interpretation by an observer, but also an expression of "the professional-is-the-expert" attitude. Furthermore, it is an example of how medically trained professionals think in terms of causes, while patients express themselves in terms of the motives or reasons for the action. Buss (1978, 1979) argued that it is crucial for researchers to make a distinction between cause-related explanations and reason-related explanations. Reasons are used to explain an action by stating the intentions behind it, while causes explain an action in terms of the properties of the environment that brought it about or made it take place (Hinkle and Schmidt, 1984). In fact, patients are very able to distinguish between reasons and causes (Michel et al, 1994).

ACTION THEORY

Alternatives to the traditional biomedical model have been proposed including, among others, the infomedical model (Foss and Rothenberg, 1988), and the anthropological model of von Uexküll and Wesiack (1988). Both models are based on a systemic developmental view of living organisms, in which processes of adaptation to the environment at biological, psychological and social levels are seen as basic conditions of life. These models imply that health in a biological as well as psychological sense is not a static condition, but a process. Antonovsky (1987) used the concept of "sense of coherence" to describe the ability of organisms to differentiate between environmental elements that enhance or threaten the internal homeostasis. von Uexküll and Wesiack maintain that the term "environment" always reflects a subjective experience, which is invisible for the external observer. Exchange with the environment takes place in the form of actions, which include verbal communication. Similarly, communication between patient and medical professional is seen as a joint action of two participants engaged in a discourse.

Actions can best be understood in the context in which they develop. Action theory, or the theory of goal-directed action, represents a developmental systems theory to explain actions in terms of goals. There are various psychological models incorporating an action-theoretical stance including cognitive psychology and social psychological theories of social control (von Cranach and Harré, 1982). These theories have been influential in Europe and North America (Kuhl, 1986; Von Cranach and Valach, 1986; Polkinghorne, 1990; Gollwitzer, 1996; Young et al, 1996), and particularly useful when applied to areas of everyday knowledge and experience.

In action theory, human behaviour is seen as goal directed, and regulated by social and cognitive forces. It uses concepts that appear in the common language of everyday life, including goal, intention, plan, strategy, decision, evaluation, choice, success and failure. However, actions are embedded in comprehensive systems, which include mid-term projects (Valach et al, 1996) and long-term life projects, such as establishing a family (Valach, 1990), and thus relate to biographical goals (i.e. life–career aspects).

At the individual level, actions are understood as being carried out by agents (i.e. by persons who are able to shape their environment and behaviours). They do this by pursuing projects, setting goals, making plans and monitoring their own behaviour, thoughts and emotions. Actions can only be understood against the background of the patient's short-term and long-term (life) projects, which involve their environment. Social meaning therefore plays a special role in goal-directed action. Actions are the fabric of social interaction and have social consequences (Von Cranach and Valach, 1983; Valach et al, 1988; Valach, 1995). One of the best examples of social action is group or joint action. The first applications of joint-action theory were related to illness and patient career (Noack and Valach, 1985) and later developed further (Valach, 1990; Valach et al, 1996). Thus, career and project are conceptualized as joint goal-directed processes. Career is seen as a complex joint process consisting of long-term, medium-term and short-term system organization. It is a process of social groups and individual agents and actions. Consequently, joint actions present decisive points in a career. Depending on the structure of the group task, the career can be steered by another faculty other than the person whose career is involved.

Actions are the result of conscious, unconscious and semi-conscious, goal-directed, planned and intended processes, which are cognitively and socially steered, controlled and regulated. They are motivated and accompanied by emotions. Conscious cognition is the highest system of self-monitoring in the human knowledge-processing system followed by emotional monitoring. Cognitions are represented via language. These ideas were elaborated in a series of publications (Von Cranach et al, 1982; Von Cranach and Valach, 1983; Kalbermatten and Valach, 1985; Valach et al, 1988). This conceptualization of action therefore implies that people make sense of the actions of others and communicate their own actions by using action-theoretical terms. In the patients' narratives life–career aspects and short-term projects as well as concepts related to action, such as intention, strategy, decision and choice, can be distinguished. Furthermore, actions are usually explained as joint actions, indicating that narratives include a person's social system.

AN ACTION-THEORETICAL MODEL OF SUICIDAL BEHAVIOUR

Developmental models to explain suicidal behaviour are not new. Several authors have stressed the importance of a developmental approach to suicide, as opposed to a traditional static-illness model. The concept of a "suicide career" has been introduced convincingly by Maris (1981). Using path analysis Maris showed that salient failures for male suicides tend to be work, achievement and sex related, while for female suicides they tended to be marriage, family and sex related. The failure to achieve a major goal of the ego-ideal may result in a sense of being useless, and particularly in shame. This may lead to withdrawal and isolation. Maris stressed the need to develop dynamic developmental models of suicide: ". . . the suicide's biography or 'career' is always relevant to his or her self-destructive reaction to crises and (. . .) it is precisely this history, individual or group, which tends to be neglected". Shneidman (1991) underlined that "suicide is an act of volition and frustrated psychological needs" and listed 10 psychological characteristics of suicide, which he called "the ten commonalities of suicide". These include (1) the common purpose of suicide is to seek a solution, (2) the common goal of suicide is cessation of consciousness, (3) the common stimulus of suicide is intolerable psychological pain, (4) the common stressor of suicide is frustrated psychological needs and (7) the common action of suicide is escape (egression). Leenaars (1993) pointed out that the driving force often is the result of unconscious processes, and that suicidal development is usually related to attachment dynamics, and thus to key significant others.

A developmental system-theoretical model implies that there is a story behind each suicide action, and not a simple cause. In an earlier publication, we have proposed a model of suicidal behaviour based on action theory (Michel and Valach, 1997). In this model suicide is seen as an alternative to original life–career goals, which may relate to relationship (to maintain a good marriage) or work (to achieve a secure income to support the family), in critical times when a person's self-evaluation is negative ("I am a failure"). Suicide thus may be a possible solution to a subjectively unbearable situation and may emerge repeatedly throughout life as a possible goal ("to end a bad story") in critical life situations. Suicide may then temporarily occupy the top position in the hierarchy of goals, replacing the original life–career goals. After a suicide attempt, life goals may re-emerge as alternative priorities (it is not uncommon for a patient to want to go to work the next morning). As described in Chapter 1, a suicide career consists of several steps, which may include repeated contemplation of suicide as a goal, suicide attempts, increasing suicidal intention, putting it down in writing, planning, devising a strategy, taking the final decision, starting the sequence of necessary actions to commit suicide. In critical life situations individuals may move closer towards suicide action on this developmental scale but they may not reach the level of action. Often, an emotional reaction to a triggering event serves as an energizer, which helps to transform an intention into a final action.

Like other actions, suicide action must be regarded as a component of a system consisting of mid-term or long-term projects. Many patients describe suicidal developments in their suicide career that are closely related to, for example, repeated problems of affect regulation, repeated contemplation or actual performance of self-harm, and substance abuse (Maris, 1981).

As the conscious representation of goal-directed processes is an integral aspect of intention building and goal setting, individuals are capable of giving their accounts of the processes which precede suicidal behaviour, and thus are relevant to explain a suicide action. These accounts are presented as narratives representing the way people explain the beliefs, desires, intentions and choices that shape human action. In a narrative, actions are put in relation to those of others, and are thus given a meaning (Sarbin et al, 1986). The narrative has the function to develop and maintain the unity of a career, or, in other words, the identity of a person. It includes the subjective interpretation of life events according to a person's beliefs and goals.

Narratives represent a series of events and their associated meanings for the teller, and without this evaluative component there can be no narrative. Meaning is accomplished interactionally, between teller and listener (Riessman, 1991). A listener enters into the world the narrator constructs, helps in the telling, and thus narratives are jointly accomplished, according to shared knowledge and interaction rules, and thus the discourse about projects and actions becomes a joint action by itself. The validity of the narrative is ascertained precisely through the narrative because it represents actual events and experiences in which goals, plans and strategies were employed.

THE NARRATIVE OF THE SUICIDAL PATIENT

Narratives have a certain structure in the way they are told, and they allow an investigator to see in what way human experience is organized. This organization of narratives can be studied by means of video-recorded and transcribed interviews with suicide attempters, followed by a video playback and a video self-confrontation interview. In the following, the authors' experiences with this method of studying narratives will be described and exemplified by means of two case studies.

The rationale of a video-playback interview is to present the video-recorded interaction to the actors individually. The video is stopped after short intervals (i.e. every 1–3 minutes), and the interviewed person is asked to report their cognitions, feelings and sensations as experienced during the interval. This interview is recorded and the content is analysed, thus allowing the researchers to monitor the ongoing events in a more comprehensive manner. The comments of the participants help in the reconstruction of the relevant individual projects and career processes. The self-confrontation itself is a practical example of a joint action of patient and interviewer, with the patient's story and feelings being the centre of attention. This method has been used in several research projects (Von Cranach et al, 1982; Breuer, 1991; Thommen et al, 1992; Young et al, 1994; Valach et al, 1996).

The recorded narratives of the patients are then transcribed and structured in a hierarchical way using the patient's own verbal reports. The research team in a consensual process formulates a summary of the narrative (i.e. a summary of the action and the self-confrontation), which is written from the perspective of goal-directed action while making use of the language of the patient as much as possible.

In addition, patients fill in the Beck Depression Inventory (BDI, Beck, 1961), and both patient and therapist fill in the Penn Helping Alliance Questionnaire (Alexander and Luborsky, 1986). To monitor autonomous vegetative processes during the interview, skin-conductance re-activity of patient and interviewer are measured simultaneously and recorded throughout the interview.

Case study 1

Mrs M., a 38-year-old mother of a boy aged 13 and a girl aged 15, is divorced and lives with her children. She jumped from the balcony of her sister's flat on the third floor. She suffered from a cerebral commotion and fractures of the pelvis, ribs, foot and a lumbar vertebra. She had orthopaedic surgery and was seen by the duty psychiatrist 3 days after the suicide attempt. A diagnosis of depression of medium severity with signs of derealization was made. The following day she was wheeled to the psychiatric department for the interview procedure described above. The BDI on the day of the interview was 16, indicating the existence of a mild depression.

The content of her narrative is presented here in an abridged version, using a hierarchical system in order to distinguish three different levels: long-term life–career aspects, projects related to the suicide action and the suicide action itself. The interview started with the opening question which is typically used to elicit the patient's narrative: "Could you describe to me how it came about that you harmed yourself?". The sequences have been rearranged according to a hierarchical structure based on an action-theoretical approach.

Life–career aspects

"This has followed me throughout my life, the problem of losing people whom I love. It doesn't matter who it is. I always had breakdowns, for instance after moving to another place I got cardiac symptoms or attacks of anxiety. I have great problems in coping with separation and loss". She maintains that she does not know the meaning of "we will part" as she does not know if it is for hours or for ever. "My children mean a lot to me and are very close to me, and when I don't know for sure that we meet again, this is very difficult for me". She suggests that it could be related to an experience in her early life: when she was 7 years old her mother told her that she had to go away. She had said that she was going to a spa, but she never came back. She had left the family for another man.

Relationship projects indeed play a substantial role in life–career aspects. Mrs M. had stayed with a man while her children were away during the school holidays. "And yes, there was a boyfriend. He said that he needed time, and I wasn't sure what it meant—if this meant separation, never meeting again, or anything else (. . .). This happened before and I was totally preoccupied with it, although now he said he just needed time for himself. But for me it could have been years or never again or no time for me, or I don't want to have anything to do with you any more. Since then, there was this nervousness in me".

The day of her suicide attempt Mrs M. was unable to go to work because she was so full of anxiety that she thought she might lose consciousness. She therefore went to her sister and was joined by her children after school.

"My son had the same way to school, so we went together. He took the bicycle and I was in the car. He then took a shortcut, which I hadn't noticed. And this was terrible for me, because I didn't know if he would come back and whether I would see him again, as I hadn't said good-bye to him. Why I had these thoughts I don't know; I simply wanted to see him once more". [Cries] . . . "already in the morning I had found it difficult to say good-bye to my daughter". "I felt as if the end of the world was near, and then I had this thought that I would not see my son again".

Projects related to suicide action

Suicide appears as a possible solution in the story of the patient. The children later came back from school and they met at her sister's flat. She tried to help her daughter with her homework. "Suddenly I realized that it was too much for all of us, this dragging along from one thing to another. There were so many thoughts and they had such a power over me that I developed the feeling that I would really go mad. I then said to myself that I didn't want my children to end up with a disturbed mother whom they would have to visit in a psychiatric hospital, but that they should rather have no mother at all, then. This was very strong, rather something else, dead or unconscious or I don't know what. This I felt very strongly. There were so many thoughts and they had such a power over me that I developed the feeling that I would really go mad".

"Actually, I wanted to flee from these thoughts, not from the too heavy demands but from the many thoughts because they did what they wanted. I couldn't live with them any longer. I wanted to kind of kill them".

"In the morning, when going to my sister, I was afraid that I would go into the lake, the water seemed to pull me in. And there was a sunbeam on the water. I thought of God and of coming out of the water again, as a new creature, maybe as an animal. Later she said that she had heard that recently a woman had drowned herself in the lake after she had seen a psychiatrist who had prescribed medication. I also had a fear of this, and although the doctor had prescribed tablets, I hadn't taken them because I didn't know what they would do to me.

"In the evening I was very agitated. My sister had a terrace to which the door was open, and I thought that the door should be closed, because I had the feeling that I was like being pushed out through this door. And always this thought, you can't live with the children if you end up in a psychiatric hospital. And then I knew that I had to keep myself occupied, because of this restlessness. So, I started to do some arithmetic and thought 'you know this already', and it was soon finished, and the agitation was still there, and it was as if I was driven without knowing where to and what for. Apparently I also spoke to my mother on the phone and she said something about suicide and that I shouldn't harm myself, but somehow it didn't reach me. And my daughter said something but I couldn't concentrate and I thought it would be best if nobody said anything because I couldn't follow any more".

Suicide action

"And then, I can't remember what happened after that. They say that I got up and walked straight out to the terrace and jumped down from it as if this had always been clear to me. My sister saw me at the last moment and asked what I was doing and then I jumped".

Additional information was gathered during the self-confrontation interview, which is conducted by a second interviewer in order to gain information about how the patient experienced the interview.

Interviewer: How was it for you to talk to the doctor?

Mrs M: Two insights: I realized how immensely I was preoccupied by the separation and how painful it had been for me. Separation is a very strong issue. Whenever I have to say good-bye to someone or whenever someone goes away from me. This has come out really strong.

Interviewer: And when you talked about it you became tearful?

Mrs M: Yes. In a way this surprises me. You see, before it happened I felt that I didn't have any emotions in me any more. I wasn't able to laugh or to cry. I had only been able to cry when my daughter had told me that she wasn't able to follow school any more, and that I should really understand that the music lessons and sports training was too much for her and that she couldn't cope with the situation any more. And the tears came when I realized that so far I hadn't really understood how it was for her. And these were the same emotions that came up in the interview now. When talking about these two things: separation, and I feel that this is deep in me, my voice gets sort of blocked, and the inability to cope, that I hadn't realized it in my daughter. It makes me feel sad to talk about separation and the crisis of my daughter. [The patient cries.]

Interviewer: It is the children who are important?

Mrs M: Yes, but not only the children. This has followed me throughout my life, saying good-bye to people I love. (. . .) It is possible that this has to do with my childhood, when mother left, and simply said she had to go. Sometimes I say to the children that they must say good-bye like we would never see each other again, because we never know if we are going to see each other again.

Interviewer: What happened with your mother?

Mrs M: My mother left the house when I was seven. She left the family. She first said that she had to go to a sanatorium, but she never came back. In fact she left for another man. Then I knew that she would never come back, although she said she only left to go to this cure.

Thus, Mrs M presents the suicide action as part of longer term projects or life–career aspects. Key significant persons are clearly involved in this process. Mrs M describes interactions, cognitions, emotions and pain in the preceding days and hours. She mentions goal-consideration and goal-setting processes, and she describes her state of mind immediately prior to the action. She gives a clear account of intensive (cognitive and emotional) monitoring and of alternative choices to suicide. She describes how, immediately prior to the action, monitoring and control became impossible. The main themes in Mrs M.'s narrative are:

- loss of her mother in childhood;
- the fear of separation;
- the need to be a good mother for her children;
- increasing cognitive disorganization and the urge to put an end to this state of mind;
- attempts to keep control;
- the suicide action (which she cannot remember).

A CLOSE LOOK AT SUICIDE ACTION

When patients are asked specifically about their motives for attempting suicide, the most frequent answer is "to escape from an unbearable situation or state of mind" (Bancroft et al, 1976; Michel et al, 1994). It appears that the typical mental state immediately before the initiation of deliberate self-harm is characterized by an acute state of anxious emotional perturbation which the individual experiences as unbearable and which has to be distinguished from the underlying, and often long-lasting and commonly interpersonal problems. This is consistent with Shneidman's cubic model of suicide (Shneidman, 1987), which distinguishes three forces called "pain", "perturbation" and "press". Shneidman (1991) stressed the importance of unbearable mental pain, or "psychache", and of the thought that the cessation of consciousness is the solution for this unbearable condition, by stating that "psychological pain and the urge (and will) to stop that pain are the core of suicide". This is reflected in the case of Mrs M. by her statement that she could not live with these thoughts any longer, so that she simply wanted to kill them.

However, the study of a number of narratives of attempted-suicide patients showed a striking similarity in the descriptions given by a majority of patients. They described their state of mind in association with the suicide action as "automatic, robot-like, trance-like", without any feelings of pain or anxiety. Such experiences are typical for dissociative states. In the frame of a homeostatic model of self-conservation, dissociation is to be regarded as a defence against pain, distress or humiliation (Shalev, 1996), or a defence against the collapse of the self. Many patients reported having felt humiliated by important others prior to their suicide attempt, which resulted in a feeling of worthlessness and a loss of self-respect, while others reported having felt emotionally abused, treated like an object and devalued as a human being. Dissociation is known to occur in acute traumatic conditions because of external threats (Holen, 1988; Marmar et al, 1994). However, what it is perceived as a threat depends on a person's earlier traumatic experiences, so that we can speak of an "inner" traumatization.

Dissociative states are typically associated with a history of sexual abuse, which indeed is commonly reported by deliberate self-harm patients. Coll and colleagues (1998) found that 72 per cent of women admitted because of a drug overdose reported some form of sexual abuse. It is known that early and repeated traumatic experiences in childhood, such as sexual abuse, are associated with an impaired capacity to regulate affective responses, and with aggression against the self and against others (Van der Kolk et al, 1991). Orbach (1994) described dissociative states related to acute suicidal crises in an intriguing paper, in which he suggests that dissociation may be the result of intra-psychic splitting. Such a splitting of consciousness may in some individuals become a habitual way of coping with negative emotions. Patients commonly report that they did not feel pain at the moment of the suicidal action (e.g. when cutting). Several authors have described such automatism and feelings of numbness immediately prior to self-injury (Kincel, 1984; Roy, 1985; Demitrack et al, 1990; Orbach et al, 1993). The "dissociation–pain–analgesia–suicide hypothesis" states that unbearable traumatic life events can lead to dissociation, analgesia and suicidal behaviour or deliberate self-harm, which in a number of cases may be associated with amnesia of the event. Such a functional amnesia was also reported by Mrs M who reported that she had no recollection of the suicidal action.

Case study 2

The following interview contains a part of the narrative of Mrs C, a 24-year-old patient who had cut her wrists. She describes a threat originating from a primarily intra-psychic experience in a similar way as Mrs M. described her inner experiences.

> *Mrs C:* I knew that I hurt my mother very much. I knew that I inflicted even more suffering on her. It was a pain for me, and I simply wanted to know whether there is a possibility to stop this pain. And I was listless, for months I

had been crying and now even this; she meant well. I did not see any way out. I could not go any further.

Interviewer: And what did you do afterwards?

Mrs C: Afterwards I went to the bathroom. (...) I know it doesn't look appetizing, but it works well, and then I tried at first here (upper lower arm) and it did not hurt. Then I watched how it was bleeding, and it was nothing particular. And then I cut myself in the strategic places (wrist) and put the arm into water and watched the rings, which was pretty. I was more or less simply watching myself. In the previous months when I was feeling so low after the breakdown of the relationship with my boyfriend, I had often looked at myself from outside, like now while I was cutting myself.

Interviewer: The way you tell it, it sounds as if you were separated from your feelings.

Mrs C: Yes, completely. I was watching myself even then, I know it sounds schizophrenic, but it was like that, "it's simply bleeding now". And then I cut again. I cut three times and then once more ... and then, suddenly, I was not outside of myself any more.

Interviewer: Then you were what?

Mrs C: Not outside of myself anymore. It was this last deep cut and it really did not look nice anymore and I knew that, if I did not do anything, I would die. As stupid as it sounds.

Interviewer: It is clear.

Mrs C: Then I dressed the wound, went to the telephone to call my mother and asked her to forgive me by saying that I was sorry and that she should help me. And my mother was somehow expecting it.

During the self-confrontation interview, Mrs C, who is a psychology student, said: "I felt out of myself and I know that it sounds crazy, schizophrenic, and it fits into DSM and I don't want to be taken for a schizophrenic. There was a difference with the first cuts, which I made to myself, more or less out of interest. I began to put myself out of my body because of the sorrow. I really watched myself. The last cut I made was really deep."

Maltsberger (1993) argues that patients who resort to self-harm have a disturbed relationship between the body and the rest of the self. The body is experienced as "escapable". In a transcript of a conversation Maltsberger gives an example of a patient's description of alienation from the body, numbness and analgesia. Similar to Mrs C, this patient describes an unusual state of mind, which she finds difficult to explain: "it feels swollen somehow, numb ... That's why it doesn't feel that it is really mine because it has a strange kind of feeling when I touch it. It is like an imitation arm. And even when I bleed it doesn't hurt. It is interesting ... it is interesting. It is actually very, very interesting ... I feel the warm blood. That always feels kind of nice. It is just interesting."

It has been suggested that self-destructive behaviour is an attempt at self-regulation (Van der Kolk, 1996). The goal would therefore be to 'reset' the emotional system. Indeed, many people who habitually engage in self-harming behaviour report that self-mutilation makes them feel better and restores a sense of being alive. Furthermore, self-mutilation is thought to be a common reaction to social isolation and fear, both in human and non-human primates (Van der Kolk, 1996).

It is possible that, once dissociation and self-harm as a form of regulation have been experienced, this coping pattern, in behaviouristic terms, gets positively reinforced, and is therefore more likely to be repeated in situations that are experienced as unbearable. This may explain why psychotherapies, which do not focus on different coping strategies, probably have little effect on the frequency of suicidal behaviour. Patients with a borderline personality disorder, who frequently have a history of sexual abuse, commonly avoid emotions, which typically leads to tension and anxiety (Linehan, 1991, 1993). Aggression, dissociation and self-harm can thus be understood as reactions aimed at reducing the suffering from an unbearable state of mind.

THE INTERVIEW AS A JOINT GOAL-DIRECTED ACTION

Patients who are seen after a suicide attempt are very vulnerable and expect that nobody will be able to understand why they harmed themselves. In routine clinical practice, usually little emphasis is put on a personal discourse about the reasons for self-harm. Therefore, patients commonly do not feel understood. Interviewing a suicidal patient with an action-theoretical approach can be seen as a joint action between patient and helper. The main features of such a joint action are (1) the requirement of a joint goal directing the joint performance of the interview and (2) the dual structure of the interview process (i.e. the joint action and the individual action, Von Cranach et al, 1986). This means that the actions of the professional and patient are directed by a joint goal; it is interesting how different the contents of their goals might be. If the individual goals cannot be adjusted to provide an agreeable content for a joint goal, it will be impossible to achieve the goal of both parties in the interview. The dual nature of such a system of joint action means that the action of the professional–patient dyad and the actions of the participating individuals have to be distinguished.

A typical opening sequence of the interview based on a joint action approach would look like:

> *Interviewer:* Now, could you describe to me how it came about that you harmed yourself?
>
> *Patient:* How far back do you want me to go?
>
> *Interviewer:* You can start where you want.
>
> *Patient:* I have been seeing a therapist for about two years—because two years ago I made another suicide attempt . . .

When patients feel respected as individuals who have respectable reasons for their actions, they are interested to participate in the interview as a joint action. They then will be willing to explain what happened, and create a picture of how they want to be seen by the health professional. The interviewer therefore should seek to enable the patient to deliver their story, and his behaviour should be complementary to the goals of the patient. Too many interpretations by the interviewer may be seen by the patient as an uncooperative gesture, and may thus decrease the motivation of the patient to engage in a meaningful therapeutic relationship.

The following is an example of how the interviewer may block the development of a meaningful interaction between him and the patient:

> *Interviewer:* What strikes me is that in the first part of your account of what happened that day you talked kind of very distanced about these events, as if this was all caused by something other than you: that you were restless, that the lake called, that you suddenly might have gone into the water, or into the light or that you would become unconscious and nobody would find you. It is like a notion that something different had a power over you and decided over you. And the first time when you talked about the way your son disappeared, and you became anxious because of the separation, you said it was as if you had planned everything. And then you suddenly reacted emotionally very strongly. How do you explain this?
>
> *Mrs M:* I don't know where it comes from. No idea.

This is an example of how the therapist's intervention is not complementary to the patient's goals. The interviewer's intervention can be understood as "there must be something wrong in what you tell me, because it doesn't make sense to me". This may be because the interviewer was not familiar with an action-theoretical concept of the patient's narrative. The patient should feel that he or she is not primarily evaluated as being mentally ill, but seen as an individual who is well able to explain the implicit goals in his or her actions. A readiness for goal-directedness should therefore be salient in such a way that patients can sense it. A more helpful intervention would probably have been: "I didn't understand this, could you please explain this to me again?"

Self-confrontation and video-playback are typical joint interactions, in which the patient indeed is the main person and the expert in commenting on himself. Based on Hermans and Hermans-Jansen's (1995) manual for self-confrontation interviews, the following skills can be considered as helpful in interviewing suicidal patients. The interviewer should be able to:

- invite the patient to tell in his own words how he came to the point that he decided to harm himself (initiate);
- be open for the narrative of the patient;
- listen actively in silence (being responsive);
- seek detailed accounts of the suicidal development when necessary (specify);
- seek clarification when the meaning is insufficiently understood (clarify);
- remain faithful to the patient's words when paraphrasing;
- only give interpretations when they contribute to the patient's own interpretations.

An action-theoretical approach requires newly defined roles of the patient and the therapist, a therapeutic relationship in which the patient's own narrative is the main joint goal, and interviewing is a joint goal-directed action. An interview in which goals are conflicting (e.g. when the interviewer's main goal is to assign a diagnosis and to decide upon the management of this patient) will lead the patient to closely monitor what to reveal and what not. Interruptions or questions, which do not promote his particular story, are seen as uncooperative gestures, thus blocking the development of the patient's story, and decreasing the motivation of the patient to engage in a meaningful therapeutic relationship. The basic assumption is that as much as the psychiatrist or psychotherapist possesses the techniques and skills to conduct a good interview, the patient has the skills to contribute to a good interview.

CONCLUSIONS

Communication is a form of an interactive or joint action, and thus is the key issue in the therapeutic relationship with suicidal patients. In order to be able to join a patient in a discourse about his or her action of deliberate self-harm we have to understand the individual way patients explain their suicidal actions. Action theory states that actions are goal directed and that in explaining their actions patients do so by using terms stressing the developmental process in which a specific action, such as attempted suicide, occurred. The traditional medical model does not encourage patients to tell their stories (i.e. narratives that belong to the action of attempting suicide). A new approach to the suicidal patient requires a new definition of the re- lationship between patient and health professional.

Many aspects of the story of Mrs M. can be regarded as a typical example of the narratives of attempted-suicide patients, when they are encouraged to explain the background of their suicidal action. These aspects include the following:

- Typically, Mrs M. does not explain her suicide attempt by describ- ing a single cause. She tells a story which explains the cognitions and emotions before the attempt, but which early in her account links these thoughts and emotions with earlier experiences, without any significant probing by the interviewer.
- Like most patients, Mrs M. has a good narrative competence. In order to encourage her to tell her own story, a model is used in which the patient, and not the health professional, is seen as the expert of his or her own story. The patient must sense that the interviewer's main goal is to understand the narrative about the suicidal action. Ideally, when the patient feels that he is understood, the interview becomes a joint action, in which the goals of both partners of the discourse are compatible. The technique of video- playback underlines and exemplifies the joint action of the interview (i.e. patient and interviewer literally looking together at the patient's suicidality).
- The presentation of attempted suicide as an action that is goal directed and integrated in a series of goal-directed behavioural systems shows that patients understand their actions as part of larger systems such as long-term projects and life–career aspects,

which themselves are goal oriented and meaningful to the patient. A suicide action often appears to be related to a failed identity project, which results in a threat to a person's sense of the self, with a subsequent loss of self-regulation. The regulation of affect or emotion appears to be a frequent life–career aspect in many suicide attempters. Patients suffering from clinical depression and hopelessness continue to show a particularly negative perception and persistent suicidal ideation even after a suicide attempt, while non-depressed individuals typically abandon self-harm as a goal and are ready to go back to pursue other (life-oriented) goals and projects such as going back to work.

- The majority of suicide attempters describe a state of mind immediately prior to and during the suicidal action, which is characterized by an altered state of consciousness, automatism and, often, analgesia. The dissociative nature of the acute suicidal state may suggest that a situation, or the actual state of mind, is experienced as a threat to identity or sense of coherence. Similar to traumatic stress as a result of an external event, which is overpowering and cannot be controlled, a form of traumatization because of inner conditions is conceivable. Individuals may be vulnerable because of earlier traumatic experiences, often in childhood. Early and repeated traumatic experiences in childhood are associated with an impaired capacity to regulate affective responses, and with aggression against the self and against others. The short-term and long-term neurophysiological mechanisms involved in suicidal behaviour are described in detail in Chapters 3 and 4. A stressful situation that is experienced as a threat to (biological or psychological) integrity arouses high levels of anxiety, agitation and even pain, which is linked with the urge to escape, or attack, which may be turned against the person's own body. In the patient's narrative, as described in this chapter, it can be seen that she repeatedly tried to regulate her affect and control her thoughts, in which suicide clearly emerged as a possible solution.

The suicidal process is a very individual and private project. Suicide as an alternative action to a person's life projects is often something that is not put to the test by others, whose answers are known in advance. In a way, suicide has to do with the dignity of the individual, the attempt to save the vulnerable self from a total catastrophe. To talk about this, patients need a secure base in the form of a therapist who is sensitive to their own and very subjective logic. Many patients have been traumatized earlier in their lives and are unable to trust anybody to talk about their problems and suicidal plans. They will only open up when they feel understood. Action theory provides a blueprint for suicide action. More than this, it is a basis for a therapeutic relationship focusing on a discourse about the patient's suicidality.

What are the possible implications of a model based on action theory for the treatment and prevention of suicidal behaviour? Apart from the assignment of a psychiatric diagnosis, the value of which is not questioned, our task must be to engage in a meaningful interaction with the suicidal patient, who is in a fragile state. In order to establish a good therapeutic relationship we must encourage the patient to tell us his or her story that is behind the suicide goal. *Without this there can be no meaningful therapeutic intervention.* Our interventions should then relate to the goal-directed organization of the suicidal process as it is presented by the patient. We have to keep in mind that patients see suicide as a possible solution for a seemingly unbearable situation or state of mind, a situation which is perceived as a threat to the self, and that this experience is related to life projects and life goals in which patients feel that they have failed or been hurt. Therefore, behind a suicidal action are other goal-directed systems, which are part of various life–career aspects (e.g. these may include relational or professional careers). The main objective in a therapeutic relationship must be to look, together with the patient, at the meaning of the crisis in the context of his or her life story and to investigate alternatives to suicide as a goal (i.e. to change the order of goals by moving suicide to a lower level in the hierarchy of goals). Such a model is compatible with Shneidman's recommendations, which are indeed clearly goal-directed: "reduce the hurt, widen the blinders, pull back from action. Let me help you generate more possibilities, to rethink and restate the problem, then look at possible courses of action other than the only one you have in mind" (Shneidman, 1991).

ACKNOWLEDGEMENTS

This project was supported by a 3-year grant from the Swiss National Science Foundation (grant No. 32-49313.96).

REFERENCES

Alexander, L.B. and Luborsky, L. (1986) The Penn Helping Alliance Scales. In L. S. Greenberg and W. M. Pinsof (Eds), *The Psychotherapeutic Process: A Research Handbook.* New York, Guilford Press.

Antonovsky, A. (1987) *Unraveling the Mystery of Health: How People Manage Stress and Stay Well*. San Francisco, Jossey-Bass.

Appleby, L., Amos, T., Doyle, U., Tommenson, B. and Woodman, M. (1996) General Practitioners and Young Suicides. *British Journal of Psychiatry*, **168**: 330–333.

Bancroft, J., Hawton, K., Simkin, S., Kingston, B., Cumming, C. and Whitwell D. (1979) The reasons people give for taking overdoses: a further enquiry. *British Journal of Medical Psychology*, **52**: 353–365.

Bancroft, J., Skrimshire, A. and Simkin S. (1976) The reasons people give for taking overdoses. *British Journal of Psychiatry*, **128**: 583–588.

Beck, A.T., Ward, C.H. and Mendelson, M. (1961) An inventory for measuring depression. *Archives of General Psychiatry*, **4**: 561–571.

Breuer, F. (1991) *Analyse beraterischer Tätigkeiten (Analysis of counselling activity)*. Münster, Aschendorff Verlag.

Buss, A. (1978) Causes and reaons in attribution theory. A conceptual critique. *Journal of Personality and Social Psychology*, **36**: 1311–1321.

Buss, A. (1979) On the relationship between causes and reason. *Journal of Personality and Social Psychology*, **37**: 1458–1461.

Cannon, W.B. (1923) *Bodily Changes in Pain, Fear, and Rage*. New York, Appleton.

Choquet, M. and Menke, H. (1989) Suicidal thoughts during early adolescence: prevalence, associated troubles and help-seeking behaviour. *Acta Psychiatrica Scandinavica*, **81**: 170–177.

Coll, X., Law, F., Tobias A. and Hawton K. (1998) Child sexual abuse in women who take overdoses: I. A study of prevalence and severity. *Archives of Suicide Research*, **4**: 291–306.

Demitrack, M.A., Putnam, F.W., Brewerton, T.D., Brandt, H.A. and Gold, P.W. (1990) Relation of clincal variables to dissociative phenomena in eating disorders. *American Journal of Psychiatry*, **147**: 1184–1188.

Ennis, J., Barnes, R.A., Kennedy, S. and Trachtenberg, D.D. (1989) Depression in self-harm patients. *British Journal of Psychiatry*, **154**: 41–47.

Foss, L. and Rothenberg, K. (1988) *The Second Medical Revolution: From Biomedicine to Infomedicine*. Boston, New Science Library Shambhala.

Gollwitzer, P.M. (1996) The volitional benefits of planning. In P.M. Gollwitzer and J.A. Bargh (Eds), *The Psychology of Action. Linking Cognition and Motivation to Behavior*. New York, Guilford Press.

Hawton, K., Arensman, E., Townsend, E., Bremner, S., Feldman, E., Goldney, R., Gunnell, D., Hazell, P., van Heeringen, K., House, A., Owens, D., Sakinofsky, I. and Träskman-Bendz, L. (1998) Deliberate self-harm: systematic review of efficacy of psychological and pharmacological treatments inpreventing repetition. *British Medical Journal*, **317**: 441–447.

Hawton, K. and Blackstock, E. (1976) General practice aspects of self-poisoning and self-injury. *Psychological Medicine*, **6**: 571–575.

Hermans, H.J.M. and Hermans-Jansen, E. (1955) *Self-Narratives: The Construction of Meaning in Psychotherapy*. New York, Guilford Press.

Hinkle, S. and Schmidt, D. (1984) The Buss cause/reason hypotheses: An empirical investigation. *Social Psychology Quarterly*, **47**: 358–364.

Holen, A. (1988) The North Sea oil rig disaster. In J.P. Wilson and B. Raphael (Eds), *International Handbook of Traumatic Stress Syndromes*. New York, Plenum Press.

Isometsä, E.T., Heikkinen, M.E., Marttunen, M.J., Henriksson, M.M., Aro, H.M. and Lönnqvist, J.K. (1995) The last appointment before suicide: Is suicide intent communicated? *American Journal of Psychiatry*, **152**: 919–992.

Kalbermatten, U. and Valach, L. (1985) Methods of an integrative approach for the study of social interaction. *Communication and Cognition*, **18**: 281–315.

Kincel, R.L. (1984) Suicide attempt: Clinical assessment and mode of intervention. *Crisis*, **5**: 1–8.

Kuhl, J. (1986) Motivation and information processing: A new look at decision making, dynamic change, and action control. In R.M. Sorrentino and E.T. Higgins (Eds), *Handbook of Motivation and Cognition: Foundation of Social Behavior*. New York, Guilford Press.

Kurz, A., Möller, H.J., Bürk, F., Torhorst, A., Wächtler, C. and Lauter H. (1988) Evaluation of two different aftercare strategies of an outpatient aftercare program for suicide attempters in a general hospital. In H.J. Möller, A. Schmidtke and R. Welz (Eds), *Current Issues in Suicidology*. Berlin, Springer.

Leenaars, A.A. (1993) Unconscious processes. In A.A. Leenaars (Ed.), *Suicidology: Essays in Honour of Edwin S. Shneidman*. Northvale, Jason Aronson Inc.

Linehan, M.M. (1993) *Cognitive-Behavioral Treatment of Borderline Personality Disorder*. New York, Guilford Press.

Linehan, M.M., Armstrong, H.E., Suarez, A., Allmon, D. and Heard, H. (1991) Cognitive-behavioral treatment of chronically parasuicidal borderline patients. *Archives of General Psychiatry*, **48**: 1060–1064.

Maltsberger, J.T. (1993) Confusions of the body, the self, and others in suicidal states. In A.A. Leenaars (Ed.), *Suicidology: Essays in Honour of Edwin S. Shneidman*. Northvale, Jason Aronson Inc..

Maris, R.W. (1981) *Pathways to Suicide: A Survey of Self-destructive Behaviors*. Baltimore, Johns Hopkins University Press.

Marmar, C.R., Weiss, D.S., Schlenger, W.E., Fairbank, J.A., Jordan, K., Kulka, R.A. and Hough, R.L. (1994) Peritraumatic dissociation and post-traumatic stress in male Vietnam theater veterans. *American Journal of Psychiatry*, **151**: 902–907.

McGaughey, J, Long, A. and Harrisson, S. (1995) Suicide and parasuicide: a selected review of the literature. *Journal of Psychiatric and Mental Health Nursing*, **2**: 199–206.

Michel, K., Valach, L. and Waeber, V. (1994) Understanding deliberate self-harm: The patients' views. *Crisis*, **15**: 172–178.

Michel, K. and Valach, L. (1997) Suicide as goal-directed bahaviour. *Archives of Suicide Research*, **3**: 213–221.

Michel, K., Runeson, B., Valach, L. and Wasserman, D. (1997) Contacts of suicide attempters with GPs prior to the event; a comparison between Stockholm and Bern. *Acta Psychiatrica Scandinavica*, **95**: 94–99.

Möller, H.J. (1990) Evaluation of aftercare strategies. In G. Ferrari, M. Bellini and P. Crepet (Eds), *Suicidal Behaviour and Risk Factors*. Bologna, Monduzzi Editore.

Noack, H. and Valach, L. (1985) Zur Rekonstruktion von Krankheitslaufbahnen in der ambulanten Versorgung (Reconstruction of illness careers in outpatient services). *Sozial- und Präventivmedizin*, **4–5**: 237–238.

Orbach, I., Palgi, Y., Stein, D., Har-Even, D., Lotem-Peleg, M. and Asherove, J. (1993) *Pain Tolerance in Suicidal, Psychiatric, and Normal Subjects*. Ramat-Gan, Department of Psychology, Bar-Ilan University.

Orbach, I. (1994) Dissociation, physical pain, and suicide: A hypothesis. *Suicide and Life-Threatening Behavior*, **24**: 68–79.

Polkinghorne, D. E. (1990) Action theory approaches to career research. In R.A. Young and W.A. Borgen (Eds), *Methodological Approaches to the Study of Career*. New York, Praeger Publishers.

Riessman, C. K. (1991) Beyond Reductionism: Narrative genres in divorce accounts. *Journal of Narrative and Life-History*, **1**: 41–68.

Roy, A. (1985) Self-destructive behavior. *Psychiatric Clinics of North America*, **8** (special issue).

Sarbin, T.R. (Ed.) (1986) *Narrative Psychology: The Storied Nature of Human Conduct.* New York, Praeger Publishers.

Shalev, A.Y. (1996) Stress versus traumatic stress. From acute homeostatic reactions to chronic psychopathology. In B.A. van der Kolk, A.C. McFarlane and L. Weisaeth (Eds), *Traumatic Stress*. New York, Guilford Press.

Shneidman, E.S. (1991) The commonalities of suicide across the life span. In A.A. Leenaars (Ed.), *Life Span Perspectives of Suicide*. New York, Plenum Press.

Shneidman, E.S. (1987) A psychological approach to suicide. In G.R. VandenBos and B.K. Bryant (Eds), *Cataclysms, Crises, and Catastrophes*. Washington, DC, American Psychological Association.

Suominen, K., Henriksson, M., Suokas, J., Isometsä, E., Ostamo, A. and Lönnqvist J. (1996) Mental disorders and comorbidity in attempted suicide. *Acta Psychiatrica Scandinavica*, **94**: 234–240.

Thommen, B., Von Cranach, M. and Ammann, R. (1992) The organization of individual action through social representations: A comparative study of two therapeutic schools. In M. von Cranach, W. Doise and G. Mugny (Eds), *Social Representations and the Social Base of Knowledge*. Lewinston, Hogrefe & Huber.

Treolar, A.J. and Pinfold, T.J. (1993) Deliberate self-harm: An assessment of patients' attitudes to the care they receive. *Crisis*, **14**: 83–89.

Valach, L. (1990) A theory of goal-directed action in career analysis. In R.A. Young and W.A. Borgen (Eds), *Methodological Approaches to the Study of Career*. New York, Praeger Publishers.

Valach, L. (1995) Coping and human agency. In I. Markova and R. Farr (Eds), *Representation of Health, Illness and Handicap*. London, Harwood Academic Publishers.

Valach, L., Von Cranach, M. and Kalbermatten, U. (1988) Social meaning in the observation of goal directed action. *Semiotica*, **71**: 243–259.

Valach, L., Young, R.A. and Lynam, J. (1996) The family's health promotion project. *Journal of Health Psychology*, **1**: 49–63.

Van der Kolk, B.A. (1996) The complexity of adaptation to trauma. Self-regulation, stimulus, discrimination and characterological development. In B.A. van der Kolk, A.C. McFarlane and L. Weisaeth (Eds), *Traumatic Stress*. New York, Guilford Press.

Van der Kolk, B.A., Perry, J.C. and Herman, J.L. (1991) Childhood origin of self-destructive behavior. *American Journal of Psychiatry*, **148**: 1665–1671.

Von Cranach, M. and Harré, R. (Eds) (1982) *The Analysis of Action. European Studies in Social Psychology*. Cambridge, Cambridge University Press.

Von Cranach, M., Kalbermatten, U., Indermuehler, K. and Gugler, B. (1982) *Goal Directed Action*. London, Academic Press.

Von Cranach, M., Ochsenbein, G. and Valach, L. (1986) The group as a self active system: outline of a theory of a group action. *European Journal of Social Psychology*, **16**: 193–229.

Von Cranach, M. and Valach, L. (1983) The social dimension of goal directed action. In H. Tajfel (Ed.), *The Social Dimension of Social Psychology*. Cambridge, Cambridge University Press.

Von Cranach, M. and Valach, L. (1986) Action theory. In R. Harré and R. Lamb (Eds), *The Dictionary of Personality and Social Psychology*. Oxford, Blackwell Reference.

Von Uexküll, Th. and Wesiack, W. (1988) *Theorie der Humanmedizin. Grundlagen*

Ärztlichen Denkens und Handelns (Theory of Human Medicine. The Basis of Medical Reasoning and Acting). München, Urban & Schwarzenberg.

Wolk-Wasserman, D. (1987) Contacts of suicidal neurotic and prepsychotic/psychotic patients and their significant others with public care institutions before the suicide attempt. *Acta Psychiatrica Scandinavica*, **75**: 358–372.

Young, R.A., Valach, L., Dillabough, J.-A., Dover, C. and Matthes, G. (1994) Career research from an action perspective: The self-confrontation procedure. *Career Development Quarterly*, **43**: 185–196.

Young, R.A., Valach, L. and Collin, A. (1996) A contextualist approach to career analysis and counselling. In D. Brown and L. Brooks (Eds), *Career Choice and Development* (Third edition). San Francisco, Jossey-Bass.

Chapter 13

PSYCHOPHARMACOLOGICAL APPROACHES TO THE SUICIDAL PROCESS

Kevin M. Malone and Maeve Moran

INTRODUCTION

Suicidal behaviour is a serious public-health concern, and associated with increased morbidity and mortality. Suicide is one of the main causes of death among young people, especially young men. There is a consensus that approximately 90 per cent of individuals who commit suicide have a psychiatric illness. However, because suicide is a relatively rare event and the majority of individuals with psychiatric illness will not die as a result of suicide, a psychiatric diagnosis has high sensitivity but low specificity. According to current knowledge the best clinical predictor of completed suicide is a history of previous attempts, but such a history is present in only 20–40 per cent of suicides.

This chapter will outline how psychopharmacological approaches may be useful in the management of the suicidal process. Preceding a discussion of the psychopharmacotherapeutic opportunities provided by the process approach to suicidal behaviour, recent findings regarding its psychobiological underpinnings will be reviewed. Thus the focus will be particularly on trait-dependent characteristics, which define an underlying vulnerability, and less on stressor-related state-like conditions. Based on these findings a model of suicidal behaviour

Understanding Suicidal Behaviour. Edited by Kees van Heeringen
© 2001 John Wiley & Sons Ltd.

in psychiatric patients will be described that may guide clinicians in their choice of treatment options.

PYSCHOBIOLOGICAL TARGETS FOR PSYCHOPHARMACOLOGICAL TREATMENT

Post-mortem studies have found altered levels of serotonin in association with suicide, independent of psychiatric diagnosis (for a review see Mann et al, 1996). Moreover, Arango and colleagues (1996) found fewer pigmented neurones in the locus coeruleus in the brains of suicide victims, with a right/left asymmetry in all cases. As the locus coeruleus is an area with a high density of noradrenergic neurones, this finding has led to a putative theory that there may be reduced amounts of noradrenergic neurones initially, while the exposure to pre-suicide stressors may lead to further noradrenaline depletion. As was described in Chapter 3, the findings with regard to noradrenaline may thus reflect stress effects.

Psychopharmacological studies have provided further evidence of the involvement of the noradrenergic system in the suicidal process. A French placebo-controlled study compared the effects of maprotiline and placebo in a cohort with depressive illness over one year. Although the doses of maprotiline used in this study (i.e. 37.5 mg and 75 mg) were lower than the generally accepted and usual thera-peutic dose of 150 mg, maprotiline had a significant effect in prevent-ing relapse of depression in patients who recovered from the acute episode when compared with placebo. The higher dosage of maproti-line was significantly more efficacious than the lower dosage. Despite this effect on the recurrence of depressive episodes, maprotiline was associated with a significantly higher number of suicide attempts than placebo over the study period. Among the patients who received maprotiline, nine suicide attempts and five completed suicides occurred, compared with one completed suicide in the placebo group (Rouillon et al, 1989). The mechanism underlying the increased number of suicide attempts has been the subject of extensive discussions. The potent noradrenergic effects of maprotiline have been suggested to play a role in the triggering of suicide attempts (Baldwin et al, 1991).

Functional changes in the serotonergic system have also been reported in *biological studies of attempted-suicide patients*, and particularly in those who have made serious suicide attempts and who suffer from major depression (Malone et al, 1996; Mann and Malone, 1996). A 1-year follow-up study showed that low levels of 5-hydroxy indoleacetic acid (5-HIAA), a metabolite of serotonin, in the cerebrospinal fluid (CSF) of suicide attempters significantly predicted completed suicide. Suicide attempters with low CSF 5-HIAA levels had a four- to six-fold increased risk of suicide in the year after discharge (Nordström et al, 1994). Given the poor predictive power of current clinical indicators of risk, further research work needs to be conducted on promising biological markers such as CSF 5-HIAA.

Recent *neuroimaging studies* indicate that altered brain-serotonin neurotransmission can be seen in depressed patients (Mann et al, 1997) and attempted-suicide patients (Audenaert et al, in press; Van Heeringen et al, submitted). Using Positron Emission Tomography (PET) to examine changes in regional brain-glucose metabolism in response to serotonin release by fenfluramine, lower glucose metabolism was found in the prefrontal cortex in depressed patients when compared with normal controls, suggesting reduced serotonin activity. This cortical area has been identified in post-mortem brain studies as being involved in suicide (Arango et al, 1996). This is the area of the brain that mediates behavioural inhibition, and thus may be involved in impulsivity. Brodsky and colleagues (1997) found that impulsivity was the only criterion of borderline personality disorder that correlated with past suicide attempts after controlling for lifetime depression and substance abuse.

More recently, the binding potential of the 5-HT_{2a} serotonin receptor was studied in attempted-suicide patients and controls by means of SPECT (Single Photon Emission Computerized Tomography), using a highly selective receptor-ligand. The results show that the binding potential of these receptors in the prefrontal cortex was significantly lower in attempted-suicide patients than in controls, and that the decrease in binding potential was significantly more prominent in individuals who attempted suicide by means of deliberate self-poisoning than in those who used self-injury (Audenaert et al, in press). The binding potential of the 5-HT_{2a} serotonin receptor in the prefrontal cortex thereby correlated significantly and negatively with the levels of hopelessness and harm avoidance, the latter being a measure of behavioural inhibition (Van Heeringen et al, submitted).

TOWARDS A MODEL OF SUICIDAL BEHAVIOUR IN PSYCHIATRIC PATIENTS

As described in Chapters 1 and 3, a stress–diathesis model has been suggested (Mann et al, 1999) which postulates that suicidal behaviour may be understood as a function of the interplay between state-dependent factors (i.e. illness or life events) and trait-dependent factors, which include putative biological markers for suicidal behaviour. This model has the merit of including biological, social and psychological factors within a single model. Thus, there is a growing consensus among health-care professionals that effective strategies to prevent suicide require a multidimensional approach. Current neuropsychopharmacological research is focused in particular on the brain neurotransmitter serotonin as a possible biological marker for suicidal behaviour, independent of psychiatric illness. Based on recent research findings, which were reviewed in Chapter 4, it can be hypothesized that serotonin has a key role in the regulation of restraint (i.e. the mechanism for suppressing action on (whether or not unwanted) thoughts) in the central nervous system. Restraint varies from individual to individual, and also within an individual, as, for example, a lower level of restraint may typically be unmasked by depression or alcohol, culminating in a suicidal act.

A growing body of research evidence thus indicates that serotonergic activity is deficient in individuals who show suicidal behaviour, thus lowering the threshold for suicidal behaviour, suggesting that the serotonergic system is a target for psychopharmacological approaches to the treatment and prevention of suicidal behaviour. Moreover, there is indirect evidence to suggest that psychopharmacology may contribute to halting or reversing the suicidal process by promoting the neuroregulatory pathways of restraint, or by aborting or suppressing neuroregulatory pathways. Dysfunctions may kindle or accelerate the suicidal process, which may become manifest as insomnia and anxiety. Psychopharmacological approaches may further address the deficient neuroregulatory pathways central to triggering and sustaining a depressive episode, or modify neuroregulatory pathways relevant to psychotic episodes, particularly when persecutory or somatic delusions and/or hallucinations predominate. A final target of psychopharmacological intervention includes the prophylactic-maintenance treatment for major recurrent psychiatric syndromes such as major depression, bipolar-mood disorder and schizophrenia.

CLINICAL ASSESSMENT OF AT-RISK POPULATIONS

The first logical stage of assessment of any patient should include a detailed and frank exploration of any suicidal thoughts or acts. In view of the suicidal-process concept the assessment of patients should also address their history of suicidal ideation or behaviour. We previously compared clinical assessment of suicide risk with research methods of assessment, and found that clinicians failed to document a history of suicidal behaviour in 12 out of 50 patients in whom such a history was identified by research tools. Furthermore, assessment was more accurate when it was done using a semi-structured procedure in comparison with discharge summaries, which were not semi-structured. These findings suggest that the use of semi-structured screening instruments as tools for the clinician improves the identification of individuals who may be at risk of suicidal behaviour (Malone et al, 1995).

A recent study by Barber and colleagues (1998) specifically examined the correlates of a history of aborted suicide attempts (see also Chapter 1). They concluded that aborted attempts were highly associated with actual attempts with comparable intent scores. The findings of both the above studies suggest that introduction of a standardized screening tool for use by clinicians may improve assessment procedures.

It is also important for the mental-health professional to be aware of potential sources of bias. Lewis and Appleby (1998) found that, following a diagnosis of personality disorder, psychiatrists were more likely to view an individual's suicidal impulses as under their control. In addition, their suicidal behaviour was more likely to be regarded as manipulative or attention seeking. Morgan and Priest (1984) found that staff often perceived future suicides as being provocative and assuming of disabilities. Morgan and Priest (1991) subsequently discussed in this context the concept of "malignant alienation" of the patient as a risk factor for suicide.

Additionally, there is a necessity to focus research attention on improving the skills of clinicians in both the diagnosis and effective treatment of mental illness, and on reducing barriers to early consultation for patients who experience suicidal ideas. Between 10 and 25 per cent of all suicides consult a clinician in the week before a completed suicide, and up to 40 per cent in the month before death (Pirkis and Burgess, 1998). However, clinicians fail to recognize and treat up to 50 per cent of cases of moderate to severe depression (Oquendo et al, 1999). This represents a missed opportunity for early clinical intervention in order to stop the suicidal process. Moreover, studies using the psychological-autopsy method have found that many individuals suffering from depressive illness who completed suicide were not receiving any or adequate antidepressant pharmacotherapy prior to death.

PHARMACOTHERAPEUTIC OPTIONS

As shown in Table 13.1 pharmacotherapeutic approaches to intervene in the suicidal process may aim at influencing traits that underlie this process, which may be responsible for symptoms such as anxiety,

Table 13.1 Psychopharmacological strategies for modifying suicidal processes

Suicidal process components	Neuroregulatory pathways	Pharmacological interventions
Restraint/suppression/ inhibition of suicidal ideas	Serotonin	SSRI, lithium, sodium valproate
Anxiety/agitation/insomnia	GABA, dopamine, norepinephrine	(Preferably non-) benzodiazepine hypnotics, buspirone, flupenthixol, tranylcypromine
Depression	Norepinephrine, serotonin, dopamine	TCA, SSRI, MAOI, NARI, ECT
Substance-dependence withdrawal	GABA, dopamine	Methadone, clonidine for opiate
Akathisia	Dopamine	Benztropine, propanolol
Psychosis with command delusions/hallucinations	Dopamine	Typical neuroleptics such as chlorpromazine or haloperidol. Preferably atypical neuroleptics such as clozapine

ECT	Electroconvulsive therapy.
NARI	Noradrenaline re-uptake inhibitors.
SSRI	Selective serotonin re-uptake inhibitors.
TCA	Tricyclic anti-depressant.

aggression or impulsivity, or focus on the treatment and prevention of chronic or recurrent psychiatric disorders, such as depression, substance abuse and/or schizophrenia. Particular attention should be paid to the co-morbid occurrence of these disorders, as has been described in Chapter 6.

Impulsivity, aggression and anxiety

Evidence for a pharmacological effect on measures of restraint or impulsivity has been found for neuroleptics, lithium, carbamazepine, tranylcypomine and antidepressants, including MAO inhibitors and SSRIs (Selective Serotonin Re-uptake Inhibitors) In a 2-month study among adolescents who suffered from borderline personality disorder, Kutcher and colleagues (1995) found evidence for an effect of flupenthixol (3 mg per day) on measures of impulsivity, dysphoria and global functioning. In borderline patients carbamazepine and tranylcypromine have been found to reduce behavioural dyscontrol and impulsivity, respectively (Cowdry and Gardner, 1998). The beneficial effect of lithium on the occurrence of suicidal behaviour among patients suffering from borderline personality disorder (see p. 265) has been attributed to a so-called "reflective delay" effect of lithium, referring to an increased capacity to "reflect" and thus to reduce impulsive behaviour. In an earlier placebo-controlled study it was found that lithium significantly reduced aggressive behaviour. Links and colleagues (1990) showed a more common improvement on ratings of anger in borderline patients who received lithium than in those who received desipramine or placebo.

There is some evidence that MAO inhibitors and SSRIs may modify traits, which are assumed to be associated with suicidal behaviour. Soloff and colleagues (1993) found an effect of phenelzine on ratings of anger and hostility in a placebo-controlled study in borderline patients. Salzmann and colleagues (1992) examined the effect of fluoxetine on patients with a diagnosis of borderline personality disorder in a double blind, placebo-controlled trial. Subjects were randomized to either placebo or fluoxetine (dosage range 20–40 mg). Anger, hostility and impulsiveness were significantly reduced in the patients who were treated with fluoxetine. Several small and open studies have shown positive effects of the SSRI fluoxetine (Norden, 1989; Markovitz et al, 1991) and sertraline (Kavoussi et al, 1994) on measures of impulsive aggression. More recently, fluoxetine was found to produce a sustained improvement in measures of irritability and aggression when compared with placebo (Coccaro and Kavoussi, 1997).

The effects of low-dose neuroleptics on measures of anxiety and irritability have been assessed in a limited number of studies. Serban and Siegal (1984) studied the effects of thiothixene and haloperidol in borderline and schizotypal patients. They showed that cognitive disturbance, derealization, anxiety, self-esteem and ideas of reference improved significantly with both neuroleptics. Soloff and colleagues (1993) found beneficial effects of 4 months of maintenance treatment with haloperidol (up to 6 mg per day) on irritability in patients suffering from borderline personality disorders. However, almost three-quarters of the patients dropped out of the study during the maintenance phase. More recently, an open study showed an effect of sodium valproate on measures of agitation in borderline disordered patients (Wilcox, 1995).

Depressive disorder

Antidepressants

It is estimated that at least 50 per cent of completed suicides have a major depressive illness (Isometsä et al, 1998). The lifetime mortality of unipolar affective disorder is 15 per cent (Lönnqvist, 2000). Approximately 25 per cent of individuals who suffer from unipolaraffective disorder will attempt suicide during their lives. Therefore, adequate diagnosis and management of depressive illness is important in any discussion of the prevention of suicide. The steps in effective management are early diagnosis, selection of a safe antidepressant, the prescription of an adequate antidepressant dosage for adequate duration in order to ensure complete therapeutic response and to avoid early relapse, and regular clinical monitoring to enhance the therapeutic alliance and advise about side effects.

When selecting an antidepressant, it is good practice to consider its safety in the eventuality of an overdose. Another issue in the choice of an antidepressant for suicidal patients concerns the duration of the latency period, which precedes actual antidepressant activity. SSRIs may be more effective than other antidepressants in terms of early (up to 4 weeks) improvement in suicidal ideation, as was demonstrated in four of the six double-blind studies that have looked at this issue (Montgomery et al, 1981; Mullin et al, 1988; Gonella et al, 1990; Nathan et al, 1990; Perez and Ashford, 1990). This early improvement may have important therapeutic implications by giving an extra protective factor in advance of the full onset of antidepressant effect. There have been a number of reports in the literature about emergent suicidality in patients on antidepressant treatment, and fluoxetine in particular (Dasgupta, 1990; Teicher et al, 1990; Hoover, 1991; Masand et al, 1991). These were mostly case reports, which did not distinguish between the relative contributions of the disease process, external stressors and/or concurrent medication. Moreover, it should be noted that a similar emergence or worsening of suicidal ideation has been reported in association with treatment by means of antidepressants of other classes, ECT (Electroconvulsive Therapy) and light therapy (Verkes and Cowen, 2000). In a consensus statement by the American College of Neuropsychopharmacology Council it was concluded that there was no evidence that SSRIs were associated with emergent suicidality over the rates already associated with depression and other antidepressants (Mann et al, 1993). According to this statement it was clear that many patients benefit significantly from these drugs.

As mentioned above, phenelzine may reduce anger and hostility in selected patients, under careful supervision (Soloff, 1993). Although no controlled studies have been conducted on the effects of ECT on the suicidal process, Avery and Winokur (1972) reported reduced suicidal acts in depressed patients who received ECT. However, in patients with depression with psychotic features, and delusional suicidal ideation, ECT may be life saving in inducing a rapid amelioration of psychotic suicidal ideation. To date, there have been no direct studies on the effectiveness of noradrenaline re-uptake inhibitors (NARIs) in the treatment of suicidal depression. Their reported relatively rapid onset of antidepressant action and safety in overdose suggest they may be useful.

With regard to the need for regular clinical monitoring particular attention should be paid to the period immediately following in-patient discharge, which represents a high-risk period for the re-emergence of the suicidal process (Flood and Seager, 1968; Roy, 1982; Appleby, 1992). It is therefore essential that all members of the multidisciplinary team working in conjunction with the patient, including the sector team in the community, conduct careful discharge planning. It should also be noted that patients with recurrent major depression who attempt suicide do so relatively early in the course of the illness (Malone et al, 1995), so this is a period of risk, which is important to monitor.

Bipolar affective disorder

Lithium

As indicated by a lifetime prevalence of 1 per cent, bipolar disorder affects only a small proportion of the population. However, the consequences can be fatal, as the lifetime risk of suicide has been estimated at 19 per cent (Jamison et al, 1986; Goodwin et al, 1990; Lönnqvist, 2000). Early open and double-blind studies have shown promising effects of lithium, which is the principal mood stabilizer used in the treatment and prophylaxis of bipolar affective disorder. However, the results of these studies have been questioned as they could be due to selection biases (e.g. based on compliance with drug regimens). Compliance has indeed been found to vary between 18 and 53 per cent. Although compliance with treatment thus is a major issue in the treatment of bipolar disorder with lithium, it has received insufficient attention in clinical studies, as less than 50 of 10 000 reviewed articles about lithium looked at compliance in any substantial way (Goodwin and Jamison, 1990). This obviously is relevant to establish the clinical effectiveness of lithium. The available evidence suggests that maintenance therapy with lithium significantly reduces the risk of suicide in patients with bipolar disorder. It remains unknown, however, whether lithium has a specific neurochemical anti-suicide effect, or whether the reduced risk is a consequence of prolonged mood stabilization. Evidence in favour of a specific anti-suicide effect has been provided by Müller-Oerlinghausen and colleagues (1992) who showed that rates of suicidal behaviour were significantly decreased in patients with recurrent mood disorders who took lithium, even when mood stabilization had not occurred.

Anticonvulsants

Anticonvulsants now have an established role as mood stabilizers in the treatment of bipolar disorder (McElroy et al, 1987). There are, however, no placebo-controlled trials to examine the extent to which mood stabilizers actually reduce the risk of suicide in bipolar disorder. Thies-Flechtner and colleagues (1996) compared the effects of lithium and carbamazepine in a 2-year randomized study in 378 patients suffering from recurrent mood disorders or schizoaffective disorder. No patients on lithium showed suicidal behaviour, while among patients taking carbamazepine five attempted suicide and four committed suicide. Optimal management of bipolar disorder should include well-organized easy-access clinics, with experienced staff that have the psychopharmacological expertise in the most effective use of lithium and other mood stabilizers.

Borderline personality disorder

Patients with borderline personality disorder represent a group at high risk of completed suicide. Corbitt and colleagues (1996) estimated that approximately 10 per cent of patients suffering from this disorder die as a result of suicide. The treatment of personality disorders is regarded as largely ineffective by many clinicians. However, there has been some work done in recent years, which shows promise from both psychotherapeutic and psychopharmacological points of view. Psychotherapeutic approaches are described in detail in Chapter 14. This section addresses findings with regard to psychopharmacological-treatment options.

Neuroleptics

Montgomery and Montgomery (1982) compared the effects of placebo, mianserin 30 mg daily, and 20 mg of depot flupenthixol monthly in a cohort of patients with personality disorder. Inclusion criteria for the trial were a history of two suicide attempts and no concurrent axis-I disorder. The results showed no difference between study groups at 3 months, but by 6 months the group who received flupenthixol had made significantly less suicide attempts than the placebo-treated group. Mianserin had no beneficial effects. These results suggest that low-dose neuroleptics should be considered as a treatment option in preventing repeat suicide attempts among patients with borderline personality disorder. Replication of these findings with regard to antipsychotic drugs is clearly needed. In view of the promising effects of the newer, atypical neuroleptics on the occurrence of suicidal behaviour among patients suffering from schizophrenia, their use in patients with borderline personality disorder should receive urgent research attention.

Lithium

There are some reports in the literature that lithium can be effective in subjects with severe personality disorders (Verkes and Cowen, 2000). Stone (1990) found that 8 per cent of a large cohort with borderline personality disorder responded to lithium. As described on pp 263–264, this effect may be attributable to an increased capacity of reflective delay.

Anticonvulsants

The effects of carbamazepine on measures of behavioural dyscontrol have been described on p. 264. As in lithium, these effects have been ascribed to an increased capacity of "reflective delay", enabling patients to think about the consequences of their actions rather than acting immediately.

Antidepressants

While there has been a much-needed increase in trials looking at the efficacy of antidepressant therapy in patients suffering from borderline personality disorder, there has been a paucity of controlled studies on the effectiveness of antidepressant pharmacotherapy in reducing suicidal activity. No effect of mianserin (Hirsch et al, 1983; Montgomery et al, 1983) or nomifensine (Hirsch et al, 1983) on the rate of repetition of suicide attempts was found in placebo-controlled studies in patients who were characterized by borderline features. Verkes and colleagues

(1998) studied the effect of paroxetine (40 mg daily) on the repetition of attempted suicide by means of a placebo-controlled study in a group of 91 recurrent suicide attempters without a major axis-I psychiatric disorder, but with predominantly borderline characteristics. Although the overall effect of paroxetine did not differ from that of placebo, there was a significant decline in the occurrence of repeated attempts in so-called "minor repeaters", who had a history of less than five previous attempts, and in a subgroup of patients meeting less than 15 criteria for cluster-B personality disorder. Paroxetine also had a beneficial effect on measures of anger, which however disappeared after 2 weeks of treatment.

Psychoactive substance abuse

Evidence about a strong association between substance abuse and suicidal behaviour with a non-fatal or fatal outcome is accumulating. Hawton and colleagues (1993) reported that substance misuse among attempted-suicide patients is among the best predictors of completed suicide. While substance misuse is associated with a seven-fold increased risk of attempted suicide, it is also associated with a 15-fold increased risk of completed suicide (Deykin and Buba, 1994; Shaffer et al, 1996). It has been postulated that much of the secular rise in young male suicides is related to substance misuse (Neeleman and Farrell, 1997). Future research needs to focus on the link between suicidal behaviour and substance misuse. Questions that need to be addressed include: Is substance abuse secondary to a primary mental illness such as depression, or are both depression and substance misuse secondary to underlying personality-related psychopathology? Does substance abuse stand alone as a risk factor in the absence of psychiatric co-morbidity (Neeleman and Farrell, 1997)? Suicide by self-poisoning, a method frequently used by addicts, is under registered (Neeleman and Wessely, 1997). Therefore, studies of official suicide statistics will suffer from selection bias. In addition, non-fatal acts are also underreported, and opiate addicts who experience non-fatal overdoses are less likely to seek help (Drake et al 1996).

Thus, more rigorous epidemiological studies on the association between substance abuse or dependence and suicidal behaviour are clearly needed. However, the effects of treatment of substance-abusing or dependent patients on the occurrence of suicidal behaviour are poorly understood. Suicide in individuals with psychoactive substance-abuse disorder is associated with the negative consequences of the abuse, so that it can be expected that the cessation of abuse is an important issue in the prevention of suicide (Murphy, 2000). The efficacy of current approaches to obtain such a cessation is, however, still a matter of debate. In view of the common co-morbid presence of other psychiatric disorders such as affective disorder (see p. 267), treatment of such co-morbid disorders can also be expected to contribute to the prevention of suicidal behaviour.

Psychiatric co-morbidity

Finally, while psychological-autopsy studies indicate that co-morbidity of psychiatric disorders is common among people who commit suicide (see Chapter 6), little is known about effective pharmacological treatment of these conditions aiming at the prevention of suicidal behaviour. General-population studies indicate that co-morbidity of the disorders that are commonly associated with suicidal behaviour, and which were described on pp. 262–267, is common. For example, the Epidemiological Catchment Area study showed odds ratios of 4.0 and 7.9 for co-morbid substance abuse among people with schizophrenia and bipolar affective disorder, respectively (Regier et al, 1990). Individuals suffering from the co-morbid presence of psychiatric disorders are more commonly male, of younger age and at higher risk of homelessness (Drake and Wallach, 1989). They tend to be hospitalized more often, and to have poorer compliance with treatment while living in the community. They are more likely to be violent than if they suffered from a single mental illness (Swanson et al, 1990; Bartels et al, 1993). Johnson (1997) suggested that these individuals constitute a high-risk group of patients who frequently fail to meet the requirements of either a general or a specialized addiction service. Many general units do not deal with people who are intoxicated and many specialist units may feel unskilled in the management of psychosis. Drake and Wallach (1989) have indicated that the path to successful outcome is one that achieves engagement of the patient in the setting in which they live. Johnson (1997) suggested that perhaps a way forward for service planners would be to include a specialist nurse in this type of co-morbidity as an integrated member of the community team.

PSYCHOPHARMACOLOGY AND THE SUICIDAL PROCESS: THE FUTURE

As one facet of a multi-dimensional approach, developments in psychopharmacology have made a significant contribution to the challenge of more efficacious management of the processes underlying suicidal behaviour. This chapter described the current state of our knowledge of the effects of neurochemicals on impulsivity or restraint, mood regulation and suicidal behaviour. Further elucidation of the brain mechanisms involved in the threshold for suicidal behaviour should lead to more specific pharmacological therapies in the future, and offer the potential to tailor more specific anti-suicide pharmacological therapies for high-risk populations. This needs to be coupled with clinical and public-health strategies for earlier recognition of high-risk groups, aiming at, among others, a reduction in current barriers to early treatment.

There has been a disappointing lack of studies examining clinical-intervention strategies for suicidal behaviour, as was recently concluded on the basis of a systematic review of treatment studies of suicide attempters (Hawton et al, 1998; see also Chapter 11). In other branches of medicine and surgery, such as cardiology and cancerology, large treatment trials have been conducted in which thousands of patients were enrolled and followed up for years following a particular clinical intervention. It is a failure of modern psychiatry that clinical-intervention studies in suicidal patients are either small or non-existent and for the most part uninformative. It is difficult to understand that, although modern antidepressant treatment, and psychopharmacotherapy in general, have been available for 30 years, no study has been conducted which is sufficiently large in scale, comprehensive in nature, or prospective and randomized in design, to examine the efficacy of modern antidepressant or antipsychotic treatment in modifying suicidal acts including suicide. Indeed, suicidal patients are routinely excluded from treatment trials. Therefore clinicians hardly have evidence-based guidelines for the pharmacological treatment of suicidal patients. This needs to be rectified as a matter of the utmost urgency in modern psychiatric research. There is an urgent need for collaborative standardized studies, which include the recruitment and follow-up of numbers of patients that are sufficiently large to have the statistical power needed to detect treatment differences. The results of these studies will provide guidelines for clinical practice in the treatment and prevention of suicidal behaviour.

REFERENCES

Appleby, L. (1992) Suicide in psychiatric patients: risk and prevention. *British Journal of Psychiatry*, **161**: 749–758.

Arango, V., Underwood, M.D. and Mann, J.J. (1996) Fewer pigmented locus coerulus neurones in suicide victims. *Biological Psychiatry*, **39**: 112–120.

Audenaert, K., Van Laere, K., Dumont, F., Slegers, G., Mertens, J., Van Heeringen, C. and Dierckx, R.A. (2001) Decreased frontal serotonin 5-HT$_{2a}$ receptor binding potential in deliberate self harm patients. *European Journal of Nuclear Medicine*, **28**: 175–182.

Avery, D. and Winokur, G. (1972) Suicide, attempted suicide, and relapse rates in depression: occurrence after ECT and antidepressant therapy. *Archives of General Psychiatry*, **35**: 749–753.

Baldwin, D., Bullock, T., Montegomery, D. and Montgomery, S.A. (1991) Serotonin reuptake inhibitors, Tricyclic antidepressants and suicidal behaviour. *International Journal of Clinical Psychopharmacology*, **6**: 49–56.

Barber, M., Marzuk, P.M., Leon, A.C. and Portera, L. (1998) Aborted suicide attempts: A new classification of suicidal behaviour. *American Journal of Psychiatry*, **155**: 385–389.

Bartels, S.J., Teague, J.B., Drake, R.E., Clark, R.E., Bush, P.W. and Noordsy, D.L. (1993) Service utilisation and costs associated with substance use disorder among severely mentally ill patients. *Journal of Nervous and Mental Disease*, **181**: 227–232.

Brodsky, B.S., Malone, K.M., Ellis, S.P., Dulit, R.A. and Mann, J.J. (1997) Characteristics of borderline personality disorder associated with suicidal behavior. *American Journal of Psychiatry*, **154**: 1715–1719.

Coccaro, E.F. and Kavoussi, R.J. (1997) Fluoxetine and impulsive aggressive behavior in personality-disordered patients. *Archives of General Psychiatry*, **54**: 1081–1088.

Cookson, J. (1997) Lithium: balancing the risks and benefits. *British Journal of Psychiatry*, **171**: 120–124.

Corbitt, E.M., Malone, K.M., Haas, G.L. and Mann, J.J. (1996) Suicidal behaviour in patients with major depression and comorbid personality disorders. *Journal of Affective Disorders*, **39**: 61–72.

Cowdry, R.W. and Gardner, D.L. (1988) Pharmacotherapy of borderline personality disorder: alprazolam, carbemazepine, trifluoperazine and tranylcypromine. *Archives of General Psychiatry*, **45**: 111–119.

Dasgupta, K. (1990) Additional cases of suicidal ideation associated with fluoxetine. *American Journal of Psychiatry*, **147**: 207–210.

Deykin, E.Y. and Buba, S.L. (1994) Suicidal ideation and attempts among chemically dependant adolescents. *American Journal of Public Health*, **84**: 634–639.

Drake, S., Ross, J. and Hall, W. (1996) Overdose among heroin users in Sydney, Australia: 2. responses to overdose. *Addiction*, **91**: 413–417.

Drake, R.E. and Wallach, M.A. (1989) Substance abuse among the chronically mentally ill. *Hospital and Community Psychiatry*, **40**: 1041–1046.

Flood, R.A. and Seager, C.P. (1968) A retrospective examination of psychiatric case records of patients who subsequently committed suicide. *British Journal of Psychiatry*, **114**: 443–450.

Gardner, D.L. and Cowdry, R.W. (1986) Positive effects of carbemazepine on behavioral dyscontrol in borderline personality disorder. *American Journal of Psychiatry*, **143**: 519–522.

Goetzl, V. (1977) Lithium carbonate in the management of hyperactive aggressive behaviour of the mentally retarded. *Comprehensive Psychiatry*, **18**: 509–606.

Gonella, G., Baignoli, G. and Eccri, U. (1990) Fluvoxamine and imipramine in the treatment of depressive patients: A double blind controlled study. *Current Medical Research Opinions*, **12**: 177–184.

Goodwin, F.K. and Jamison, K.R. (1990) *Manic-Depressive Illness*. New York, Oxford University Press.

Hawton, K., Fagg, J., Platt, S. and Hawkins, M. (1993) Factors associated with suicide after parasuicide in young people. *British Medical Journal*, **306**: 1641–1644.

Hawton, K., Arensman, E., Townsend, E., Bremner, S., Feldman, E., Goldney, R., Gunnell, D., Hazell, P., Van Heeringen, K., House, A., Owens, D., Sakinofsky, I. and Träskman-Bendz, L. (1998) Deliberate self harm: systematic review of efficacy of psychosocial and pharmacological treatments in preventing repetition. *British Medical Journal*, **317**: 441–447.

Hoover, C.E. (1991) Additional cases of suicidal ideation associated with fluoxetine. (letter) *American Journal of Psychiatry*, **147**: 1570–1571.

Isometsä, E.T. and Lönnqvist, J.K. (1998) Suicide attempts preceding completed suicide. *British Journal of Psychiatry*, **173**: 531–535.

Jamison, K.R. (1986) Suicide and bipolar disorders. *Annals of the New York Academy of Science*, **487**: 301–315.

Johnson, S. (1997) Dual diagnosis of severe mental illness and substance misuse: a case for specialist services? *British Journal of Psychiatry*, **171**: 205–208.

Kavoussi, R.J., Liu, J. and Coccaro, E.F. (1994) An open trial of sertraline in personality disordered patients with impulsive aggression. *Journal of Clinical Psychiatry*, **55**: 137–141.

Kutcher, S., Papatheodorou, G., Reiter, S. and Gardner, D. (1995) The successful pharmacological treatment of adolescents annd young adults with borderline personality disorder: a preliminary open rial of flupentixol. *Journal of Psychiatry and Neuroscience*, **20**: 113–118.

Lewis, G. and Appleby, L. (1988) Personality disorders: the patients psychiatrists dislike. *British Journal of Psychiatry*, **153**: 44–49

Links, P.S., Steiner, M., Boiago, I. and Irwin, D. (1990) Lithium therapy for borderline patients: preliminary findings. *Journal of Personality Disorder*, **4**: 173–181.

Lönnqvist, J. (2000) Psychiatric aspects of suicidal behaviour: depression. In K. Hawton and K. Van Heeringen (Eds), *The International Handbook of Suicide and Attempted Suicide*. Chichester, Wiley.

Malone, K.M., Corbitt, E.M., Li, S. and Mann, J.J. (1996) Prolactin response to fenfluramine and suicide attempt lethality in major depression. *British Journal of Psychiatry*, **168**: 324–329.

Malone, K.M., Haas, G.L., Sweeney, J.A. and Mann, J.J. (1995) Major depression and the risk of attempted suicide. *Journal of Affective Disorders*, **34**: 173–185.

Malone, K.M., Szanto, K., Corbitt, E.M. and Mann, J.J. (1995) Clinical assessment versus research method in the assessment of suicidal behavior. *American Journal of Psychiatry*, **152**: 1601–1607.

Mann, J.J., McBride, P.A., Brown, R.P., Linnoila, M., Leon, A.C., DeMeo, M., Mieczkowski, T., Myers, J.E. and Stanley, M. (1992) Relationship between central and peripheral serotonin indexes in depressed and suicidal psychiatric inpatients. *Archives of General Psychiatry*, **49**: 442–446.

Mann, J.J., Goodwin, F.K., O'Brien, C.P. and Robinson, D.S. (1993) Suicidal behavior and psychotropic medication. *Neuropsychopharmacology*, **2**: 177–183.

Mann, J.J., Underwood, M.D. and Arango, V. (1996) Post-mortem studies of suicide victims. In S.J. Watson (Ed.), *Biology of Schizophrenia and Affective Disease*. Washington, DC, American Psychiatric Press.

Mann, J.J. and Malone, K.M. (1997) Cerebrospinal fluid amines and higher-lethality suicide attempts in depressed inpatients. *Biological Psychiatry*, **41**: 162–171.

Mann, J.J., Malone, K.M., Diehl, D.J., Perel, J., Cooper, T.B. and Mintun, M.A. (1997) Demonstration in vivo of reduced serotomin responsivity in the brain of untreated depressed patients. *American Journal of Psychiatry*, **153**: 174–182.

Mann, J.J., Waternaux, C., Haas, G.L. and Malone, K.M. (1999) Toward a clinical model of suicidal behavior in psychiatric patients. *American Journal of Psychiatry*, **156**: 181–189.

Markovitz, P.J., Calabrese, J.R., Schultz, S.C. and Meltzer, H.Y. (1991) Fluoxetine in the treatment of borderline and schizotypical personality disorders. *American Journal of Psychiatry*, **148**: 1064–1067.

Masand, P., Gupta, S. and Damon, M. (1991) Suicidal ideation related to fluoxetine treatment. *New England Journal of Medicine*, **324**: 420.

McElroy, S.L. et al. (1987) Sodium valproate: its use in primary psychiatric disorders. *Journal of Clinical Psychopharmacoogy*, **7**: 16–24.

Montgomery, S.A., McAuley, R., Rani, S.J., Roy, D. and Montgomery, D. (1981) A double-blind comparison of zimeldine and amitriptyline in endogenous depression. *Acta Psychiatrica Scandinavica*, **290**: 314–327.

Montgomery, S.A. and Montgomery, D. (1982) Pharmacological prevention of suicidal behaviour. *Journal of Affective Disorders*, **4**: 291–298.

Morgan, H.G. and Priest, P. (1984) Assessment of suicide risk in psychiatric inpatients. *British Journal of Psychiatry*, **145**: 467–469.

Morgan, H.G. and Priest, P. (1991) Suicide and other unexpected deaths among psychiatric inpatients. The Bristol Confidential Inquiry. *British Journal of Psychiatry*, **158**: 368–374.

Müller-Oerlinghausen, B., Müser-Causemann, B. and Volk, J. (1992) Suicides and parasuicides in a high-risk patient group on and off lithium long-term medication. *Journal of Affective Disorders*, **25**: 261–270.

Mullin, J.M., Pandita-Gunawardena, V.R. and Whitehead, A.M. (1988) A double blind comparison of fluvoxamine and dotheipin in the treatment of major affective disorder. *British Journal of Clinical Practice*, **42**: 51–55.

Murphy, G.E. (2000) Psychiatric aspects of suicidal behaviour: substance abuse. In K. Hawton and K. Van Heeringen (Eds), *The International Handbook of Suicide and Attempted Suicide*. Chichester, Wiley.

Nathan, R.S., Perel, J.M., Pollock, B.G. and Kupfer, D.J. (1990) The role of neuro-pharmacologic selectivity in antidepressant action: fluvoxamine versus desipramine. *Journal of Clinical Psychiatry*, **51**: 367–372.

Neeleman, J. and Farrell, M. (1997) Suicide and substance misuse. *British Journal of Psychiatry*, **171**: 303–304.

Neeleman, J. and Wessely, S. (1997) Changes in classification of suicide in England and Wales: time trends and associations with coroners professional backgrounds. *Psychological Medicine*, **27**: 467–472.

Norden, M.J. (1989) Fluoxetine in borderline personality disorder. *Progress in Neuropsychopharmacology and Biological Psychiatry*, **13**: 885–893.

Nordström, P., Samuelsson, M., Åsberg, M., Träskman-Bendz, L., Aberg-Wistedt, A., Nordin, C. and Bertilsson, L. (1994) CSF 5-HIAA predicts suicide risk after attempted suicide. *Suicide and Life-Threatening Behavior*, **24**: 1–9.

Oquendo, M.A., Malone, K.M., Ellis, S.P., Sackeim, H.A. and Mann, J.J. (1999) Inadequacy of antidepressant treatment for patients with major depression who are at risk of suicidal behavior. *American Journal of Psychiatry*, **156**: 190–194.

Perez, A. and Ashford, J.J. (1990) A double blind randomised comparison of fluvoxamine with mianserin in depressive illness. *Current Medical Research Opinions*, **12**: 234–241.

Pirkis, J. and Burgess, P. (1998) Suicide and recency of the health care contacts: a systematic review. *British Journal of Psychiatry*, **173**: 462–474.

Regier, D. A., Farmer, M.E., Rae, D.S., Locke, B.Z., Keith, S.J., Judd, L.L. and Goodwin, F.K. (1990) Comorbidity of mental disorders with alcohol and other substances: results from the Epidemiological Catchment Area. *Journal of the American Medical Association*, **164**: 2511–2518.

Rihmer, Z. (1995) Studies of suicide and suicidal behaviour in Hungary. *Homeostasis*, **36**: 35.

Rouillon, F., Phillips, R., Serrurier, D., Ansart, E. and Gerard, M.J. (1989) Rechutes de depression unipolaire et efficacité de la maprotiline. *L'Encephale*, **15**: 527–534.

Roy, A. (1982) Risk factors for suicide in psychiatric patients. *Archives of General Psychiatry*, **39**: 1089–1095.

Salzman, C., Schatzberg, A.F. and Miyawaki, E. (1992) Fluoxetine in borderline personality disorder. Presented at *145th Annual Meeting of the American Psychiatric Association*, Washington, DC, American Psychiatric Association.

Serban, G. and Siegal, S. (1984) Response of borderline and schizotypal patients to small doses of thiothixene and haloperidol. *American Journal of Psychiatry*, **141**: 1455–1458.

Shaffer, D., Gould, M.S., Fisher, P., Trautman, P., Moreau, D., Kleinman, M. and Flory, M. (1996) Psychiatric diagnosis in child and adolescent suicide. *Archives of General Psychiatry*, **53**: 339–348.

Soloff, P.H., Cornelius, J., George, A., Nathan, S., Perel, J.M. and Ulrich, R.F. (1993) Efficacy of phenelzine and haloperidol in borderline personality disorder. *Archives of General Psychiatry*, **50**: 377–385.

Stone, M. (1990) *The Fate of Borderline Patients*. New York, Guilford Press.

Swanson, J., Holzer, C. and Ganju, V. (1990) Violence and psychiatric disorder in the community: evidence from the Epidemiological Catchment Area survey. *Hospital and Community Psychiatry*, **41**: 761–770.

Teicher, M.H., Slod, C. and Cole, J.O. (1990) Emergence of intense suicidal preoccupation during fluoxetine treatment. *American Journal of Psychiatry*, **147**: 207–210.

Thies-Flechtner, K., Müller-Oerlinghausen, B., Seibert, W., Walther, A. and Greil, W. (1996) Effect of prophylactic treatment on suicide risk in patients with major affective disorders. *Pharmacopsychiatry*, **29**: 103–107.

Van Heeringen, C., Audenaert, K., Van Laere, K., Dumont, F., Slegers, G., Mertens, J. and Dierckx, R.A. (submitted) Prefrontal 5-HT$_{2a}$ receptor binding potential, hopelessness and personality characteristics in attempted suicide.

Verkes, R.J. and Van der Mast, R.C., Hengeveld, M.W., Tuyl, J.P., Zwinderman, A.H., Van Kempen, G.M. (1998) Reduction by paroxetine of suicidal behavior in patients with repeated suicide attempts but not major depression. *American Journal of Psychiatry*, **155**: 543–547.

Verkes, R.J. and Cowen, P.J. (2000) Pharmacotherapy of suicidal ideation and behaviour. In K. Hawton and K. Van Heeringen (Eds), *The International Handbook of Suicide and Attempted Suicide*. Chichester, Wiley.

Wilcox, J.A. (1995) Divalproex sodium as a treatment for borderline personality disorder. *Annals of Clinical Psychiatry*, **7**: 33–37.

Chapter 14

PSYCHOTHERAPEUTIC IMPLICATIONS OF THE SUICIDAL PROCESS APPROACH

Ineke Kienhorst and Kees van Heeringen

INTRODUCTION

While a vast amount of scientific literature is available concerning either suicidal behaviour or psychotherapy, far less information is available regarding the combined topic—psychotherapy and suicidal behaviour. This discrepancy is even more marked with regard to scientific information concerning the efficacy of the psychotherapeutic treatment of suicidal persons. This can be illustrated by means of a literature search (e.g. using PsycLit or Medline). A PsycLit search covering the period between 1993 and 1998 using "suicid*" and "psychotherapy" resulted in 3974 and 10 595 titles, respectively. The combination of both terms revealed only 269 titles. A search using Medline revealed a similar pattern.

In addition to the limited amount of information, the use of divergent definitions in scientific studies of the psychotherapy of suicidal persons poses substantial problems. This applies not only to what is meant by "suicidal", but also to the word "psychotherapy". This term is sometimes used to describe a complete therapeutic system, while in other studies the term may refer only to a particular technique. The interpretation of the results of studies in which no detailed descriptions of

Understanding Suicidal Behaviour. Edited by Kees van Heeringen
© 2001 John Wiley & Sons Ltd.

experimental treatments or control conditions are given can thus be difficult or even impossible.

With regard to the treatment of patients, Linehan (1997) has pointed out that "all treatment interventions attempt to change or improve the factors presumed to underlie or control the problem behaviours or symptoms of the patient". She makes a difference between two basic strategies for treating suicidal behaviour (i.e. indirect and direct strategies). The first strategy is based on the assumption that suicidal behaviour is a symptom of some underlying disorder, and that the treatment of the disorder will thus reduce suicidal behaviour. In this way reduction of suicidality is an *indirect* benefit of the therapy aimed at the disorder. She claims that this approach is the model underlying most psychodynamic and biological approaches. The second strategy aims at a direct reduction of suicidal behaviour as an explicit goal of the treatment and the target of the intervention. The underlying assumption is that suicidal behaviour can be reduced independently of other disorders. According to Linehan (1997), this second strategy is favoured by crisis interventionists and particularly used in behavioural approaches.

This chapter provides a "state of affairs" with regard to the role of psychotherapy in the treatment and prevention of suicidal behaviour. As an introduction, however, two related but different forms of treatment of suicidality will be discussed (i.e. psychotherapy and crisis intervention). In addition, psychotherapeutic views and treatments of suicidal behaviour will be reviewed. The efficacy of psychotherapies using direct and indirect approaches to suicidal behaviour will be examined. The indirect strategy will be addressed in more detail by describing psychotherapeutic approaches to the treatment of two psychiatric problems which are commonly associated with suicidal behaviour. These include an axis-I disorder (i.e. depression) and an axis-II disorder (namely borderline personality disorder). Finally, conclusions and recommendations will be offered.

SIMILARITIES AND DIFFERENCES REGARDING CRISIS INTERVENTION AND PSYCHOTHERAPY

Psychotherapy is defined by Strupp (1978) as "an interpersonal process designed to bring about modifications of feelings, cognitions, attitudes and behaviours which has proved troublesome to the person seeking help from a trained professional". According to this definition, crisis intervention can be considered as a form of psychotherapy. However, crisis intervention is a psychosocial treatment, which is used only in very specific circumstances and employing very specific and direct techniques. By definition, crisis intervention is applied only during an emotionally overwhelming situation induced by internal or external stressors, which cannot be managed by the usual coping mechanisms of the person (Caplan, 1964). As pointed out by Parad and Parad (1990), crisis intervention in general is a process to alleviate the impact of the stressful event by immediate emotional and environmental first aid. Moreover, crisis intervention aims at strengthening the person in his or her coping and integrative struggles by means of immediate clarification and guidance during the crisis period.

A suicidal crisis is similar to a non-suicidal crisis with regard to most characteristics, but it differs in one aspect. In contrast to a person in a non-suicidal crisis, the person in a suicidal crisis conceptualizes a solution to the problematic and painful situation (Kienhorst, 1995). This solution is to attempt or commit suicide. If the probability of such behaviour is high, the crisis will turn into an emergency, which demands immediate intervention aimed at decreasing the suicide risk. Leenaars (1994) describes this immediate intervention as "keeping the person alive . . . by lowering lethality".

Consequently, in crisis intervention the direct aim is *reducing the immediate suicidal threat*. Psychotherapy *seeks to prevent the occurrence of a suicidal crisis* and should therefore be aimed at the patient's *tendency* to react with suicidal behaviour. In other words, if a suicidal crisis is compared with a fire, crisis intervention is aimed at fighting the fire, while psychotherapy tries to prevent the occurrence of the fire.

A distinction between chronic and acute styles of suicidal behaviour has been made (Kernberg, 1994; Lester, 1994). According to this distinction, acute states will be treated using crisis-intervention techniques, while chronic states will be approached with psychotherapeutic strategies. Rudestam (1985, 1986) observed that a crisis-oriented approach is rarely useful for chronically suicidal patients. One may agree with this view, but something needs to be added. Psychotherapeutic treatment should be offered after reduction of a suicidal crisis, even in non-chronically suicidal persons, because a suicidal person apparently has *propensity to react* with suicidal behaviour, and may do so in the future as well. This inclination has not been the main target of crisis intervention, and is left untreated as such. Psychotherapy will be the appropriate-treatment approach to this propensity.

PSYCHOTHERAPEUTIC VIEWS OF SUICIDAL BEHAVIOUR

Applicability of the main psychotherapeutic systems to suicidal patients has scarcely been described. Exceptions include Lester (1994), and, with regard to specific age groups, Berman and Jobes (1994) and Richman (1994) who address adolescents and older adults, respectively.

This section addresses two major psychotherapeutic-treatment approaches to suicidal behaviour (i.e. psychoanalysis and cognitive behaviour therapy). Two examples of cognitive behaviour treatments will be discussed in more detail (i.e. dialectical behaviour therapy and mindfulness-based cognitive therapy). However, these latter treatment approaches cannot be regarded as general psychotherapeutic systems, as they were developed for the treatment of a particular group of patients (i.e. females with a borderline personality disorder) and a particular cognitive characteristic, respectively.

Psychoanalysis

Freud's major hypothesis concerning suicide can be regarded as an extension of his theory of depression. When a person loses someone whom he has ambivalently loved and hated, and introjects that person, aggression is directed towards himself. If these feelings are strong enough, he or she will commit suicide (Davison and Neale, 1996). Following Freud, Menninger (1938) thought that suicide represented the translation of a wish to kill, a wish to be killed and a wish to die. Other psychoanalytical concepts view suicide as an attempt to punish specific external forces or objects.

What has psychoanalysis to offer to suicidal patients? Lester (1994) has stated that a possible goal of the psychoanalytical treatment of a suicidal patient is to make conscious to the patient what is unconscious. He observes that this may not be an easy process, which may produce anxiety, even to the point of panic. To avoid this panic, increasing the client's awareness must be achieved slowly and carefully. His conclusion is that, since psychoanalysis is a slow process, documenting the use of its techniques for dealing with suicidal persons is difficult.

Additionally, Roth and Fonagy (1996) noted that "classical psychoanalysis is not aimed at removing single symptoms or problem behaviours, but at attempting to restructure the entire personality". More recent dynamic approaches focus on the provision of conscious understanding. This is achieved primarily by interpretation of the patient's verbalizations and behaviour during sessions (Roth and Fonagy, 1996). Based on their review of psychotherapy research, Roth and Fonagy (1996) conclude that psychodynamic psychotherapy, although still not proven to be effective, is promising in the treatment of depression and personality disorders. Whether and how it affects suicidal behaviour is still unknown.

Cognitive behaviour therapy

Cognitive behaviour therapy shares with psychodynamic approaches the assumption of irrational cognitive processes. However, Roth and Fonagy (1996) point out that "within cognitive therapy, cognitions are seen as having been learned and maintained through reinforcement. Challenges to these assumptions may therefore be made directly rather than via unconscious determinants as implied by dynamic theory".

Cognitive theory states that negative emotions and behaviours do not result from unpleasant events, but from irrational evaluations of these events. Ellis (1962, 1996) and Beck (1976) have formulated a system of cognitive therapy. Although there are reasons to consider the therapy of Ellis as more profound, both have the same main goal (i.e. to replace irrational ways of thinking by more rational ways in order to change negative emotions and dysfunctional behaviours). This is done by disputing irrational ideas and to replace them with rational ones.

Based on their overview of the main findings of cognitive psychological research on suicidal behaviour Williams and Pollock concluded in Chapter 5 that relevant psychological mechanisms involve attention, memory and judgement. In short, these mechanisms are reflected by a hypersensitivity to stimuli signalling defeat or rejection, overgeneral memories that prevent solutions for current problems and a lack of fluency in generating positive events leading to hopelessness. Overgeneral memory may be particularly important in the context of this chapter, as this dysfunctional cognitive style can be changed by a specific treatment, as will be discussed below. Hypersensitivity to affectively toned aspects of events (positive and negative), whether present as an aspect of temperamental style (see Chapter 8) or because of negative experiences, gives rise to a tendency to encode specific aspects of the environment in terms of their more general schematic aspects. This leads to a habitual use of encoding and retrieval strategies in which more general aspects of events are represented in memory, with poorer strategic access to specific episodic exemplars. This style affects the processing of further events (positive, negative or neutral), but has particular implications for the satisfactory emotional processing of any new negative event that occurs. The retrieval of specific aspects of events may thus become effortful and unsatisfactory, leading to attempts to avoid specific retrieval. Evidence accumulates indicating that patients, who have difficulty in specific retrieval, experience interpersonal problem-solving deficits (Williams et al, 2000). As was discussed in Chapter 8, such deficits may play a crucial role in the development of suicidal behaviour.

In case of suicidal persons, Weishaar (1996) assumes that cognitive characteristics such as hopelessness, dichotomous thinking and problem-solving deficits, may play a role as acute and chronic risk factors in the development of suicidal behaviour. She is not the only author who considers the recognition of cognitive organization of self-destructive people as a critical variable in suicidal behaviour (Weishaar and Beck, 1990; Schmidtke and Schaller, 1992).

In their review of the literature on cognitive styles and suicidal behaviour, Diekstra and colleagues (1995) noted that according to some authors (e.g. Neuringer and Lettieri, 1982; Weishaar and Beck, 1990) research has convincingly shown that, when compared with non-suicidal persons, suicidal individuals have impoverished internal-judgement processes, a stronger tendency towards polarized (dichotomous) thinking, are more rigid and constricted in their thinking and have poorer problem-solving capacities. Finally, they are more present oriented and have an impaired ability to project themselves into the future. However, based on their review Diekstra and colleagues (1995) stated that "several reasons exist to hesitate before drawing conclusions. Most of the suicidal subjects were patients tested at some time soon after the suicidal act. The question is whether the observed patterns of thought that are assumed to be characteristic of suicidal patients are indeed associated with a tendency to suicide rather than with the high level of stress during the period following a suicidal act. In other words, these patterns of thought might be shared with persons under high levels of stress in general, instead of being specific to persons with a tendency to suicide". Reasons for a cautious interpretation are found in the discrepancy of findings, which may be illustrated by two examples. Based on a daily follow-up of individuals at high risk, medium risk, low risk and absent risk of suicide following a suicidal crisis during a period of 3 weeks, Neuringer and Lettieri (1982) reported that high-risk suicidal subjects were far more extreme in their polarized thinking than the others. Moreover, this extreme dichotomous thinking did not diminish over time. Neuringer and Lettieri (1982) thus concluded that extreme polarization of thinking found in suicidal individuals is not a temporary state induced by stress, but a dispositional or trait characteristic. On the other hand, Schmidtke and

Schaller (1992) compared cognitive characteristics of individuals following a suicide attempt with those of non-suicidal psychiatric patients and normal controls, and found that cognitive rigidity was a common feature of persons in a crisis and in a depressive state. This finding led them to conclude that dichotomous thinking probably is a state-dependent rather than a trait-like characteristic.

However, Williams's review (1996) of research on overgeneral memory, a core cognitive characteristic in association with suicidal behaviour as described above, suggests that such a memory style starts early in development and can thus be regarded as a trait marker of vulnerability.

Thus, while some issues regarding their trait- or state-dependent nature need to be resolved, there is no doubt that suicidal behaviour is associated with particular cognitive characteristics. Cognitive therapy with suicidal persons generally focuses on their tendency to evaluate events, the presence and the future in such a way that this results in feelings of being entrapped (based on deficient problem-solving skills) and in hopelessness (because of a lack of fluency in generating positive future events). In the following, two examples of cognitive therapy-based psychotherapeutic approaches will be described, which can be applied in the treatment of suicidal individuals (i.e. dialectical behaviour therapy and mindfulness-based cognitive therapy). As described by Hawton in Chapter 11, studies in several patient samples have shown a significant positive effect of dialectical behaviour therapy on rates of repetition of attempted suicide. Mindfulness-based cognitive therapy will be described, first, because it targets a core trait-dependent characteristic of suicidal behaviour (i.e. overgeneral memory), and, second, because its efficacy was recently demonstrated in formerly depressed patients (Williams et al, 2000).

Dialectical behaviour therapy

Dialectical behaviour therapy is a form of cognitive behaviour psychotherapy, which was developed by Linehan for the treatment of borderline personality disorder, including suicidal behaviour. The major premise is that "borderline personality disorder is primarily a dysfunction of the emotion regulation system, which results from biological irregularities combined with certain dysfunctional environments, as well as from their interaction and transaction over time" (Linehan, 1993). In general, borderline behaviours are considered as attempts by the individual to regulate intense affect or as outcomes of emotional dysregulation. On one hand, Linehan's treatment approach aims at increasing the tolerance for distress and at developing the resources for reducing the impact of stress. On the other hand, dialectical behaviour therapy aims at teaching affect regulation, self- and behaviour management, interpersonal problem-solving skills, and developing and maintaining social support.

Linehan perceives suicidal behaviour as the consequence of aversive affective states, which may be caused by negative environmental events, self-generated dysfunctional-behaviour patterns and deficiencies in both the tolerance for distress and the resources for reducing distress (Berman and Jobes, 1994). According to this line of reasoning, suicidal behaviour is explicitly regarded as a way of problem solving (Linehan, 1993). In dialectical behaviour therapy, several treatment modes can be offered to the patient concurrently. Such a mode may consist of weekly individual treatment sessions, in which the focus will primarily be on motivational issues and on the improvement of problem-solving skills. A second mode may consist of weekly group sessions of behavioural-skills training, according to a psycho-educational format. In addition to this multi-modal approach, dialectical behaviour therapy is divided in stages. In the first stage, a hierarchy of treatment goals is specified in which the reduction of suicidal behaviours is the first target. In this first stage, the focus will thus be on decreasing suicidal behaviours, and on behaviours which may interfere with therapy or with quality of life. Treatment aims at replacing these aversive behaviours by skilful interpersonal responses, adequate emotion-regulation responses, distress-tolerance responses and mindful behavioural responses (Linehan, 1993).

According to Linehan (1993), the first task of the therapist is to keep track of and focus treatment on the reduction of suicidal behaviours. The approach to these behaviours depends on their nature, as they may range from suicide-crisis behaviours, parasuicidal acts or intrusive suicidal urges, images and communications, to suicidal ideation, expectations and emotional responses. These behaviours are targeted immediately and discussed directly during treatment, except for those connected with suicidal ideation. Ideation is not addressed directly in the case of continuous, or "background", suicidal ideation. Such ongoing suicidal ideation is regarded as the consequence of a low quality of life, and treatment should thus focus on increasing this quality.

The effects of dialectical behaviour therapy on the occurrence of suicidal behaviour have been evaluated in several patient samples (for an overview see Heard, 2000). The evaluation showed, in general, significant positive effects on rates of repeated suicide attempts and on medical severity of repeated attempts.

Mindfulness-based cognitive therapy

This form of cognitive therapy was developed to treat one of the core dysfunctional cognitive characteristics associated with suicidal behaviour (see Chapter 5 and above) (i.e. overgeneral memory, Teasdale et al, 1995). The mindfulness technique aims at increasing patients' awareness of present, moment-to-moment experience. Patients receive extensive practice in learning to bring their attention back to the present, using a focus on the breath as an anchor, whenever they notice that attention has been diverted to streams of thoughts, worries or general lack of awareness. Mindfulness-based cognitive therapy combines this technique with some techniques drawn from cognitive therapy in a comprehensive treatment package specifically tailored to train patients in skills relevant to the prevention of depressive relapse (Williams et al, 2000). Its efficacy in changing overgeneral memory was recently demonstrated in a sample of formerly depressed patients. A potential effect in preventing the occurrence of suicidal behaviour remains to be shown.

DEPRESSION AND BORDERLINE PERSONALITY DISORDER IN RELATION TO SUICIDAL BEHAVIOUR

As stated above, the indirect treatment of suicidality is based on the assumption that treating the underlying mental disorder will lead to the reduction of suicidal behaviour. However, Linehan (1997) concludes in her review that indirect treatment of suicidal behaviour by treating depression with antidepressants has failed to show conclusively its effectiveness in reducing the occurrence of suicide or suicide attempts. This may also be the case for psychotherapeutic treatment of depression, as was noted by Kerkhof and Diekstra (1995). They concluded that psychotherapeutic treatment might reduce symptoms of depression, including suicidal ideation, but that it is not possible to state anything definite with regard to its effects on the incidence of suicide and suicide attempts.

At face value, these conclusions do not seem reasonable. In *DSM IV* suicidal behaviour is listed as a symptom of major depression

(American Psychiatric Association, 1994). From this point of view, it seems only logical that by treating depression the depressive symptoms will diminish, including suicidal behaviour. However, there is currently no research-based evidence for this assumption, which may be due to, among others, the fact that it might not be clear what the "underlying disorder" actually is.

It is obviously true that depression and suicidal behaviour are highly interrelated, but it is also true that not every depressed patient is suicidal. Moreover, all mental disorders are associated with an increased risk of suicidality, including schizophrenia and borderline personality disorder (in which suicidal behaviour is also one of the constituting symptoms). Additionally, co-morbidity, particularly affective disorder and conduct or substance-abuse disorder, will increase the occurrence of suicidal behaviours (see Chapter 7; Kovacs, 1993; Bronisch, 1996; Wagner et al, 1996). To complicate matters even more, evidence is accumulating which indicates that some symptoms of a specific disorder are more commonly associated with suicidal behaviour than others. Three studies have shown that some characteristics of depressed individuals who attempted or completed suicide differ from those of non-suicidal depressed persons. These characteristics included anhedonia and hopelessness in adolescents and adults, and insomnia in adults (Kienhorst et al, 1992; Wolfersdorf, 1995; Fawcett et al, 1987, 1990). In their study of the association between suicidal behaviour and characteristics of borderline personality disorder, Brodsky and colleagues (1997) found that, after controlling for lifetime diagnoses of depression and substance abuse, impulsivity was the only symptom of borderline personality disorder associated with a higher number of suicide attempts. These four studies suggest that not the disorder as a whole, but only particular symptoms of the disorders under study are associated with suicidal behaviour.

Thus, it seems justifiable to conclude that suicidal behaviour is not caused by one of the categorical DSM disorders. Nevertheless, the probability of occurrence will increase in the presence of a specific disorder. From this point of view, some questions are waiting to be answered. Is the development of suicidal behaviour mediated by a disorder, or does such behaviour develop independently from such a condition? Is it possible that both the disorder and the development of suicidal behaviour are expressions of a third, underlying and unknown state? Or is this all true at the same time? Considering our present understanding of the ontogenesis of suicidal behaviour these questions cannot be answered conclusively. The study of suicidal behaviour by different disciplines, including biological research (see Chapters 3 and 4), and an integration of the results (see Chapter 8) may provide more insight. We are currently left with hypotheses, including the hypothesis that different subgroups of suicidal persons exist, for which the pathway to suicidal behaviour is different. Based on their overview of epidemiological findings Kerkhof and Arensman indeed suggest in Chapter 2 that the suicidal process can become manifest in divergent ways.

CONCLUSIONS AND RECOMMENDATIONS

Considering that suicidal behaviour exists since manhood and psychotherapy only since the beginning of the previous century, the number of studies on the efficacy of psychotherapy to suicidal behaviour will hopefully increase. Two issues need, however, to be taken into account. First, as described by Hawton in more detail in Chapter 11, the study of the efficacy of treatment is not without a number of methodological problems. Second, the *efficacy* of a treatment is something other than its *clinical effectiveness*.

Roth and Fonagy (1996) have underlined the fact that, if a clear and specific intervention is evaluated, it may be unrepresentative of the quality of that intervention as it is generally offered in clinical practice. Moreover, patients are generally included in clinical trials according to their categorical DSM diagnosis. Although such classification systems have their merits in promoting comparative research, individuals hardly ever fit exactly in the proposed diagnostic categories. Tucker (1998) is thus more than probably right in stating that comparisons of two different groups of patients in the same diagnostic category or similar groups in different diagnostic categories may blur the outcomes of the efficacy studies.

With regard to the second issue, Roth and Fonagy (1996) have pointed out that efficacy is the result of a form of therapy in the setting of a research trial, while clinical effectiveness is the outcome of therapy in routine practice. Most psychotherapists have had the experience that clients became less suicidal during their treatment. Nevertheless, the problem in such cases is that it is hard to tell what actually produced the improvement. Was improvement due to the quality of the therapeutic relationship? Was it due to a spontaneous remission? Was the choice of a combination of techniques by the therapist responsible? Thus, if *clinical effectiveness* is achieved, it is hard to tell which component of the treatment was responsible for the improvement. It is thus not known if the treatment will be effective in the treatment of other patients.

The *indirect* treatment of suicidal persons, based on the assumption that suicidal behaviour will be reduced if the underlying disorder is treated, is not supported by research-based evidence. One reason for this is that it is far from clear what should be considered as the "underlying disorder". Moreover, suicidal behaviour may indeed be associated with particular disorders, but more so with particular symptoms, the occurrence of which may not be limited to these disorders. Strictly speaking, the assumption that treating the underlying disorder will lead to a reduction in suicidal behaviour is neither confirmed nor rejected by the arguments provided in this chapter. However, this might be due to the incapacity of research to prove the efficacy of indirect treatment of suicidal patients. More convincing evidence is available in support of the *direct* treatment of suicidal behaviour by means of cognitive behavioural therapy, but more research is clearly needed.

From a clinical perspective, the excitement of some therapists when they cry out, referring to *DSM* criteria: "finally I have found a pure borderline", suggests that the focus of attention is not on the patient, but on the fact that finally one of their numerous patients perfectly fits in the diagnostic system. Tucker (1998) warns that, by using the *DSM* system, clinicians are sometimes treating the diagnosis and not the patient, and that they are not looking at or studying the patient's phenomenology any more, but looking for the symptoms needed to make the diagnosis.

What can be learned from this? First of all we should try to understand why this specific person reacts with suicidal behaviour. A diagnosis of depression, borderline personality disorder or any other disorder will not provide the answer. As elegantly described by Michel and Valach in Chapter 12, the story which patients tell about themselves, their motives and their lives can give us clues as to why this individual reacts with suicidal tendencies. This suggests that we should look for those characteristics of the patient which in his or her specific case will facilitate suicidal behaviour. These characteristics may include poor problem-solving skills, unresolved traumatic experiences, recent losses, an aversive environment, cognitive rigidity, low frustration tolerance, physical diseases, a self-defeating reaction pattern, entrapment and/or impulsivity.

Fortunately, research provides us with many characteristics which discriminate between suicidal and non-suicidal people. It offers us clues about what therapists have to look for. However, when dealing in the therapy room with a suicidal individual, we never know which characteristic will apply to this specific patient. From this perspective, in spite of the diagnosis the patient has to live with, psychotherapeutic treatment may be different in every suicidal person, or at least in subgroups of suicidal patients.

Therapists thus have to rely on their clinical experience, on results of research about prediction of suicidal behaviour and, last but not least, on careful understanding of the reasons why this particular person engages in suicidal behaviour. Given the current scientific state of affairs, the integration of knowledge in these three areas will provide the information needed to influence suicidal tendencies by psychotherapy.

REFERENCES

Allard, R., Marshall, M. and Plante, M.C. (1992) Intensive follow-up does not decrease the risk of repeat suicide attempts. *Suicide and Life Threatening Behavior*, **22**: 303–314.

American Psychiatric Association (1994) *Diagnostic and Statistical Manual of Mental Disorders* (Fourth Edition). Washington, DC, American Psychiatric Association.

Beck, A.T. (1976) *Cognitive Therapy and the Emotional Disorders*. New York, International Universities Press.

Berman, A.L. and Jobes, D.A. (1994) Treatment of suicidal adolescents. In A.A. Leenaars, J.T. Maltsberger and R.A. Neimeyer (Eds.), *Treatment of Suicidal People*. Washington, Taylor & Francis.

Bronisch, T. (1996) The relationship between suicidality and depression. *Archives of Suicide Research*, **2**: 235–254.

Brodsky, B.S., Malone, K.M., Ellis, S.E., Dulit, R.A. and Mann, J.J. (1997) Characteristics of borderline personality disorder associated with suicidal behavior. *American Journal of Psychiatry*, **154**: 1715–1719.

Caplan, G. (1964) *Principles of Preventive Psychiatry*. New York, Basic Books.

Davison, G. and Neale, J.M. (1996) *Abnormal Psychology* (Sixth Revised Version). Chichester, Wiley.

Ellis, A. (1962) *Reason and Emotion in Psychotherapy*. New York, Lyle Stuart.

Ellis A. (1996) *Better, Deeper and More Enduring: Brief Therapy. The Rational Emotive Behavior Therapy Approach*. New York, Brunner/Mazel.

Diekstra, R.F.W., Kienhorst, C.W.M. and de Wilde, E.J. (1995) Suicide and suicidal behaviour among adolescents. In M. Rutter and D.J. Smith (Eds), *Psychosocial Disorders in Young People; Time Trends and Their Causes*. Chichester, Wiley.

Fawcett, J., Scheftner, W., Clark, D., Hedeker, D., Gibbson, R. and Coryell, W. (1987) Clinical predictors of suicide in patients with major affective disorders. A controlled prospective study. *American Journal of Psychiatry*, **144**: 35–40.

Fawcett, J., Scheftner, W., Fogg, L., Clark, D., Young, M.A., Hedeker, D. and Gibbson, R. (1990) Time-related predictors of suicide in patients with major affective disorder. *American Journal of Psychiatry*, **147**: 1189–1194.

Hawton, K., Brancroft, J., Catalan, J., Kingston, B., Stedeford, A. and Welch, N. (1981) Domiciliary and out-patient treatment of self-poisoning patients by medical and non-medical staff. *Psychological Medicine*, **11**: 169–177.

Hawton, K., Arensman, E., Townsend, E., Bremmer, S., Feldman, E., Goldney, R., Gunnel, D., Hazell, P., van Heeringen, K., House, A., Sakinofsky, I. and

Träskman-Bendz, L. (1998) Deliberate self-harm: A systematic review of the efficacy of psychosocial and pharmacological treatment in preventing repetition. *British Medical Journal*, **137**: 441–447.

Heard, H.L. (2000) Psychotherapeutic approaches to suicidal ideation and behaviour. In K. Hawton and K. van Heeringen (Eds), *The International Handbook of Suicide and Attempted Suicide*. Chichester, Wiley.

Kerkhof, A.J.F.M. and Diekstra, R.F.W. (1995) The prevention of suicidal behaviour. In R. Diekstra, W, Gulbinat, I. Kienhorst and D. de Leo (Eds), *Preventive Strategies on Suicide*. Leiden, E.J. Brill.

Kernberg, O.F. (1994) Psychological interventions for the suicidal adolescent. *American Journal of Psychotherapy*, **48**: 52–63.

Kienhorst, C.W.M., de Wilde, E.J., Diekstra, R.F.W. and Wolters, W.H.G. (1992) Differences between adolescent suicide attempters and depressed adolescents. *Acta Psychiatrica Scandinavica*, **85**: 222–228.

Kienhorst, C.W.M. (1995) Crisis intervention and a suicidal crisis in adolescents. *Crisis, The Journal of Crisis Intervention and Suicide Prevention*, **4**: 150–151.

Kovacs, M., Goldston, D. and Gatsonis, C. (1993) Suicidal behaviors and childhood onset depressive disorders: a longitudinal investigation. *Journal of the American Academy of Child and Adolescent Psychiatry*, **32**: 8–20.

Leenaars, A.A. (1994) Crisis intervention with highly lethal suicidal people. In A.A. Leenaars, J.T. Maltsberger and R.A. Neimeyer (Eds), *Treatment of Suicidal People*. Washington, DC, Taylor & Francis.

Lester, D. (1994) Psychotherapy for suicidal clients. In A.A. Leenaars, J.T. Maltsberger and R.A. Neimeyer (Eds), *Treatment of Suicidal People*. Washington, DC, Taylor & Francis.

Linehan, M. (1993) *Cognitive-Behavioral Treatment of Borderline Personality Disorder*. New York, Guilford Press.

Linehan, M., Heard, H.L. and Armstrong, H.E. (1993) Naturalistic follow-up of behavioral treatment for chronically parasuicidal borderline patients. *Archives of General Psychiatry*, **50**: 971–975.

Linehan, M. (1997) Behavioral treatments of suicidal behaviors. In D.M. Stoff and M.J. Mann (Eds), *The Neurobiology of Suicide*. New York, The New York Academy of Sciences.

Menninger, K.A. (1938) *Man Against Himself*. New York, Harcourt, Brace & Co., Inc.

Neuringer, C. and Lettieri, D. (1982) *Suicidal Woman. Their Thinking and Feeling Patterns*. New York, Gardner Press.

Parad, H.J. and Parad, L. (1990) *Crisis Intervention: Yesterday, Today and Tomorrow*. In N. Rao Punukollu (Ed.), *Recent Advances in Crisis Intervention*. Huddersfield: International Institute of Crisis Intervention and Community Psychiatry.

Richman, J. (1994) Psychotherapy with older adults. In A.A. Leenaars, J.T. Maltsberger and R.A. Neimeyer (Eds), *Treatment of Suicidal People*. Washington, DC, Taylor & Francis.

Roth, A. and Fonagy, P. (1996) *What Works for Whom? A Critical Review on Psychotherapy Research*. New York: Guilford Press.

Rudestam, K.E. (1985; 1986) Suicide and the selfless patient. *Emotional First Aid*, **3**: 5–8.

Tucker, G.J. (1998) Putting DSM-IV in perspective. *American Journal of Psychiatry*, **155**: 159–161.

Salkovskis, P.M., Atha, C. and Strorer, D. (1990) Cognitive-behavioural problem solving in the treatment of patients who repeatedly attempt suicide: A controlled trial. *British Journal of Psychiatry*, **157**: 871–876.

Schmidtke, A. and Schaller, S. (1992) Covariation of cognitive styles and mood factors during crisis. In P. Crepet, G. Ferrari, S. Platt and M. Bellini (Eds), *Suicidal Behaviour in Europe*. Rome, Libbey.

Strupp, H.H. (1978) Psychotherapy research and practice—an overview. In A.E. Bergin and S.L. Garfield (Eds), *Handbook of Psychotherapy and Behavior Change* (Second Edition). Chichester, Wiley.

Teasdale, J.D., Segal, Z.V. and Williams, J.M.G. (1995) How does cognitive therapy prevent depressive relapse and why should attentional control (mindfulness) training help? An information processing analysis. *Behaviour Research & Therapy*, **33**: 25–39.

Van Heeringen, C., Jannes, S., Buylaert, H., de Bacquer, D. and van Remoortel, J. (1995) The management of non-compliance with referral to out-patient aftercare among attempted suicide patients: a controlled intervention study. *Psychological Medicine*, **25**: 963–970.

Wagner, B.M., Cole, R.E. and Schwartzman, P. (1996) Comorbidity of symptoms among junior and senior highschool suicide attempters. *Suicide and Life-Threatening Behavior*, **26**: 300–307.

Weishaar, M.E. (1996) Cognitive risk factors in suicide. In P.M. Salkovskis (Ed.), *Frontiers of Cognitive Therapy*. New York, Guilford Press.

Weishaar, M.E. and Beck, A.T. (1990) Cognitive approaches to understanding and treating suicidal behavior. In S. Blumenthal and D. Kupfer (Eds), *Suicide over the Life Cycle*. Washington, DC, American Psychiatric Press.

Williams, J.M.G. (1996) Autobiographical memory in depression. In D. Rubin (Ed.), *Remembering Our Past: Studies in Autobiographical Memory*. Cambridge, Cambridge University Press.

Williams, J.M.G., Segal, Z.V., Teasdale, J.D. and Soulsby, J. (2000) Mindfulness-based cognitive therapy reduces overgeneral memory in formerly depressed patients. *Journal of Abnormal Psychology*, **109**: 150–155.

Wolfersdorf, M. (1995) Depression and suicidal behaviour. Psychopathological differences between suicidal and non-suicidal patients. *Archives of Suicide Research*, **1**: 273–288.

Chapter 15

THE PROCESS APPROACH TO SUICIDAL BEHAVIOUR: FUTURE DIRECTIONS IN RESEARCH, TREATMENT AND PREVENTION

Kees van Heeringen

INTRODUCTION

The chapters in Part II of this book have reviewed potential consequences of the process approach for the understanding, treatment and
prevention of suicidal behaviour. As may become clear from these
reviews, many questions still remain unanswered. In this chapter, implications of the psychobiological approach to the suicidal process will
be addressed in terms of future directions in research, treatment and
prevention. In particular, this chapter will address strategies for further
study of the mechanisms which may underlie many forms of suicidal
behaviour. It can be expected that knowledge of these mechanisms will
contribute to the development of new approaches to treatment and
prevention.

The description of these implications is based on the hypothetical
psychobiological stress–diathesis model, as elaborated in Chapter 8.
In short, according to this model the probability of occurrence of
suicidal behaviour is determined by the interaction between (particular)
stressful life events and a persistent predisposition or diathesis. This
diathesis is hypothesized to consist of at least two components, which

Understanding Suicidal Behaviour. Edited by Kees van Heeringen
© 2001 John Wiley & Sons Ltd.

were described as the "social-interaction component" and the "behavioural-inhibition component". This diathesis is not to be regarded as a stable characteristic, but rather as a dynamic organization of psychobiological mechanisms, which can be influenced by adverse circumstances but also by treatment. Several chapters in the second part of this book have described treatment approaches. This chapter will address potential developments in treatment based on the psychobiological process model of suicidal behaviour.

POTENTIAL DEVELOPMENTS IN TREATMENT

Gabbard (2000) has recently pointed at the unfortunate tendency towards dichotomization of psychiatric treatment, based on the poorly supported view that psychotherapy is a treatment for "psychologically based" disorders, while "biologically based" disorders should be treated with medication. The psychobiological model of suicidal behaviour as described in Chapter 8 is based on integration of biological and psychological approaches, which is consistent with the view that "mind" is an activity of the brain (Andreasen, 1997). The growing awareness that the brain possesses more plasticity than most of the other organs in the body allows us to begin to conceptualize a neurobiologically informed perspective on treatment that reflects the dynamic nature of the interaction between genes and environment (Gabbard, 2000). The psychobiological approach of the suicidal process model may have a number of important consequences for the treatment and prevention of suicidal behaviour. These relate to the three basic assumptions which underlie the model and which were described in Chapter 8 (i.e. the role of stressors in (particularly early phases of) the process, the interaction of these stressors with the diathesis and the changes in the diathesis over time). The psychobiological process approach implies, first, that the choice among psychotherapeutic and psychopharmacological treatment options may depend upon the phase of the process, and second, that psychological and biological strategies in the treatment and prevention should be combined as much as possible.

In several chapters in this book it has been argued that the study of suicidal behaviour needs to be separated from the study of associated psychiatric disorders. In a very similar way, it can be stated that the treatment of suicidal behaviour should be separated from that of associated psychiatric disorders such as depression, schizophrenia or substance-abuse disorder. While it can be assumed that adequate treatment of these disorders will contribute to the prevention of suicidal behaviour, the inclusion of trait-dependent characteristics related to the suicidal process indicates that additional targets for treatment can be described. The following sections will focus on such potential additional targets.

Stress-related aspects as a target of treatment

If findings from research on the evolving nature of mood disorders are indeed applicable to the suicidal process, psychotherapeutic and psychopharmacological treatments of early manifestations of this process will have to address the fact that stressors play a particularly crucial role in triggering (early manifestations of) the suicidal process, and that stressor-induced biochemical changes may have a detrimental effect on resilience to future stressors. In Chapter 4 Van Praag addressed the potential psychopharmacological implications for the prevention of suicidal behaviour, and concluded that there may well be a role for drugs which influence the (consequences of) hyperresponsivity of the hypothalamic–pituitary–adrenal axis. Anecdotal studies indeed suggest that interfering with steroid synthesis may have antidepressant properties (Deakin, 1996). The use of steroid-synthesis inhibitors and corticotropin-releasing hormone-receptor antagonists or steroid antagonists has been shown to have at least some efficacy in lowering depressive symptoms (Murphy, 1997; Zobel et al, 2000). Moreover, it was recently demonstrated that the serotonergic antidepressant fluoxetine reduces corticosterone concentrations in major depression (Ströhle et al, 2000). It has been hypothesized that chronic treatment with antidepressants may protect neurons in the hippocampus and prefrontal cortex from further damage or even reverse the atrophy and damage that has occurred (Duman et al, 1999). Much more work has to be done in order to assess to what extent such drugs have the potential to prevent the development of the suicidal process, as can be predicted from the psychobiological model as described in Chapter 8 of this book.

Early phases of the process may particularly be characterized by symptoms owing to a disturbed regulation of anxiety (see Chapters 4 and 8), and it thus follows that anxiolytics may have their place in treatment. However, clinical and research evidence suggests a detrimental effect of benzodiazepines on the recurrence of attempted suicide (e.g. see Verkes et al, 1998), but little is known about the neuropharmacological mechanisms involved. The GABA-stimulating effects of benzodiazepines may well be responsible for this effect, potentially by suppressing glutamate function and thus by interfering with memory processes and learning capacities. As described in Chapter 8, glutamate is involved in processing of sensory input and encoding of factual or autobiographical memory. The consequences of stress are probably mediated by down-regulation of the GABA system, allowing an excessive activation of the glutamate system that results in the laying down of autobiographical memory (Nutt, 2000). Taking benzodiazepines (or alcohol) at the moment of the occurrence of stressors may prevent the development of stressor-related emotional or behavioural problems, as suggested by the finding that intoxication with alcohol reduces the risk of developing post-traumatic stress disorder (McFarlane, 1998). However, administration of a benzodiazepine between 2 and 18 days after trauma has been shown to increase the likelihood of developing a post-traumatic-stress disorder (Gelpin et al, 1996), probably by interfering with cognitive processing. Benzodiazepines and alcohol thus may block curative processes and impair learning from new experiences, whether or not in therapeutic situations. These considerations, as far as they are applicable to the development of suicidal behaviour, add to the clinical evidence that the use of benzodiazepines in the treatment of attempted suicide patients should be avoided, probably even in the management of problems shortly after a precipitating stressful event.

With regard to psychotherapeutic treatments which focus on the role of stressors in the suicidal process, and more particularly in the early stages of the process, it has been suggested that psychodynamic therapy, which primarily uses limbic memory systems, is appropriate for early, stress-related dysphorias or initial episodes of major depression (see also below; Post, 1992). Cognitive, behavioural or interpersonal therapies may be more effective in patients with repeated episodes in which stressors may play a less outspoken role. Cognitive and behavioural therapies may deal with this developing automaticity by targeting habit or striatal memory systems (Post, 1992).

Diathesis as a target of treatment

The psychobiological process approach to suicidal behaviour (see Chapter 8) may guide the planning of treatment, suggesting the use of a combined psychotherapeutic and psychopharmacological approach. Preceding a discussion of the treatment options, which can be derived from this model, some general remarks can be made. From a psychotherapeutic point of view, insight learning, which is the mechanism involved in the process of maturation related to character development (see Chapters 5 and 8), may contribute to the control over temperament-driven reactions to environmental stimuli (e.g. including impulsive self-harming behaviour following exposure to (perceived) interpersonal problems). While this psychotherapeutic treatment approach may thus be useful in developing mastery over environmental stimuli by increasing self-directedness, medication can target temperament-related trait-dependent symptoms, aiming in a very similar way at reduction in reactivity to environmental stimuli. Although evidence is accumulating of a detrimental effect of certain drugs (e.g. benzodiazepines, see above) on learning, it is not yet clear if and to what extent drugs may enhance the capacity to learn (e.g. from psychotherapeutic treatment).

A dysfunction of the first component, which was called *the social-interaction component*, referring to the sensitivity or resilience to social stressors, may become manifest following confrontation with social (e.g. interpersonal) stressors as emotional turmoil, under the form of anxious or aggressive symptoms in early stages of the process and depressed mood in later stages, with suicidal ideation. From a neuro-biological point of view noradrenaline and the serotonin 5-HT_{1a} system appear to play a mediating role. Psychopharmacological studies have suggested a role of the noradrenergic system in the development of suicidal behaviour by showing an increased risk of attempted suicide in association with noradrenergic drugs (see also Chapter 13). It is, however, not yet clear in which way this system can be influenced in order to prevent the occurrence of suicidal ideation or behaviour (see also below for a discussion of strategies for further study of this issue). Van Praag discussed in Chapter 3 the potential benefits of drugs which target the 5-HT_{1a} system in the prevention of suicidal behaviour.

The psychobiological process model, and more particularly the "social-interaction component", may be important in the planning and provi-sion of treatment in at least three additional ways. These are related to temperament dimension reward dependence, a core aspect of the social-interaction component of the diathesis for suicidal behaviour (see Chapter 8). First, it has been shown that temperament-related characteristics may predict the response to treatment with antidepres-sants (Cloninger et al, 1994). Of particular importance is the demon-stration of a positive correlation between scores on reward dependence and percentage of change in severity of depression during treatment with serotonergic antidepressants found in one study (Joyce et al, 1994), suggesting that individuals with low scores on reward depen-dence are less likely to respond to serotonergic drugs. This finding was confirmed in a study of the effects of paroxetine and pindolol (Tome et al, 1997), but Nelson and Cloninger (1995) failed to replicate this finding using nefazodone. It remains to be demonstrated whether such observations may explain the fact that it is still unclear whether (serotonergic) antidepressants have an impact on suicidal behaviour (Verkes and Cowen, 2000). Second, it can be hypothesized that low scores on reward dependence have a negative influence on the capability of individuals to engage in and/or be compliant with treatment. As described by Hawton in Chapter 11, compliance-related problems are common in attempted suicide patients, and may interfere substantially with treatment. Although there is no research-based evidence in support of this consideration, it is indeed conceivable that a detached and distant personality style, as a manifestation of low reward dependence and thus part of the proposed diathesis for suicidal behaviour, will interfere with the capacity to engage in (particularly psychotherapeutic) treatment. An increase in reward dependence could thus well be an extremely important and primary goal of treatment. Although temperament constructs such as reward dependence, at least theoretically, can be influenced by means of medication (Gabbard, 2000), it is currently not known how such an increase in reward dependence can be achieved, thus indicating the need for further study of the biological underpinnings of this personality dimension (see below). Third, it is conceivable that reward dependence is involved in the important concept of self-disclosure. As described in Chapters 1 and 6, self-disclosure refers to the ability to communicate personal thoughts and feelings such as those related to suicide. While Chapter 12 has made clear that the therapist may play an important role in providing the circumstances for the communication of personal feelings, it may be clear that a lack of self-disclosure may prevent individuals from getting adequate treatment.

Relatively more is known about the efficacy of psychopharmacological and psychotherapeutic treatment approaches to the second component of the diathesis (i.e. *the behavioural-inhibition component*). Chapter 13 has reviewed studies into the efficacy of psychopharmacological approaches to the involved serotonergic and dopaminergic neurotransmission systems, while psychotherapeutic approaches with demonstrated efficacy were described in Chapter 14. Deakin's (1996) model of depression, which served as the basis for description of the psychobiological process model of suicidal behaviour, states that this component serves to modulate approach to or avoidance of future incentives, which may become clinically manifest as impulsivity and aggression, or anxiety-driven inhibition, respectively. As will be described on page 298, the complex relationship between anxiety, aggression and impulsivity is, however, not yet totally clear.

The evolving nature of the suicidal process as a target of treatment

Taking into account the similarities between the suicidal process and the sequentially evolving nature of the affective disorders, Post's (1992) suggestions with regard to stage-dependent pharmacological and psychotherapeutic treatment of depression may well be applicable to the treatment and prevention of suicidal behaviour. With regard to psychosocial or psychotherapeutic interventions he has postulated that psychodynamic therapy, by primarily using the limbic-memory system, may be appropriate for early, minor stress-related dysphorias or initial episodes of major depression. Cognitive, interpersonal or behavioural therapies may be more appropriate for the treatment of subsequent episodes, in which stressors may have a less prominent role, by dealing with increasing automaticity through the use of striatal memory-based habit mechanisms (Post, 1992).

With regard to pharmacotherapy, Post (1992) has pointed at the critical role of psychopharmacological prophylaxis, possibly preventing triggered episodes leading to untriggered episodes. Early initiation and long-term treatment of attempted suicide patients thus appears to be necessary to reduce the probability of an increasing vulnerability to repeated suicidal behaviour, whether or not with a fatal outcome. However, Post (1992) also postulates that responsivity to treatment may differ as a function of the stage in the longitudinal course of a disorder. In addition he has pointed at the possibility that not only may episodes engender vulnerability to recurrences, but that recurrence may also trigger new mechanisms that can overwhelm or circumvent a previously effective treatment. Patients may thus become resistant to previously effective treatments, particularly when effective prophylaxis is discontinued and restarted after a relapse. This may well be applicable to the effect of drugs on the course of the suicidal process, as can be derived from results of the study of Verkes and colleagues (1998) on the effect of paroxetine on recurrence of attempted suicide. While this study could not demonstrate an overall effect of paroxetine on rates of repetition, or an effect in so-called "major repeaters" (i.e. patients with a history of five attempts or more), this antidepressant appeared to be effective in reducing repetition in a subgroup of attempted suicide patients with a history of less than five attempts. This finding indicates that drugs such as paroxetine may be effective in earlier phases of the suicidal process, and suggests that patients with more recurrent episodes become resistant to this form of treatment. Based on their pre-clinical model of mood disorder, Post and Weiss (1999) predict that institution of effective pharmacotherapy early in the course of illness may be more effective than the same treatment later in the course of illness. In view of the highly speculative character of these considerations and their potential dramatic consequences, the development of tolerance to treatment clearly needs to be studied in the context of the suicidal process.

In addition to the potential advantages of psychological and pharmacological approaches, like those described in Chapter 14 and above, recent animal studies suggest that additional psychosocial interventions might be an important component of treatment. As described by Goldney in Chapter 7, a recent study in mice indeed suggests that a so-called enriched environment overcomes genetic deficits by causing the brain to exploit other mechanisms that circumvent the genetic defect (Rampon, 2000). While the enrichment of the environment of the mice could easily be standardized in terms of frequently changed toys, running wheels and small houses, the equivalent of this enrichment for humans remains to be defined. In view of the interpersonal nature of stressors, which are thought to affect the involved brain structures, it can be hypothesized that aspects of enrichment with relevance for humans must involve interpersonal relations. In this respect it is interesting to note Deakin's (1996) speculation that touch may be an all-important modality by which social contact maintains 5-HT neurotransmission. This speculation is based, among others, on the observation of the pro-social effects of substances, such as ecstacy and fluoxetine, which influence the serotonergic system in animal and human studies.

Many of the findings like those described above suggest that the brain indeed possesses more plasticity than most of the other organs in the body (Gabbard, 2000), a consideration which should act as a stimulant for further research on the suicidal process and the ways in which it can be stopped.

IMPLICATIONS OF THE PROCESS APPROACH FOR THE STUDY OF SUICIDAL BEHAVIOUR

Many aspects of the psychobiological model of the suicidal process as described in Chapter 8 are currently regarded as hypothetical and thus in need of further study. However, the model may provide a number of research targets, which can be discussed in terms of the extent to which stress-related aspects or diathesis-dependent characteristics of the process model are addressed.

Further study of stress-related aspects of the suicidal process

With regard to the study of the effects of stressors on the triggering and course of the suicidal process, there is a great need for longitudinal studies of individuals who are in the initial phases of the process. Such studies will allow for the description of psychological, biological, social and psychiatric characteristics which determine the course of the process. In order to study the mechanisms involved in triggering the suicidal process, subjects should be included even before the suicidal process as such has started. Selection of the subjects for such studies could be based on behavioural characteristics, which may fit in the category of risk-taking behaviours, as proposed by O'Carroll and colleagues (1998) and described in Chapter 1. Unfortunately, based on current knowledge such characteristics are highly unspecific, so that large samples would be required.

In the psychobiological process approach to suicidal behaviour (see Chapter 8) it is hypothesized that stressors play a particularly important role in early phases of the process, which may be characterized by relatively low intent of self-harming behaviour, but which may substantially increase the risk of repetition and completed suicide. Our knowledge of the role of stressors in the course of the suicidal process could thus benefit from a careful monitoring of characteristics of stressful events and those of suicidal behaviour. While we know, for example, that attempted suicide in general is commonly associated with particular life events (see Chapter 11), it is currently not known whether there is an association between the occurrence or severity of such events and certain characteristics of suicide attempts such as suicidal intent or lethality of the attempt. These research questions can also be addressed from a biological point of view by means of the study of the stress system (see Chapter 3) in different stages of the process. For example, we have recently demonstrated a substantially increased cortisol secretion in violent suicide attempters (Van Heeringen et al, 2000). It is, however, not yet clear whether this increase is due to the exposure to particularly stressful events, or to a severe hyperreactivity of the neuroendocrine stress system. The psychobiological process approach suggests the latter mechanism to be responsible for the increase in cortisol secretion, but this remains to be demonstrated.

Issues which require further study are, first, related to the interactive nature of the proposed stress–diathesis component of the process model, and thus concern the way in which stress and diathesis affect each other. For example, as described in Chapters 4 and 8, there is evidence for the detrimental effect of the activation of the stress system on the diathesis for suicidal behaviour. The potential protective effects of drugs, which influence the (consequences of the) activation of the neuroendocrine system, on the course of the suicidal process thus need to be studied.

Second, relatively little is known about the evolution of psychopathological manifestations of stressor-induced conditions in the course of the suicidal process. From a cognitive psychological point of view Williams and Pollock in Chapter 5 have described how initial phases of the process may be characterized by signs of "protest", while in later phases signs of "despair" may become predominant. In psychopathological terms it can be hypothesized that this evolution will become manifest as a more or less gradual change from anxiety- or aggression-related symptoms to increasing levels of hopelessness. From a behavioural point of view the process model assumes that this change may become manifest as an increase in suicidal intent, lethality of the method used or medical severity of physical consequences of self-harming behaviour. Studies of failed suicides may be particularly instructive in the understanding of later phases of the process (see also Chapter 6). The detailed study of the timing and severity of stressors and of the psychopathological characteristics of stressor-induced conditions in psychological-autopsy studies may provide important insight into the ways suicidal processes may develop.

Further study of a diathesis for suicidal behaviour

As described in Chapter 2, the process approach to suicidal behaviour has a heuristic value for our understanding of suicidal behaviour. However, as many of the considerations, which have led to the development of the psychobiological process model as described in Chapter 8, are still hypothetical, much more research is needed to determine the aetiological validity of the model, in particular with regard to the proposed components of the diathesis.

First component: the psychobiology of social interaction

The first component of the diathesis concerns social interaction in the sense that this component is hypothesized to reflect resilience to social or interpersonal stressors and to modulate interaction with others. Thus, this component can be considered responsible for what Williams and Pollock in Chapter 5 have called "sensitivity to signals of defeat". Moreover, studies of temperamental characteristics have indicated that this sensitivity may also have a profound effect on the way in which individuals engage in interpersonal relations, thus leading to a detached personality style. This component thus not only reflects sensitivity to interpersonal problems, but may also influence their occurrence. As described in Chapters 4, 5 and 8, currently available knowledge allows for definition of characteristics of this component in psychological and biological terms (i.e. attentional biases and the noradrenergic and serotonergic ($5-HT_{1a}$) systems, respectively). In Chapter 7 Goldney reviewed ethological studies of the neurobiological basis of social attachment, and pointed at the evidence in support of a role of the neuropeptides oxytocin and vasopressin in determining affiliative capacities, including pair bonding, parental care and attachment behaviour. In view of the relevance of these behavioural characteristics for development of suicidal behaviour, the potential involvement of these neuropeptides deserves further study, in particular with regard to the modulation of temperamental dimension reward dependence, as was also suggested by Cloninger (1994). It can further be hypothesized that manipulation of this component leading to an increase in affiliative capacities may contribute to what was called an "enriched environment" earlier in this chapter.

Second component: anxiety or impulsivity?

As described above relatively more is known with regard to the second component of the diathesis (i.e. the "behavioural-inhibition component"). However, as mentioned in Chapter 8, more study is needed to unravel the psychological and biological underpinnings of anxiety, aggression and impulsivity, and their complex relationships. The regulation of anxiety is a core aspect of the "behavioural-inhibition component" of the psychobiological process model. This trait-dependent characteristic may become manifest as biases in behavioural inhibition following a confrontation with adverse events, leading to what ethologists call "arrested flight" (see Chapters 5 and 8). In Chapters 4 and 6, respectively, Van Praag and Apter described disturbances in the regulation of anxiety and aggression as prominent features of a serotonergically linked cluster. In Chapter 6 Apter and Ofek added the trait-like characteristic impulsivity to this syndrome, based on their finding of significant positive correlations between suicidality, violence, impulsivity, depression and anxiety. Moreover, Amsel and Mann described in Chapter 9 the aggression/impulsivity trait as a key component of the diathesis for suicidal behaviour. Thus, there is ample evidence of a (serotonergically linked) cluster of anxiety, aggression and impulsivity. However, while behavioural inhibition can be regarded as the mechanism involved in avoidance behaviour, impulsivity is a form of approach behaviour which can be regarded as the expression of a lack of (anticipatory) anxiety. A number of questions are thus remaining which, at least in part, can be attributed to the lack of use of unequivocal definitions of concepts such as aggression and impulsivity. For example, at least two relevant types of impulsivity can be discerned (i.e. the "motor" and "cognitive" types, Brunner and Hen, 1997). Motor impulsivity is close to the idea of impulse control and behavioural inhibition, processes that may allow decisions to be based on deeper analysis of information while initial emotional reaction is mitigated. Cognitive impulsivity affects the way in which a response outcome is evaluated, and thus can be regarded as a distorted judgement of alternative outcomes (Brunner and Hen, 1997). While it can be argued that the latter definition of impulsivity may correspond particularly to what suicidal patients experience (i.e. hopelessness as a result of perceived absence of positive events that may occur in the future, see Chapter 5), Brunner and Hen (1997), among others, clearly demonstrated an association between serotonergic function and motor impulsivity.

However, it can be hypothesized that motor impulsivity may also play a role in suicidal behaviour. As was described in Chapter 8, and in keeping with Deakin's (1996) hypothetical model of depression, the behavioural-inhibition component is probably mediated by the serotonergic system in conjunction with the dopaminergic neurotransmission system. It has been shown that serotonin acts in an antagonistic way to dopamine, so that depletion of serotonin disinhibits aggressive behaviour (Zuckerman, 1994). The combination of high dopamine and low serotonergic levels may thus lead to (outward-directed or inward-directed) aggression. This would mean that the association between approach behaviour (i.e. impulsivity and/or aggression) and decreased serotonergic functioning can be explained by a (secondary) disinhibition of the dopaminergic system.

Neuropsychological study of the process model

Neuropsychological studies of attempted suicide patients may provide further support for the psychobiological process approach to the understanding of suicidal behaviour. In Chapter 5 Williams and Pollock described examples of neuropsychological studies in suicidal patients, thus providing evidence in support of the crucial role of sensitivity to signals of defeat, the sense of being trapped and the absence of rescue factors in the development of suicidal behaviour. Early neuropsychological studies have investigated the hypothesis that cognitive rigidity mediates the relationship between stressful life events and suicidal behaviour, and provided evidence that suicidal individuals experience difficulties in identifying, generating and/or implementing divergent strategies to solve cognitive problems (Levenson and Neuringer, 1971; Patsiokas et al, 1979). Later studies focused on more specific neuropsychological tasks (e.g. showing that suicide attempters have more difficulty in generating alternative solutions on measures of verbal and non-verbal fluency, Bartfai et al, 1990). More recently, King and colleagues (2000) used a wide range of neuropsychological tests, and showed that depressed suicide attempters performed more poorly with increasing age than depressed non-attempters on a test of mental sequencing and flexibility, while no differences were found with regard to attention/concentration, and verbal or figural fluency. Their results thus challenge the broader cognitive rigidity hypothesis, but are consistent with the possibility that age-related changes in frontal or subcortical regions of the brain, which are involved in the modulation of complex cognitive processes, contribute to the development of suicidal behaviour. Becker and co-workers (1999) recently studied selective attention in suicide attempters, and found a specific attentional bias for suicide-related materials when compared with healthy controls, using a modified Stroop task. Interestingly, there was no association between the bias and measures of anxiety, depression and hopelessness, whereas the level of suicidal ideation correlated significantly with the attentional bias, suggesting that the modified Stroop task assesses in particular characteristics of the "social interaction" component of the diathesis, as described in Chapter 8. In view of accumulating evidence in support of the information-processing approach to the understanding of suicidal behaviour, neuropsychological studies can be expected to contribute further to elucidation of the mechanisms involved in the development of suicidal behaviour. Clearly, much more work needs to be done in this area (e.g. taking into account the potential confounding effects of psychiatric disorders such as substance abuse and depression, psychotropic medication and age).

Such research could benefit from recent diagnostic advances in the area of neural science, by means of which neuropsychological assessments can be combined with functional neuro-imaging strategies (for an overview see Cabeza and Nyberg, 2000), whether or not in combination with the assessment of aminergic modulation of cerebral functions.

Neurotransmitters and cognitive functions

The study of the role of neurotransmitters in modulation of higher cerebral functions may shed additional light on the mechanisms involved in the diathesis for suicidal behaviour. Such modulation is included in the psychobiological process model as described in Chapter 8 at several places. These include, for example, the noradrenergic modulation of attention, a core aspect of the "social-interaction component" of the diathesis, and the serotonergic (i.e. 5-HT_{2A}) modulation of prefrontal executive functions as an important characteristic of the "behavioural-inhibition component". Deakin (1996) has reported evidence in support of dissection of the diathesis into two components, which are mediated by the 5-HT_{1a} and 5-HT_2 systems, by showing that drugs that influence 5-HT_2 function selectively affect performance on neuropsychological tests of executive function without affecting tests of learning and memory. The reverse was the case with the 5-HT_{1a} agonist buspirone.

A second example concerns noradrenergic modulation of attention. Although there still is some controversy about the behavioural functions of the noradrenergic system (e.g. see Zuckerman, 1994), most researchers agree about a general cognitive function of this system (i.e. that it serves to focus attention on significant environmental stimuli and to filter out irrelevant stimuli, see also Southwick et al, 1999; Ressler and Nemeroff, 1999). It should be noted that reward dependence, which was described as the temperamental dimension involved in this component of the diathesis, is predicted to reflect individual differences in the brain's system for modulation of conditioned signals of reward, particularly social signals. This modulation is hypothetically mediated by the noradrenergic system (Cloninger, 1998). It has indeed been shown that the administration of drugs which decrease the release of noradrenaline (such as clonidine) impair the paired associate-learning mechanism, which is involved in the process of conditioning of social signals (Cloninger et al, 1994). Further study is clearly needed to demonstrate what role such mechanisms play in triggering and continuation of the suicidal process.

These two examples indicate the role of neurotransmitters in modulation of neuropsychological mechanisms involved in the diathesis for suicidal behaviour. Findings like these suggest that, in keeping with the psychobiological approach, a combination of psychopharmacological and psychotherapeutic approaches can be used to target this component of the diathesis for suicidal behaviour. Such findings also suggest that the inclusion of neuropsychological and behavioural assessments in the study of the effects of drugs, such as those described in Chapter 13, may contribute to our understanding of the mechanisms involved in the aetiology of suicidal behaviour.

Genetics

While there is clearly a significant genetic contribution to the risk of suicide, we are at present largely ignorant of the mechanisms underlying this. It seems inherently unlikely that suicidal behaviour itself has a genetic basis, but it is entirely credible that genetic factors may influence attributes that enhance suicide risk (Hawton and Van Heeringen, 2000). By dissecting the diathesis for suicidal behaviour into two components, the psychobiological process model as described in Chapter 8 may provide a more accurate description of such attributes, which may include the temperament dimensions harm avoidance and reward dependence and the involved neurobiological systems (i.e. the serotonergic 5-HT_{1a} and 5-HT_2), noradrenergic and dopaminergic systems).

CONCLUSIONS

In this chapter some implications of a process approach to treatment, prevention and further study of suicidal behaviour were reviewed. The combination of biological and psychological approaches with regard to the treatment and study of suicidal behaviour is an important aspect of the psychobiological approach to the suicidal process as described in Chapter 8. Such an approach opposes a Cartesian dualism that splits individuals into a mind and a brain. For example, we are just beginning to understand the ways in which biological mechanisms may interfere with the ability to learn (e.g. from psychotherapy). On the other hand, learning about oneself, which is an important ingredient of insight learning in psychotherapy and thus of gaining mastery over our temperamental drives, may in itself influence the structure and function of the brain (Kandel, 1998). This approach to the intriguing problem of suicidal behaviour is based on the observation that our knowledge of the complex interaction between brain and environment has developed to such an extent that integrative strategies for the treatment and further study of the suicidal process can be described.

By taking a psychobiological approach to the understanding of suicidal behaviour, this book also reflects a shift in the focus from psychiatric disorders to stress–diathesis and process models. This does not mean, however, that the role of psychiatric disorders in the aetiology of suicidal behaviour is underestimated, or that the contribution of the adequate treatment of these disorders to the prevention of suicide is considered as relatively unimportant. The information provided in various chapters of this book implies that the treatment of psychiatric disorders, in association with an increased risk of suicide, should be separated from the treatment of suicidal behaviour to such an extent that the involvement of trait-dependent characteristics requires additional interventions.

The chapters in this book have indicated that evidence in support of the psychobiological process model of suicidal behaviour is increasing, but also make clear that a number of aspects certainly are hypothetical at this point in time, and thus in need of further study. However, science is a system set up to challenge theories and models, ultimately reformulating or scrapping them for better ones (Popper, 1979). Even incomplete or inaccurate models are preferable to none, and without models efforts tend to be dissipated in blind, piecemeal, inductive research with no focus or direction (Zuckerman, 1994). The benefits of a model such as the proposed psychobiological process approach to suicidal behaviour include the fact that it provides an opportunity to organize currently available knowledge in such a way that it may serve as a basis for further study. It is hoped that this book will act as a stimulus for research, ultimately aiming at understanding human behaviour.

REFERENCES

Amini, F., Lewis, T. and Lannon, R. (1996) Affect, attachment, memory: contributions towards psychobiologic integration. *Psychiatry*, **59**: 213–239.

Andreasen, N.D. (1997) Linking mind and brain in the study of mental illness: a project for a scientific psychopathology. *Science*, **275**: 1586–1593.

Bartfai, A., Winborg, I.M. and Nordström, P. (1990) Suicidal behavior and cognitive flexibility: design and verbal fluency after attempted suicide. *Suicide and Life-Threatening Behavior*, **20**: 254–266.

Becker, E.S., Strohbach, D. and Rinck, M. (1999) A specific attentional bias in suicide attempters. *Journal of Nervous and Mental Disorders*, **12**: 730–735.

Brunner, D. and Hen, R. (1997) Insights in the neurobiology of impulsive behavior from serotonin receptor knockout mice. In D.M. Stoff and J.J. Mann (Eds), *The Neurobiology of Suicide. From the Bench to the Clinic*. New York, Annals of the New York Academy of Sciences, vol. 836.

Cabeza, R. and Nyberg, L. (2000) Imaging cognition II: an empirical review of 275 PET and fMRI studies. *Journal of Cognitive Neuroscience*, **12**: 1–47.

Cloninger, R.C. (1994) Temperament and personality. *Current Opinion in Neurobiology*, **4**: 266–273.

Cloninger, R.C. (1998) The genetics and psychobiology of the seven-factor model of personality. In Silk, K.R. (Ed.), *Biology of Personality Disorders*. Washington DC, American Psychiatric Press.

Cloninger, R.C., Przybeck, T.R., Svrakic, D.M. and Wetzel, R.D. (1994) *The Temperament and Character Inventory: A Guide to its Development and Use*. St Louis, Center for Psychobiology of Personality.

Deakin, J.F.W. (1996) 5-HT, antidepressant drugs and the psychosocial origins of depression. *Journal of Psychopharmacology*, **10**: 31–38.

Duman, R.S., Malberg, J. and Thome, J. (1999) Neural plasticity to stress and antidepressant treatment. *Biological Psychiatry*, **46**: 1181–1191.

Gabbard, G.O. (2000) A neurobiologically informed perspective on psychotherapy. *British Journal of Psychiatry*, **177**: 117–122.

Gelpin, E., Bonne, O., Peri, T., Brandes, D. and Shalev, A.Y. (1996) Treatment of recent trauma survivors with benzodiazepines: a prospective study. *Journal of Clinical Psychiatry*, **57**: 390–394.

Hawton, K. and Van Heeringen, C. (2000) Future perspectives. In K. Hawton and K. Van Heeringen (Eds), *The International Handbook of Suicide and Attempted Suicide*. Chichester, Wiley.

Joyce, P., Mulder, R. and Cloninger, R.C. (1994) Temperament predicts clomipramine and desipramine response in major depression. *Journal of Affective Disorders*, **30**: 35–46.

Kandel, E.R. (1998) A new intellectual framework for psychiatry. *American Journal of Psychiatry*, **155**: 457–469.

King, D.A., Conwell, Y., Cox, C., Henderson, R.E., Denning, D.G. and Caine, E.D. (2000) A neuropsychological comparison of depressed suicide attempters and nonattempters. *The Journal of Neuropsychiatry and Clinical Neurosciences*, **12**: 64–70.

Levenson, M. and Neuringer, C. (1971) Problem solving behavior in suicidal adolescents. *Journal of Consulting and Clinical Psychology*, **37**: 433–436.

McFarlane, A.C. (1998) *Addictive Behaviour*, **23**: 813–825.

Murphy, B. (1997) Antiglucocorticoid therapies in major depression—a review. *Psychoneuroendocrinology*, **22**(suppl. 1): 125–132.

Nelson, E.C. and Cloninger, R.C. (1995) The tridimensional personality questionnaire as a predictor of response to nefazodone treatment of depression. *Journal of Affective Disorders*, **35**: 51–57.

Nutt, D.J. (2000) The psychobiology of posttraumatic stress disorder. *Journal of Clinical Psychiatry*, **61**(suppl. 5): 24–29.

O'Carroll, P.W., Berman, A.L., Maris, R., Moscicki, E., Tanney, B. and Silverman, M. (1998) Beyond the Tower of Babel: A omenclature for suicidology. In R.J. Kosky, H.S. Eshkevari, R.D. Goldney and R. Hassan (Eds), *Suicide Prevention: The Global Perspective*. New York, Plenum Press.

Patsiokas, A.T., Clum, G.A. and Luscomb, R.L. (1979) Cognitive characteristics of suicide attempters. *Journal of Consulting and Clinical Psychology*, **47**: 478–484.

Popper, K.R. (1979) *Objective Knowledge: An Evolutionary Approach*. Oxford, Clarendon Press.

Post, R.M. (1992) Transduction of psychosocial stress into the neurobiology of recurrent affective disorder. *American Journal of Psychiatry*, **149**: 999–1010.

Post, R.M. and Weiss, S.R.B. (1999) Neurobiological models of recurrence in mood disorder. In D.S. Charney, E.J. Nestler and B.S. Bunney (Eds), *Neurobiology of Mental Illness*. Oxford, Oxford University Press.

Rampon, C. (2000) Enrichment induces structural changes and recovery from nonspatial memory deficits in CA1 NMDAR1–knockout mice. *Nature Neuroscience*, **3**: 238–244.

Ressler, K.J. and Nemeroff, C.B. (1999) Role of norepinephrine in the pathphysiology and treatment of mood disorders. *Biological Psychiatry*, **46**: 1219–1233.

Southwick, S.M., Brmner, J.D., Rasmusson, C.A., Morgan III, C.A., Arnsten, A. and Charney, D.S. (1999) Role of norepinephrine in the pathophysiology and treatment of posttraumatic stress disorder. *Biological Psychiatry*, **46**: 1192–1204.

Ströhle, A.W., Pasini, A., Romeo, E., Hermann, B., Spalletta, G., di Michele, F., Holsboer, F. and Rupprecht, R. (2000) Fluoxetine decreases concentrations of

3α, 5α-tetrahydrodeoxycorticosterone (THDOC) in major depression. *Journal of Psychiatric Research*, **34**: 183–186.

Tome, M.B., Cloninger, R.C., Watson, J.P. and Isaac, M.T. (1997) Serotonergic autoreceptor blockade in the reduction of antidepressant latency: personality variables and response to paroxetine and pindolol. *Journal of Affective Disorders*, **44**: 101–109.

Van Heeringen, K., Andenaert, K., Van de Wiele, L. and Verstraete, A. (2000) Cortisol in violent suicide attempters: association with monoamines and personality. *Journal of Affective Disorders*, **60**: 181–189.

Verkes, R.J. and Cowen, P.J. (2000) Pharmacotherapy of suicidal ideation and behaviour. In K. Hawton and K. Van Heeringen (Eds), *The International Handbook of Suicide and Attempted Suicide*. Chichester, Wiley.

Verkes, R.J., Van der Mast, R.C., Hengeveld, M.W., Tuyl, J.P., Zwinderman, A.H. and Van Kempen, G.M.J. (1998) Reduction by paroxetine of suicidal behavior in patients with repeated suicide attempts but not major depression. *American Journal of Psychiatry*, **155**: 543–547.

Zobel, A.W., Nickel, T., Künzel, H.E., Ackl, N., Sonntag, A., Ising, M. and Holsboer, F. (2000) Effects of the high-affinity corticotropin-releasing hormone receptor 1 antagonist R121919 in majordepression: the first 20 patients treated. *Journal of Psychiatric Research*, **34**: 171–181.

Zuckerman, M. (1994) *Psychobiology of Personality*. Cambridge, Cambridge University Press.

AUTHOR INDEX

SUBJECT INDEX

The Wiley Series in

CLINICAL PSYCHOLOGY